# THE M[ASK]

NEW
NUMBER

JUST
OUT

# Gordon Craig
## denounces
# Russian Ballet

## ORDER AT ONCE
# 7 JOHN ST. ADELPHI

TELEPHONE
REGENT 1601

The posters reproduced as endpapers were used to advertize the July 1913 number of The Mask which contained an article on the Russian ballet by Craig (reprinted in this collection). They were printed at the Chiswick Press in London. The "denounces" poster is a reconstruction from a fragment on the reverse of which Craig's son, Edward, wrote, in 1970, "The sandwich men marched around with posters contradicting each other—'Craig defends' . . . 'Craig denounces' etc. 'Craig defends' was in red—'Craig denounces' was in green—and this remnant is the only example I have come across and, of course, goes to Arnold Rood." The sketch above accompanied this description, with the further explanation that one color was worn on each side by the sandwich men. The editor is grateful to Mr. Craig for allowing the text and sketch to be reproduced here.

*Edward Gordon Craig. Vence, France, 1961. Photograph by Arnold Rood.*

# GORDON CRAIG
# ON
# MOVEMENT
# AND
# DANCE

Edited, and with an Introduction

by ARNOLD ROOD

Dance Books, London

First published 1977.
First British edition 1978.
This edition is published by arrangement
with the original publishers, Dance Horizons,
1801 East 26th Street, Brooklyn, N.Y. 11229. U.S.A.

ISBN 0 903 102 37 4
Printed in the United States of America
Dance Books Ltd., 9 Cecil Court, London WC2N 4EZ.

edicated to

Ruth Kobart

for her

friendship, loyalty, encouragement

and to the memory of

Ellen M. Gordon Craig

# ACKNOWLEDGEMENTS

he editor wishes to gratefully acknowledge the kind courtesy and cooperation he has received from *The Observer,* London; *The Argonaut Press* % Chas. J. Sawyer, 12/13 Grafton Street, London W1X 3LA; *Periodical Publications Ltd.; BBC Publications; The Dancing Times Limited;* Lincoln Kirstein for their permission to include articles originally published by them.

He is especially indebted to H.E. Robert Craig, Administrator of the E. Gordon Craig, C.H., Estate for his permission to reproduce Craig's work.

In addition, the editor wishes to acknowledge his thanks to those who own title to now defunct periodicals or which were not identifiable and so could not be specifically mentioned here.

As the editor has repeatedly learned, Edward A. Craig is a veritable endless source of information and an invaluable guide to the work of his father and so a special note of gratitude must be made to him.

# TABLE OF CONTENTS

LIST OF ILLUSTRATIONS

Signets with G. C. initials used as ornaments were cut in wood by Edward Gordon Craig.

# CAVEAT LECTOR

lthough it may seem to be careless proof-reading or idiosyncratic on the part of the Editor or, perhaps, sloppiness by the original typesetters, it was wished that Craig's spelling and punctuation, particularly in *The Mask* pieces, could be maintained throughout this volume in the hope it would offer the reader a greater feeling for Craig's style. However, it was found necessary to regularize both somewhat. Nevertheless, wherever it proved practical, the Editor has kept the original without puncturing the text with "[*sic*]."

# INTRODUCTION

s I ponder Gordon Craig's writings, as my curiosity is increasingly whetted, not only by what he says or by what he does not say, but by what he hints at, I have wondered, more and more, why Craig did not also become what we call a choreographer. "Choreography is a map of movement—patterns for action that ballet masters ordain by design. Its composition depends on human bodies schooled in a grammar of movement whose end is legible virtuosity . . . it exists as cousin to music, architecture, painting, and sculpture."[1] Certainly Craig expected the director of a play to be capable of arranging choreographed movement; he himself had done this in several productions shortly after the turn of the twentieth century.

Walter Sorell writes, ". . .that dancing is older than man. We know of early man that he moved in imitation of various animals and tried to reproduce their motions while in attack or flight, while in search for food or in courtship. The Greek Lucian, writing in the second century, thought that dancing was as old as love."[2]

Since it is obvious that the one element essential to dance and choreography is movement, it follows that choreography would have been an area in which Craig's creative ability might also have blossomed fully.

By 1900, Craig had not only been trained as an actor but had considerable professional experience behind him, with Henry Irving's company in London and on tour, and performances under other managements in the provinces. By the turn of the century he had become knowledgeable in other art forms as well: the visual arts through his friends James Pryde and William Nicholson (the Beggarstaff Brothers) and William Rothenstein; literature through Max Beerbohm; music through Martin Fallas Shaw, with whom he essayed the productions of *Dido and Aeneas, The Masque of Love* and *Acis and Galatea* under the aegis of the Purcell Operatic Society.

*Dido and Aeneas* was first presented at the Hampstead Conservatoire in May, 1900. Other than the title characters, who were played by professional performers, the cast consisted of amateurs with knowledge of singing, but none were trained in stage movement or dancing. While rehearsing the music Shaw was asked by Craig to have the chorus walk about as they sang so that when he came to stage the opera, the singers would not be reluctant to follow his directions. In a letter to Shaw, Craig writes, "I'm trying to turn dancers out while making my book. Dancers are devilish fishy things for any but professionals to attempt. One dance I'll make a dance of arms — white *white* arms — the rest of the scene dark—and out of it, the voices—with arm accompaniment—exciting if done well."[3] This idea was to be seen as the accompaniment of Dido's death at the end of the opera.

In the following year, the opera was revived. Presented on the same bill was *The Masque of Love.* Shaw arranged this work from Purcell's opera *Dioclesian,* the text for which was Thomas Betterton's version of Beaumont and Fletcher's play, *The Prophetess; or, The History of Diocletian,* with music by Purcell.[4] Craig arranged for *The Masque* to take place in

. . .a hall in a mansion. Cupid sends forth children to fetch masks, by which we understand that they are playing at being Gods and Goddesses—Flora, Comus, and the rest. Three groups, representing Blood, Riches, and Poverty, enter at different points; their wrists bound, and they are dragged in, in a typification of the stern mastery of Love. Their fetters are loosened. The rod of captivity becomes a maypole of merriment, whereon a solemn movement follows—"Hear mighty Lord!" At the conclusion of this chorus, we hear outside a rustling and the sound of feet which create mingled fear and expectation. Bacchanals enter, and the masquers flee like startled fauns. A hymn to Bacchus follows, with lively movement of hands and bodies, and an interweaving dance. While the eyes are fed, the measure of a bright country dance enchants the ear, the masque closing with the usual procession.[5]

All, however, was not of such great seriousness. In his autobiography, Martin Shaw records that "In the Masque, the children upset the infant Bacchus in his car and while the unlucky babe (where was the L.C.C.?) hung perilously downward, howling, his attendants shrilly disputed the question who was to blame for his ungodlike position."[6]

Because Ellen Terry also had appeared in a one-act play on the bill, the week's run at the Coronet Theatre was successful artistitically and financially. The resulting small profit was sufficient reason for optimism, so plans proceeded for a production of *Acis and Galatea* by Handel, with text by John Gay. After a number of months' planning, rehearsals began and continued for eight months, culminating in the first performance on March 10, 1902, at the Great Queen Street Theatre. On the same bill was a revival of *The Masque of Love.*[7]

As *Acis* has a mythological setting, Craig had a choice: to design a traditional "idyllically bucolic 'Sicilian' landscape, or to give free play to his imagination and follow where the music led him."[8] Naturally Craig chose the latter course and, by so doing, had the freedom to make continued use of simplified line, color, light and movement.

Once again Craig had successfully transmuted what might have been a stodgy, dull, unimaginative presentation into a stirring, exciting experience. Among other enthusiastic responses from artists, one finds Graham Robertson, the painter and writer, concluding a rather lengthy piece: "Mr. Gordon Craig, and Deviser and Executor of these fair imaginings had achieved his great object—that the Sister Arts of Music, Painting, and Pantomime should make up their little differences and cast away their jealousies, and, by a united effort, should create anew a Forgotten Art—the Art of the Theatre."[9]

We can see that within the first two years of the century, if only in these three productions, Craig had already laid the groundwork, through practice, for his developing ideas regarding movement. During 1902, the search became more intense. He and Elena Meo, whom he had met in 1900, wandered about London at different hours of the day with Craig recording in his notebook Elena's movements in changing light patterns in varied architectural settings.

These sketches and notes were put aside and became synthesized finally, in 1906, into the series of drawings called *The Steps,* reproduced in 1913 in *Towards A New Theatre.* Each of the four drawings is also identified as a "mood." Craig tells us that in the second mood, "You see that the steps have not changed . . . and at the very top of a flat and deep terrace we see many girls and boys jumping about like fireflies. And in the foreground, and farthest from them, I have made the earth respond to their movements. The earth is made to dance."[10]

In 1906, Craig drew two other studies for movement. In one the viewer observes a number of people toiling up a large staircase seen in profile. Of this he later wrote, "What steps have to do with movement, except as the recipient of movers, is not as clear to me on one day as it is on another . . . but when I come to think of the way some dancing school may probably plump a big flight of hard steps at the end of their room and make poor girls run up and down them, posing like the dreadful things we want to escape from, then I curse anything so material as steps in connection with movement, and regret that I ever made any record suggesting a connection between the two things."[11]

In December 1904, a few months after his arrival in Berlin, Craig met Isadora Duncan. What is of interest in their over-publicized relationship is the influence on each other within their respective arts. In Craig, Duncan found the theoretic basis for her dancing, and in Duncan, Craig found the substantiation of his ideas and dreams regarding human movement which had occupied his thinking for some time. In his description of the first time he saw her dance, he tells us:

She came through some small curtains which were not much taller than she was herself; she came through them and walked down to where a musician, his back turned to us, was seated at a grand piano; he had just finished playing a short prelude by Chopin when in she came, and in some five or six steps was standing by the piano, quite still and, as it were listening to the hum of the last notes. . . . You might have counted five, or even eight, and then there sounded the voice of Chopin again, in a second prelude or etude; it was played through gently and came to an end and she had not moved at all. Then one step back or sideways, and the music began again as she went moving on before or after it. Only just moving—not pirouetting or doing any of those things which we expect to see, and which a Taglioni or a Fanny Ellsler would have certainly done. She was speaking in her own language, not echoing any ballet master, and so she came to move as no one had ever seen anyone move before. The dance ended and again, she stood quite still, no bowing, no smiling—nothing at all. Then again the music is off, and she runs from it—it runs after her then, for she had gone ahead of it.[12]

What is of greatest importance is that, even in this comparatively recent description, the operable verb is "to move" rather than "to dance," a word occurring again and again in Craig's writing about the use of action by the performing artist. To be noted as well is the utter simplicity of the stage picture, the same sort of simplicity which was the keynote of Craig's operatic productions between 1900 and 1902.

Let us turn our attention briefly to Isadora Duncan and try to find some clues about her thoughts on dance. She was born in San Francisco on May 26, 1877. The Duncan children were introduced to music, poetry, drama and the other arts by their mother, who was an accomplished pianist. In lieu of any religious observance she had the children perform at family gatherings; it was at these functions that Isadora first recited and danced. According to her autobiography she was teaching babies to wave their arms gracefully—at the age of six. In this simple incident is to be found the genesis for Duncan's search for beauty, her revulsion towards traditional ballet training, and her devotion to children.

Even as a child, Duncan was interested in a different kind of movement from what was then traditional. Rather than formalized, constrained, ballet-ic movement, the young Duncan attempted freeflowing movement imitating nature. "My first idea of movement, of the dance, certainly came from the rhythm of the waves," she writes.[13]

It is thought that Duncan must have been exposed to the influence of Delsarte, partly because of her voracious reading habits, despite the fact that she withdrew from school at a very early age. As a teenager Duncan was not only teaching Delsarte-influenced movement, but performed with her family in a converted barn on the family property and on short tours of towns along the California coast. By the time she was twenty years old she had quite thoroughly organized her thinking almost into a creed: "This is what we are trying to accomplish, to blend together—a poem, a melody and a dance—so that you will not listen to the music, see the dance or hear the poem, but will live in the scene and the thought that all are expressing."[14]

From 1897, Duncan toured America and Europe dancing at the homes of the wealthy and, wherever she went, meeting all sorts of artists, visiting museums, and absorbing the classic arts. Her exposure to the collections of Greek art in the British Museum led her to a lasting interest in the spirit and arts of Greece. As she was discovering classic Greece, she also turned, increasingly, to the music of the masters. Both these insights brought her even closer to a theory of movement towards which she had been moving.

Despite the hit-or-miss, amateur training in Duncan's chosen vocation and the more formal, certainly much more disciplined, training Craig received as a performer, both, it must be noted, had their artistic perceptions enlarged at approximately the same time, the turn of the twentieth century. Another interesting coincidence is that, as Craig started his experimental stage work in 1900, so did Duncan begin hers at about the same time. In Paris she started her dance experiments leading to a statement of theory: "For hours I would stand quite still, my two hands folded between my breasts, covering the solar plexus. . . .I was seeking and finally discovered the central spring of all movement, the crater of motor power, the unity from which all diversities of movements are born, the mirror of vision for the creation of the dance—it was from this discovery that was born the theory on which I founded my school."[15]

Craig's vision regarding a moving scene—"the Thousand Scenes in One Scene"—so beautifully illustrated in the etchings he made in Florence in 1907 is quite familiar. This moving "Scene," as demonstrated in the etchings, called for an up-and-down movement of the cubes into which the stage was divided, requiring a vertical stage opening. Unfortunately, because he did not know how to execute this revolutionary concept, the moving scene remained a secret for the balance of Craig's life. Because of this lack of the requisite technical knowledge he compromised by executing the concept as moving screens. The screens called for side-to-side movement in a horizontal stage opening with which Craig was familiar because it was traditional. As a result of the use of the moving screens at Dublin's Abbey Theatre from 1911 until 1951, and at the Moscow Art Theatre in 1912, it was thought that these moving screens were what Craig had envisioned. Needless to say, they were not.

An integral part of the moving scene was light. From his early wood engravings, through his etchings and drawings, Craig always placed primary emphasis in these graphics on light.

However, I must not digress regarding Craig and the scenic elements of theatre. This has been documented already by Craig, his disciples and his detractors. What is of much more immediate concern is the performer and Craig's point of view toward him and, ultimately, toward dance.

In his first book, *The Art of the Theatre,* published in 1905 during the first year of the liaison with Isadora Duncan, Craig concludes that the artist of the theatre of the future would create his art "Out of ACTION, SCENE, and VOICE."[16] (In a copy, in the possession of Professor John Wesley Swanson, of Catharine Valogne's book, *Gordon Craig,* which quotes this passage, Craig wrote in the margin that "Voice" related to Yvette Guilbert, "Scene" to Adolphe Appia, and "Action" to Isadora Duncan.) Craig then goes on to say, "And when I say *action,* I mean both gesture and dancing, the prose and poetry of action."[17]

In his later essay, "The Actor and the Über-marionette," appearing in the second issue of *The Mask* in April 1908, Craig advocates the use of a super-marionette because "art arrives only by design . . . . to make any work of art it is clear we may only work in those materials with which we can calculate. Man is not one of those materials."[18] He claims that man is not a material of art because of man's desire for freedom, which causes a lack of discipline, and man's emotionality, which causes a lack of reasoning. What Craig wants are actors who ". . .must create for themselves a new form of acting, consisting for the main part of symbolical gesture."[19] Craig softened his cry for a super-marionette in 1924 when he wrote that he didn't want to replace the living actor with a marionette; he wanted poor actors to catch a little of the Devil's spirit and rid themselves of traditional mannerisms. "The Über-marionette is the actor plus fire, minus egoism: the fire of the gods and demons, without the smoke and steam of mortality."[20] What he was looking for in the performer, ". . .always and now here, again, *I ask only for the liberation of the actor that he may develop his own powers,* and cease from being the Marionette of the playwright.[21]

Although Duncan was faithful in her thinking about movement through-out her career and did a great deal of talking about her ideas she never recorded the essence very accurately, so that it is difficult to find the focus expressed in her own words. Perhaps the best indication of Duncan's point of view is the statement by John Martin:

What she was primarily concerned with can only be called basic dance—not a trade or a profession or even an art to begin with, but a biological function. She was not seeking to invent or devise anything, but only to discover the roots of that impulse toward movement as a response to every experience, which she felt in herself and which she was convinced was a universal endowment. Without benefit of formal psychology, she knew as no other dancer on record had known that spontaneous movement of the body is the first reaction of all men to sensory or emotional stimuli. Though civilization tends to dull and to inhibit this tendency, it is still the fundamental reaction of men to the universe about them. A revival of the conscious use of this faculty would mean deepening and broadening the whole range of life . . . . Only when he has developed the power to touch life at first hand does he begin to be aware of his inherent selfhood, and until he has become thus aware he cannot develop his true bent or resist the forces that would con-ventionalize him into a mass product.[22]

As stated earlier, there was, unquestionably, a mutual influence on each of these artists, the exact influence not being fully recorded yet. There is a hint of Craig's reaction to Duncan's method of work when he wrote that what he expected was to "Let the temperament of each actor develop for all that his temperament is worth, and let the sense of discipline be devel-oped in proportion to the force of his temperament. Do not let tempera-ment be an excuse for an absence of discipline. It is this that is killing the modern stage."[23] In short, Craig expected the actor to be an Isadora Duncan *with* discipline.

Craig further elaborated on this need for the performer to be disciplined when, in 1909, using Adolf Furst as his pseudonymic spokesman, he wrote in "A Note on Marionettes":

Two of the most salient characteristics which chiefly impress us in them are their simplicity and their calm. The gestures which seem so varied, so complicated as to necessitate the most elaborate mechanism are produced by means so amazingly simple, while a marionette 'green-room' between the performances . . . forms a welcome contrast to the real theatre, . . . as tranquil a spot as can be found. Each little figure, strangely human in its repose, hangs upon its nail in the dim light, gazing before it with eyes as inscrutable as those which yet meet ours from under the quiet brows of the gods of Egypt and Etruria. It is their silence, their passionless gaze, their profound indifference which give so supreme a dignity to the frail little bodies tricked out in gauze and tinsel. As in the fallen descendant of a great family some one trait may yet remain to recall a noble origin, so does that impassive gaze, that air of seeing *beyond* all the transitory and the accidental, still proclaim for the marionette his kinship with the grave stone images of the ancient eastern world. And when, in more than his former dignity and dowered with more than his former gifts, the puppet returns to our stage in the form of that Über-Marionette whom Mr. Gordon Craig has created, bringing with him his supreme quality, that of perfect obedience to the hand and mind of the master whom he serves as material, with him will come that Renaissance of the Art of the Theatre of which the first hints are even now beginning to appear.[24]

Now that Craig had seen, in Duncan, that some of his ideas were workable, it suddenly occurred to him, toward the end of his relationship with her, in 1906, that "it might be possible for an audience to derive an emotional experience from the movement of plastic forms as well . . . from three dimensional structures . . . He would use movement to express ideas in time and space."[25] As Duncan improvised her movement, as she was affected by the music being played, so Craig saw the possibility of the scene doing something similar, resulting in each performance being a unique one. This is what led to the compromise vision of the "moving scene."

The end of the relationship did not end Craig's thinking regarding the performer's movement. As a result of the money-raising efforts of Elena Meo, Craig was able to open his School for the Art of the Theatre in Florence in 1913. In the biography of his father, Edward Craig asks, "What was it that Craig wanted to study? First and foremost came MOVEMENT. 'The movements of the elements and Man.' To help with this he even thought to make use of films. . . . Connected with movement would be DANCE—ceremonials—posture, etc. Connected with dance would be MIME."[26] Also included in the curriculum was to have been light, experiments with the screens, marionettes, masks and theatre history. Although World War I terminated the school after only one year, we can see that movement and dance were still occupying a very important place in Craig's thinking.

In March, 1908, the first issue of *The Mask* had appeared. This periodical was to be Craig's spokesman demanding revolutionary changes in the theatre in its articles, its editorials, its book reviews, its letters from foreign correspondents. Because a huge amount of material was needed to keep the magazine in print, Craig reverted to a practise he had used in his earlier periodical, *The Page:* pseudonyms. And so, we find that the editor is none other than the well-known Javanese-born writer and drama critic, John

Semar. Not only did Semar write an editorial on the Russian Ballet and a piece on Nijinski but he also wrote an historical piece on Lambranzi and his book of dances. Further contributions were made by Craig in the guise of John Balance, Allen Carric, Edward Edwardovitch, François M. Florian, Adolf Furst, Lois Lincoln, Giovanni Mezzogiorno, Drury Pervil (who was also the designer of the dust wrapper for Craig's biography of Henry Irving), Giulio Piero, Rudolf Schmerz, C. G. Smith, Jan van Holt, and XYZ, all reporting at varying lengths from various parts of the world on varied occasions. Lest it be forgotten, it must be noted that Gordon Craig, in his true embodiment, also contributed a number of pieces on dance and, I suspect, he was responsible for many of the unsigned ones which also appeared in The Mask's fifteen year existence. During this time, the editor, John Semar, also encouraged other "real" people to write on dance for the magazine. Among the dance subjects covered by "real" contributors were Indian and Cambodian dance, Inigo Jones' masques, English Morris dances, Spanish dance, classic ballet and even a full, illustrated reprint of Albert Smith's "The Ballet Girl."

Craig's own articles, notes, editorials, ranged over a wide variety of material which I have loosely categorized, for convenience's sake as, first, those concerned with theory such as "The Actor and the Über-marionette," "The Artists of the Theatre of the Future," "Motion, Being the Preface to the Portfolio of Etchings," and "A Note on Masks." Interestingly, all these basic theory pieces appeared in the first year of the life of The Mask with each concerning itself, to some extent, with the performers' movement.

Another category might be titled "classic dance." In this area we find historical pieces on Francesco Clerico, Mademoiselle Guimard, Giuseppa Cortesi, Lambranzi, Taglioni. We also come across pieces on Pavlova, Nijinski and Ida Rubinstein.

There are also articles which deal with ethnic or folk dance such as Indian, Javanese, Japanese, the English folk dance, and Elizabethan dances.

In still another group, Craig deals with modern artists and their work, such as Margaret Morris, Angna Enters, Loie Fuller, Ted Shawn, Ruth St. Denis and Jacques Dalcroze, all of whom suffer Craig's ire because they did not acknowledge their indebtedness to Isadora Duncan. In a typical comment in a book review, Craig dismisses the work under consideration with the question, "Why write a book about Dancing at all unless you know all about the art?"[27]

All through this group of pieces there are bold statements, comparisons, hints at the art of Duncan. Craig, in these, is singularly disposed to be annoyed that those who came after Duncan did not acknowledge their indebtedness to her and her contribution to the art. He points out that each of these performers or teachers imitate the superficialities of Duncan's free and natural artistic expression but, at the same time, they never understand nor capture the essence of her art. In his 1952 BBC talk, he says:

She was a fore-runner. All she did was done with very great ease—or so it seemed, at least. This it was which gave her an appearance of power. She projected the dance into this world of ours in full belief that what she was doing was right and great. And it was. She threw away ballet skirts and ballet thoughts. She discarded shoes and stockings too. She put on some bits of stuff which when hung up on a peg looked more like torn rags than anything else; when she put them on they became transformed. Stage dresses usually transform the performers, but in her case it was these bits which actually became transformed by her putting them on. She transformed them into marvels of beauty and at every step she took, they spoke.

He continues,

How it is that we know she is speaking her own language? We know it, for we see her head, her hands, gently active, as are her feet, her whole person. And if she is speaking, what is it she is saying? No one would ever be able to report truly, yet no one present had a moment's doubt. Only this can we say—that she was telling to the air the very things we longed to hear and until she came we had never dreamed we should hear; and now we heard them, and this sent us all into an unusual state of joy. . .[28]

A final group of dance articles by Craig, and possibly the largest in number, are those concerning the Russian ballet in its Diaghilev manifestation. The Russian ballet seems to have been Craig's *bête-noire* in movement. His denunciation is fiery against Diaghilev, Bakst, the dancers, the choreographers. In an article concerning the Russian Ballet in the July 1913 issue of *The Mask,* Craig writes:

In Art there must be created no feeling of disharmony between the Body and the Soul, yet in creating Art, the body must be obedient, true, faithful to the Soul. . . ."Glorious," "wonderful," "brilliant," these are the words used towards the works of Art made by the Body today. By these works the mob excuses its own ignorance and comforts its cowardice. . . . for the mob, fearing the individual, stands as much for the Body today as it has always done: the mob, . . . . that which is everlastingly fickle and detests the Soul, . . . . the inspirer . . . . that which alone remains unconquerable through faith . . . . the Russian Ballet is essentially the "Art" which is created by the Body. Its perfection is physical. Its appeal is to our senses, not through them . . . . The Russian Ballet is held to be the finest achievement of the New Theatre. The Russian Ballet belongs to the Theatre of Yesterday.[29]

Not only was Craig angered by the artificial use of the human body in ballet, but he thought, as well, that native or folk dances were too often being ignored because of the fad, still with us, of admiring what is foreign to us: ". . .we can't be expected any longer to be enthusiastic about a group of foreigners who had given us quite the wrong notions of dancing. We mustn't dance that way . . . . English dances say one thing, Russian another. Would you have our coming Shakespeare writing plays to the model Tchekov offers? Are we so utterly tongue-tied, brain-frozen, leg-bound and blind that we must ape the foreigner. I know we are not. What on earth makes us do it?"[30]

What was it that Craig wanted in art, in theatre, in dance? A return to the natural, to nature. Not a slavish imitation of nature but to make use of nature as an inspiration for art rather than an arbitrary adoption of mannered artificiality. Not only did Craig seek this goal through his vision of movement in the stage picture, the lighting and the performer but other avant-garde visionaries in the performing arts did so as well. Eleonora Duse is quoted as saying: "To save the theatre, the theatre must be destroyed, the actors and actresses must all die of the plague. They poison the air, they make art impossible. It is not drama that they play but pieces for the theatre. We should return to the Greeks, play in the open air; the drama dies of stalls and boxes and evening dress, and people who come to digest their dinner."[31]

In "The Great Source" Isadora Duncan wrote: "The great and the only principle on which I feel myself justified in leaning, is a constant, absolute and universal unity between form and movement; a rhythmic unity which runs through all the manifestations of nature. The waters, the winds, the plants, living creatures, the particles of matter itself obey this controlling rhythm of which the characteristic line is the wave. In nothing does Nature suggest jumps and breaks; there is between all the conditions of life a continuity or flow which the dancer must respect in his art, or else become a mannequin—outside Nature and without true beauty."[32]

Craig, too, sought a return to nature through the spirit of ancient Greece because its art was so natural: the stage building was a real building, the spectators readily identified with the chorus because it was made up of real individuals moving, dancing, in a natural fashion. In addition, there was the natural movement of light across the stage. In unidentified manuscript notes, possibly in preparation for his 1932 *Observer* article, "Animadversions on Dancers," Craig ruminated:

Dancing is not flying . . . we realize that man is not a bird. Dancing belongs very certainly to the good earth . . . Yet I believe I am right in saying that most trainers teach the pupils to hop, to float, to do everything to get into the air. I would teach them exactly the reverse for my reason tells me that the dancer has two well made feet on which to stand firm while dancing—that these feet will carry him if he wishes to advance or retreat, go sideways or stand still—but that these feet are not meant to do more than this. When you eat a boiled egg, you do not suspend it from a string or keep it tossing in the air—you plant it firmly in that admirable invention, an egg cup—. . . It is the 4 wheels which are the essentials of the cart or the carriage or motor car. These are to be kept on the ground no matter where the body of the carriage may be dragged—whereas the flying ship is never to be on the ground at all—except for just the few moments of starting. But then flying ship and dancer are dissimilar in that the dancer has no motor to propell him through space & no helicopter to keep him suspended there.[33]

1. Lincoln Kirstein. *Movement & Metaphor.* (New York, 1970), p. 4.
2. Walter Sorell. *The Dance Through the Ages.* (New York, 1967), p. 9.
3. Edward Craig. *Gordon Craig. The Story of His Life.* (London, 1968), pp. 117-118.
4. "Dido and Aeneas" and "Diocletian." N. p. [March 24, 1901].
5. Edward Craig, p. 136.
6. Martin Shaw. *Up to Now.* (London, 1929), p. 28.
7. Denis Bablet. *Edward Gordon Craig.* (London, 1966), p. 48.
8. Bablet, p. 49.
9. Edward Gordon Craig. *The Art of the Theatre.* (Edinburgh and London, 1905), p. 8.
10. Edward Gordon Craig. *Towards a New Theatre.* (London and Toronto, 1913), p. 43.
11. *Ibid.,* p. 61.
12. Edward Gordon Craig. "Memories of Isadora Duncan," *The Listener,* XLVII, 1214 (June 5, 1952), pp. 913-914.
13. Isadora Duncan. *My Life.* (New York, 1928), p. 10.
14. Walter Terry. *Isadora Duncan. Her Life, Her Art, Her Legacy.* (New York, 1964), pp. 20-21.
15. *My Life,* p. 75.
16. *The Art of the Theatre,* p. 54.
17. *Ibid.,* p, 54.
18. Edward Gordon Craig. "The Actor and the Über-Marionette," *The Mask,* I, 2 (April, 1908), pp. 3-15.
19. *Ibid.*
20. Edward Gordon Craig. *On the Art of the Theatre.* (London, 1962), pp. ix-x.
21. Edward Gordon Craig. *The Theatre Advancing.* (London, 1921), p. 260.
22. Paul Magriel, ed. *Isadora Duncan.* (New York, 1947), pp. 3-4.
23. *The Theatre Advancing,* p. 280.

24. Adolf Furst. "A Note on Marionettes," *The Mask*, II, 4-5-6 (October, 1909), pp. 72-76.

25. Edward Craig, p. 234.

26. *Ibid.*, p. 289.

27. Unsigned. "Modern Dancing and Dancers by J.E. Crawford Flitch, M.A.," *The Mask*, V, 1 (July, 1912), pp. 81-82.

28. "Memories of Isadora Duncan."

29. Edward Gordon Craig. "The Russian Ballet," *The Mask*, VI, 1 (July, 1913), pp. 6-14.

30. Unsigned. *"The Star of Piccadilly* by Lewis Melville, *Enemies of Society* by Charles Kingston, *Souvenirs du Vieux Colombier* by Berthold Mahn, *Some Studies in Ballet* by Arnold Haskell," *The Mask*, XIV, 2 (April-May-June, 1928), p. 90.

31. Arthur Symons. *Studies in Seven Arts*. (New York, 1907), p. 336.

32. Isadora Duncan. *The Art of the Dance*. (New York, 1928), p. 102.

33. Edward Gordon Craig. *Dancing is Not Flying*. Manuscript (State I), n.d.

# PART I.

GORDON CRAIG ON THE THEORY OF MOVEMENT

## A NOTE ON MASKS by John Balance. *The Mask,* Volume I, no. 1, March, 1908.

lmost all the things which had to do with the Theatre of the ancients have so degenerated to the ludicrous that it is impossible to speak of these things of the ancient Theatre without evoking laughter, . . . laughter in the common people and a particular kind of bored drawl in many of the educated. It seems to me that I shall never forget trying to explain to a certain Doctor T . . . that a piece of work which a friend of mine had just invented for the Theatre was to be given without the use of words. He could not permit (I remember his gravity) that a serious subject should be treated on the stage without long discourses in words. And when I assured him of my friend's resolve to do this, how strange was the tone with which Doctor T . . . shot out the one word, "Ah, Pantomime?"

Dancing, Pantomime, Marionettes, Masks; these things so vital to the ancients, all parts of their respected Art of the Theatre at one time or another, have been all turned into a jest. Dancing—a straight toe like an icicle, strapped in like a 'Bambino', in an over-pink tight; something on the top of it like a powder puff, and the whole thing sent whirling at an enormous rate like a teetotum, . . . . it is the modern public dancer.

Or two persons like bears hugging one another, and slowly and heavily as bears growling their way round a room, plod, plod, plod, bump, plod bump, . . . . this is the modern private dancer. And it is permitted.

These things being permitted and being so obviously ridiculous, and being labelled as the dance, it stands to reason that when the word "Dance" is mentioned seriously one of these ridiculous pictures is conjured up by the listener. Indeed, people are even prevailed upon to smile on reading in the Bible that King David danced among the women before the Ark. They picture to themselves a fancy King David attired either as a powder puff or a bear, whirling or lumbering round on a dusty road . . . probably uphill. Why, the thing is inconceivable! It is no use for the Royal Academicians to draw a picture of the famous Artist-King as sedately advancing with a harp in his hands like a courtier of the time of Louis XIV. Here again the thing becomes inconceivable; and as the imagination of man is not very brilliant, it stands to reason that people give up the idea of serious and beautiful dancing as having really existed, and fall back into the modern distortion.

The case is even worse with Pantomime. At the best the world conceives pantomime to be what the French actors are so good at and at the worst they think it is Clown and Pantaloon. French actors are amusing and delightful; Clown and Pantaloon are entrancing, but these beings are undoubtedly not the exponents of the Art of Pantomime.

So if you point out the case of Buddah teaching symbolic gesture of ''Pantomime'' to his pupils the world will instantly think of Harlequinade or of ''L'Enfant Prodigue,'' and, dressing Buddah, (in their mind's eye) in coloured, diamond-patterned tights or the loose white costume of Pierrot, will giggle as they try to be serious about it all.

The Marionette, too; mention him in good society, even in learned society, and there will be an awkward moment or two. It seems that he has become one of those things that one must not mention; like the novels of Dumas, he is only for boys and girls; and if you remind anyone that he figured in the Feast of Bacchus when the Egyptians celebrated these rites, people will instantly think of a poor doll tied to a stick and resembling nothing so much as Aunt Sally. If you remind people of what Mr. Anatole France writes of these strange and wonderful beings, the Marionettes, they will probably put Mr. Anatole France down as an eccentric gentleman. He happens to be an artist and knows about what he is speaking, so let us hear what he says: . . .

''J'ai vu deux fois les marionnettes de la rue Vivienne, et j'y ai pris un grand plaisir. Je leur sais un gré infini de remplacer les acteurs vivants. S'il faut dire toute ma pensée, les acteurs me gâtent la comédie. J'entends les bons acteurs. Je m'accommoderais encore des autres! Mais ce sont les artistes excellents, comme il se trouvent à la Comédie-Française, que décidement je ne puis souffrir! Leur talent est trop grand; il couvre tout! Il n'y a qu'eux.'' And again: ''J'en ai déjà fait l'aveu, j'aime les marionnettes, et celles de M. Signoret me plaisent singulièrement. Ce sont des artistes qui les taillent; ce sont des poètes qui les montrent. Elles ont une grâce naïve, une gaucherie divine de statues qui consentent à faire les poupées, et l'on est ravi de voir ces petites idoles jouer la comédie . . . Ces marionnettes ressemblent à des hiérogliphes Egyptiens, c'est-à-dire à quelque chose de mystérieux et de pur, et, quand elles représentent un drame de Shakespeare ou d'Aristophane, je crois voir la pensée du poète se dérouler en caractères sacrés sur les murailles d'un temple.'' And finally: ''Il y a une heure à peine que la toile du *Petit Théâtre* est tombée sur le groupe harmonieux de Ferdinand et de Miranda. Je suis sous le charme et, comme dit Prospero, "je me ressens encore des illusions de cette île." L'aimable spectacle! Et qu'il est vrai que les choses exquises, quand elles sont naïves, sont deux fois exquises." (La "Vie Littéraire" et "Le Temps.")

So much then for Dancing, Pantomime, the Marionette; and now for Masks.

Used by the savages when making war at a time when war was looked on as an art; used by the ancients in their ceremonies when faces were held to be too weak and disturbing an element; used by those great artists of the theatre, Aeschylus, Sophocles and Euripides; rejected later on by the vanity of the actors, and relegated by them to the toy-shop and the fancy-dress ball, the Mask has sunk to the level of the Dance, of Pantomime and of the Marionette. From being a work of art carved in wood and ornamented with precious metals, it has frittered itself away into a piece of paper, badly painted or covered with black satin.

I shall not here deal historically with the Mask, as this will be fully gone into in another number and my particular wish is not to confuse the reader with the point at issue, which is the importance of the mask to the Life of the Theatre of today and of tomorrow. It is as important now as it was of old and is in no way to be included among the things we have to put aside as old fashioned, must in no way be looked upon merely as a curiosity, for its existence is vital to the Art of the Theatre.

The historical study of this question will only assist those who already perceive the value and importance of reviving in the Theatre the famous and beautiful vitality of its earlier days. To those who know nothing of this spirit the historical study of the Mask is valueless, for like antiquaries they will but collect material for the sake of collecting, and any old thing, provided it be of good craftsmanship and excessively rare, will attract them.

Gordon Craig, in his writings on the Theatre, speaks for the Mask over and over again. He sees the gain to the Theatre which is attached to this thing. What he tells us is not new, . . . it is what all artists know, but there lies intrinsic value today in hearing it definitely from the mouth of an artist sprung from one of the most productive families of the English Stage. He tells us that human facial expression is for the most part valueless, and that the laws of his Art tell him that "It is better, provided it is not dull, that instead of six hundred expressions, but six expressions shall appear upon the face." Later on he gives an example:—"the Judge sits in Judgment upon the Prisoner, and he shall display but two expressions, each of which is in just proportion with the other. He has two masks and on each mask one main *statement,* these statements being tempered by Reflections, . . . the hopes and fears and the rest of not merely the Judge, but of Justice and Injustice."

Craig "aims at taking us beyond reality; he replaces the pattern of the thing itself by the pattern which that thing evokes in his mind, the symbol of the thing." In saying this Arthur Symons recognises in Craig a descendent of the family of the ancient artists of the Theatre, for his aim was theirs, and the Mask a part of their strength,—the Mask, the symbol of the Human face.

It is this sense of being beyond reality which permeates all great art. We see it in the little clumsily painted pictures of those periods when the true *beyond* was of more importance than a right perspective, when the perspective of thought and feeling held its true value. We see it in the marvellous little Etruscan figures of but an inch high!—one faces me as I write,—a tiny little piece of bronze, charge with an overwhelming spirit, but which would be refused at the Royal Academy of today because its hand is as big as its head and the toes of the feet are not defined; because it does not wriggle itself into a pose, but is poised with firm conviction, . . . conviction, a thing detested by committees and hence refused admission in Academies.

Masks carry conviction when he who creates them is an artist, for the artist limits the statements which he places upon these masks. The face of the actor carries no such conviction: it is over-full of fleeting expression, . . . frail, restless; disturbed and disturbing, and, as Craig says elsewhere, on this account not *material* with which to make a work of art.

It is doubtful whether the actor will ever have the courage to cover his face with a mask again having once put it aside, and it is doubtful whether he shall see that it would serve as his gain. If it can be proved that it would be to the actor's loss and not his gain it will prove that the Actor and the Art of the Theatre are divided at the outset, and one of three things will happen:—either the Actor will drift further from the Art, or he will be destroyed in battling against the Art, or, finally, he will, like the phoenix, destroy himself to re-form himself, and so in a new shape advance with the Art for which he has sacrificed himself.

The mask will return to the Theatre; of that one seems to be assured; and there is no very great obstacle in the way although there is some slight danger attached to a misconception of its revival. First of all it is not the Greek mask which is going to be resuscitated; rather is it the English mask which is going to be created. There is something very depressing in the idea of groping among ruins for the remains of the past centuries. It is a great trade today, but not for the purposes of the Theatre. They dig for the marbles and the bronzes and the statuettes: they unearth tombs; they rummage even for crinolines of 1860; they admire these things.

The Theatre may admire the old Greek masks, but it must not dig in the ground for them; it must not collect them; it must not waste what power it has as a creator, attending to its fads; it must not play the antiquary.

That such a danger as this exists and needs guarding against is most evident. Some time ago, we do not know how far back, (the collector knows) the world became tired of creating and took unto itself the rage for the old fashioned.

"Pictures . . . . away with the young painters: let us fill our houses with the old paintings; drag them out of the churches, dig them out of the niches, scrape them off the walls; what does it matter! Hateful young men! Lovely old masters!"

"Sculpture . . . . quick, fly to Greece! Now's the time! Nobody's looking, . . . occupied with affairs, . . . no money in the country; a lot of money in the ground; dig it all up; let sculpture go to the dogs, and let the old remains come back from Athens to fill our collections."

"Music . . . . some young musician wants his symphony played, Nonsense, costs too much; have discovered splendid new piece in little old shop for one fife and a drum; never heard anything like it before! Wonderful discovery! Tell the young man to take up chemistry."

And so on and so on. This craze for the antique has become a general habit, and the more antique the more the craze. Old furniture, houses packed with old furniture; books, tapestries, all sorts of metal work, even down to coins,—though here the true collector, the millionaire, is careful to keep as modern as he can. And this love of the antique is growing so petty to-day that it is positively eating into the very people themselves and they are becoming as antique as that which they collect: with this difference, that the old stuff has life in it and they have none. This love of the antique has come into the Theatre now and then; it entered into England with William Poel and his Elizabethan Stage Society. Those who know Mr. Poel know him to be a man of distinction, cultivated, and an authority upon the stage of the 16th century. But what is that for the purpose of the living Theatre? All those connected with the stage should be distinguished and cultivated, and authorities on all questions pertaining to the stage; but they should possess that only as a basis, and on that basis they should build anew and not merely exhibit the basis itself, saying, "Lo, the ruins of the

16th century! tickets 6d; plan of excavation, 2d extra." There have been others besides Mr. Poel. There have been the revivalists of the so-called Greek Theatre, . . . a dreadful thing entirely in Greek; and so on.

It would be a sad thing, therefore, if masks, sham-Greek in idea, sham-Greek in their manufacture, should be brought into the Theatre, appealing to the curious only by creating a subject for small talk. No! the Mask must return to the Stage to restore expression, . . . the visible expression of the mind.

There is a second danger, . . . the danger of the innovator. As Art must not be antique, neither can it be up-to-date. I think it is Mr. Whistler who points out that Art has no period whatever. It has only vitality or affectation, and under 'affectation' come both the imitation of the antique and the up-to-date.

The vitality of the Art depends upon its artists and their willingness to work under the Laws which have ruled their Art from the commencement. Not Laws put down by committees to suit a period, but the commandments unspoken and uninscribed, the ever-living Law of Balance which is the heart of perfect Beauty and from which springs Freedom, . . . . that Freedom which we hope and believe is the soul of Truth. To move incessantly towards this is the aim of artists, and those of the Theatre must not lag behind.

As has been said many times before, this will be nothing new. It is what the men of the Theatre began thousands of years ago: it is what the men of the Theatre a few hundred years ago relinquished as beyond their strength. When we shall resume this we shall not be merely repeating: it will be no echo of a past century: the inspiration which led men to use the mask in past ages is the same now as it ever was and will never die. It is this inspiration that we shall act under and in which we trust. Therefore let no one attempt to put this thing aside as being of the antique, or an eccentric explosion of "l'Art Nouveau." I anticipate the charges so as to call attention to the class of person who is sure to have something to say against us. We all know the kind of individual who is continually heard laughing to scorn the vitality of his country and his age. He is an unhealthy creature and I am glad to find that in England he is already beginning to die out. For the last seven years a new spirit has awakened in England and everything is coming under its influence. There is a gaiety abroad and a sense of freedom which loosens the joints of our island and which gives to our dignified and solemn people an added grace of which they were much in need. Let the young men of the Theatre rememeber this and stand at ease, for there is a protective spirit abroad whom they can look to when they need support. No longer a stiff courtesy reigns in the Court, but a genial one; . . . one which I believe is friendly to all things young and vital, . . . which I hope is not to forget the young and vital Art of the Theatre.

---

## THE ARTISTS OF THE THEATRE OF THE FUTURE in two parts. *The Mask,* Volume I, no. 1, March, 1908. Volume I, nos. 3-4, May-June, 1908.

---

### PART ONE.

edicated to the young race of athletic workers in all the theatres.

Second thoughts. I dedicate this to the single coura-geous individuality in the world of the theatre who will some day master and remould it.

They say that second thoughts are best. They also say it is good to make the best of a bad job, and it is merely making the best of a bad job that I am forced to alter my first and more optimistic dedication to my second. Therefore the second thoughts *are* best. What a pity and what a pain to me that we should be obliged to admit it! No such race of athletic workers in the Theatre of today exists; degeneration, both physical and mental, is round us. How could it be otherwise? Perhaps no surer sign of it can be pointed to than that all those whose work lies in the Theatre are to be continually heard announcing that all is well and that the Theatre is today at its highest point of development.

But if all were well no desire for a change would spring up instinctively and continually as it ever does with those who visit or ponder on the modern Theatre. It is because the Theatre is in this wretched state that it becomes necessary that some one shall speak as I do; and then I look around me for those to whom I can speak and for those who will listen, and, listening, understand; and I see nothing but backs turned towards me . . . . the backs of a race of unathletic workers. Still the individual, the boy or man of personal courage, faces me. Him I see, and in him I see the force which shall create the race to come. Therefore to him I speak and I am content that he alone shall understand me. It is the man who will, as Blake says, "leave father, mother, houses and lands if they stand in the way of his art"; it is the man who will give up personal amibition and the temporary success of the moment . . . . he who will cease to desire an agreeable wealth of smooth guineas, but who shall demand as his reward nothing less than the restoration of his home, its liberty . . . . its health . . . . its power . . . . It is to him I speak.

You are a young man; you have already been a few years in a theatre, or you have been born of theatrical parents; or you have been a painter for a while but have felt the longing towards movement; or you have been a manufacturer. Perhaps you quarrelled with your parents when you were eighteen, because you wished to go on the stage, and they would not let you. They perhaps asked why you wanted to go on the stage, and you could give no reasonable answer because you wanted to do that which no reasonable answer could expain; in other words you wanted to fly. And had you said to your parents "I want to fly," I think that you would have probably got further than had you alarmed them with the terrible words, "I want to go on the stage."

Millions of such men have had the same desire, this desire for movement, this desire to fly, this desire to be merged in some other creature's being, and not knowing that it was the desire to live in the imagination, some have answered their parents, "I want to be an actor; I want to go on the stage."

It is not that which they want; and the tragedy begins. I think when walking, disturbed with this newly awakened feeling, a young man will say, "*perhaps* I want to be an actor"; and it is only when in the presence of the irate parents that in his desperation he turns the "perhaps" into the definite "I want."

This is probably your case. You want to fly; you want to exist in some other stage, to be intoxicated with the air, and to create this state in others.

Try and get out of your head now that you really want "to go on the stage." If unfortunately you are upon the stage, try and get out of your head then that you want to be an actor and that it is the end of all your desires. Let us say that you are already an actor; you have been so for four or five years, and already some strange doubt has crept upon you. You will not admit it to anyone; your parents would apparently seem to have been right; you will not admit it to yourself for you have nothing else but this one thing to cheer yourself with. But I'm going to give you all sorts of things to cheer yourself with, and you may with courage and complete good spirits throw what you will to the winds and yet lose nothing of that which you stood up for in the beginning. You may remain on, yet be above the stage.

I shall give you the value of my experience for what it is worth, and maybe it will be of some use to you. I shall try to sift what is important for us from what is unimportant; and if while I am telling you all this you want any doubts cleared or any more exact explanations or details you have only to ask me for them and I am ready to serve you.

To begin with, you have accepted an engagement from the manager of the Theatre. You must serve him faithfully, not because he is paying you a salary but because you are working under him. And with this obedience to your manager comes the first and the greatest temptation which you will encounter in your whole work.

Because you must not merely obey his words but his wishes; and yet you must not lose yourself. I do not mean to say you must not lose your personality because it is probable your personality has not come to its complete form. But you must not lose sight of that which you are in quest of, you must not lose the first feeling which possessed you when you seemed to yourself to be in movement with a sense of swinging upwards.

While serving your apprenticeship under your first manager listen to all he has to say and all he can show you about the theatre, about acting, and go further for yourself and search out that which he does not show you. Go where they are painting the scenes; go where they are twisting the electric wires for the lamps; go beneath the stage and look at the elaborate constructions; go up over the stage and ask for informations about the ropes and the wheels; but while you are learning all this about the Theatre and about acting be very careful to remember that outside the world of the Theatre you will find greater inspiration than inside it: I mean in nature. The other sources of inspiration are music and architecture.

I tell you to do this because you will not have it told you by your manager. In the Theatre they study from the Theatre. They take the Theatre as their source of inspiration, and if at times some actors go to nature for assistance, it is to one part of nature only, to that which manifests itself in the human being.

This was not so with Henry Irving, but I cannot stop here to tell you of him, for it would mean letter upon letter to put the thing clearly before you. But you can remember that as actor he was unfailingly right, and that he studied all nature in order to find symbols for the expression of his thoughts.

You will be probably told that this man whom I hold up to you as a peerless actor, did such and such a thing in such and such a way; and you will doubt my counsel; but with all respect to your present manager you must be very careful how much credence you give to what he says and to what he shows, for it is upon such tradition that the Theatre has existed and has degenerated.

When Henry Irving did is one thing; what they tell you he did is another. I have had some experience of this. I played in the same Theatre as Irving in Macbeth, and later on I had the opportunity of playing Macbeth myself in a theatre in the North or the South of England. I was curious to know how much would strike a capable and reliable actor of the usual fifteen years experience, especially one who was an enthusiastic admirer of Henry Irving. I therefore asked him to be good enough to show me how Irving had treated this or that passage; what he had done and what impression he had created because it had slipped my memory. The competent actor thereupon revealed to my amazed intelligence something so banal, so clumsy, and so lacking in distinction, that I began to understand how much value was in tradition; and I have had several such experiences.

I have been shown by a competent and worthy actress how Mrs. Siddons played Lady Macbeth. She would move to the centre of the stage and would begin to make certain movements and certain exclamations which she believed to be a reproduction of what Mrs. Siddons had done. I presume she had received these from someone who had seen Mrs. Siddons. The things which she showed me were utterly worthless in so far as they had no unity, although one action here, another action there, would have some kind of reflected value; and so I began to see the uselessness of this kind of tuition; and it being my nature to rebel against those who would force upon me something which seemed to me unintelligent, I would have nothing to do with such teaching.

I do not recommend you to do the same, although you will disregard what I say and do as I did if you have much of the volcano in you; but you will do better to listen, accept and adapt that which they tell you, *remembering* that this your apprenticeship as actor is but the very beginning of an exceedingly long apprenticeship as craftsman in all the crafts which go to make up the art.

When you have studied these thoroughly you will find some which are of value and you will certainly find that the experience as actor has been necessary. The pioneer seldom finds an easy road and as your way does not end in becoming a celebrated actor but is a much longer and an untrodden way leading to a very different end, you will have all the advantages and disadvantages of pioneering; but keep in mind what I have told you; that your aim is *not* to become a celebrated actor, it is not to become the manager of a so-called successful theatre; it is not to become the producer of elaborate and much talked of plays; it is to become an Artist of the Theatre; and as a base to all this you must, as I have said, serve your term of apprenticeship as actor faithfully and well. If at the end of five years as actor you are convinced that you know what your future will be; if, in fact, you are succeeding, you may give yourself up for lost. Short cuts lead nowhere in this world. Did you think when the longing came upon you and when you told your family that you must go upon the stage that such a great longing was to be so soon satisfied? Is satisfaction so small a thing? Is desire a thing of nothing, that a five year's quest can make a parody of it? But of course not. Your whole life is not too long, and then only at the very end will some small atom of what you have desired come to you. And so you will be still young when you are full of years.

---

## PART TWO.

---

### ON THE ACTOR.

---

As a man he ranks high . . . . possesses generosity, and the truest sense of comradeship. I call to mind one actor whom I know and who shall stand as the type. A genial companion, and spreading a sense of companionship in the theatre; generous in giving assistance to younger and less accomplished actors, . . . . continually speaking about the work, . . . . picturesque in his manner, . . . . able to hold his own when standing at the side of the stage instead of in the centre; . . . . with a voice which commands my attention when I hear it, . . . . and finally, with about as much knowledge of the art as a cuckoo has of anything which is at all constructive. Anything to be made according to plan or design is foreign to his nature. But his good nature tells him that others are on the stage besides himself, and that there must be a certain feeling of unity between their thoughts and his, yet this arrives by a kind of good natured instinct and not through knowledge, & produces nothing positive. Instinct and experience have taught him a few things, I am not going to call them tricks , which he continually repeats. For instance, he has learned that the sudden drop in the voice from forte to piano has the power of accentuating and thrilling the audience as much as the crescendo from the piano into the forte. He also knows that laughter is capable of very many sounds, and not merely Ha Ha Ha. He knows that geniality is a rare thing on the stage and that the bubbling personality is always welcomed. But what he does not know is this . . . . that this same bubbling personality and all this same instinctive knowledge doubles or even trebles its power when guided by scientific knowledge, that is to say, by art. If he should hear me say this now he would be lost in amazement and would consider that I was saying something which was finicking, dry, and not at all for the consideration of an artist. He is one who thinks that emotion creates emotion, and hates anything to do with calculation. It is not necessary for me to point out that all art has to do with calculation and that the man who disregards this can only be but half an actor. Nature will not alone supply all which goes to create a work of art, for it is not the privilege of trees, mountains and brooks to create works of art, or everything which they touch would be given a definite and beautiful form. It is the particular power which belongs to man alone, and to him through his intelligence and his will. My friend probably thinks that Shakespeare wrote Othello in a passion of jealousy and that all he had to do was to write the first words which came into his mouth; but I am of the opinion, . . . . and I think others hold the same opinion, . . . . that the words had to pass through our author's head and that it was just through this process and through the quality of his imagination and the strength of his brain that the richness of his nature was able to be entirely and clearly expressed, and by no other process could he have arrived at this.

Therefore it follows that the actor who wishes to perform . . . . Othello, let us say, must have not only the rich nature from which to draw his wealth, but must also have the imagination to know what to bring forth, and the brain to know how to put it before us. Therefore the ideal actor will be the man who possesses both a rich nature and a powerful brain. Of his nature we need not speak. It will contain everything. Of his brain we can say that the finer the brain the less liberty will it allow itself, remembering how much depends upon its co-worker, the Emotion, and also the less liberty will it allow its fellow-worker knowing how valuable to it is its sternest control. Finally, the intellect would bring both itself and the emotions to so fine a sense of reason that the work would never boil to the bubbling point with its restless exhibition of activity, but would create that perfect moderate heat which it would know how to keep temperate. The perfect actor would be he whose brain could conceive and could show us the perfect symbols of all which his nature contains. He would not ramp and rage up and down in Othello, rolling his eyes and clenching his hands in order to give us an impression of jealousy; he would tell his brain to enquire into the depths, to learn all that lies there, and then to remove itself to another sphere, the sphere of the imagination, and there fashion certain symbols which, without exhibiting the bare passions, would none the less tell us clearly about them. And the perfect actor who should do this would in time find out that the symbols are to be made mainly from material which lies outside his person. But I will speak to you fully about this when I get to the end of our talk. For then I shall show you that the actor as he is today, must ultimately disappear and be merged in something else if works of art are to be seen in our kingdom of the Theatre.[1]

Meantime do not forget that the very nearest approach that has ever been to the ideal actor, with his brain commanding his nature, has been Henry Irving. There are many books which tell you about him, and the best of all the books is his face. Procure all the pictures, photographs, drawings, you can of him, and try to read what is there. To begin with you will find a mask, and the significance of this is most important. I think you will find it difficult to say when you look on the face, that it betrays the weaknesses which may have been in the nature. Try and conceive for yourself that face in movement, . . . . movement which was ever under the powerful control of the mind. Can you not see the mouth being made to move by the brain, and that same movement which is called expression creating a thought as definite as the line of a draughtsman does on a piece of paper or as a chord does in music? Cannot you see the slow turning of those eyes and the enlargement of them ? These two movements alone contained so great a lesson for the future of the art of the theatre, . . . . pointed out so clearly the right use of expression as opposed to the wrong use, that it is amazing to me that many people have not seen more clearly what the future must be. I should say that the face of Irving was the connecting link between that spasmodic and ridiculous expression of the human face as used by the theatres of the last few centuries, and the masks which will be used in place of the human face in the near future.

Try and think of all this when losing hope that you will ever bring your nature as exhibited in your face and your person under sufficient command. Know for a truth that there is something other than your face and your person which you may use and which is easier to control. Know this, but make no attempt yet awhile to close with it. Continue to be an actor, continue to learn all that has to be learned, as to how they set about controlling the face, and then you will learn finally that it is not to be entirely controlled.

I give you this hope so that when this moment arrives you will not do as the other actors have done. They have been met by this difficulty and have shirked it, have compromised, and have not dared to arrive at the conclu-

15

sion which an artist must arrive at if faithful to himself. That is to say, that the mask is the only right medium of portraying the expressions of the soul as shown through the expressions of the face.

---

## ON THE STAGE MANAGER.

---

After you have been an actor you must become a stage manager. Rather a misleading title this, for you will not be permitted to manage the stage. It is a peculiar position and you can but benefit by the experience, though the experience will not bring either great delights to you or great results to the theatre in which you work. How well it sounds, this title, Stage manager! it indicates "Master of the science of the stage."

Every theatre has a stage manager, yet I fear there are no masters of the stage science. Perhaps already you are an under stage manager. You will therefore remember the proud joy you felt when you were sent for, and, with some solemn words, informed that your manager had decided to advance you to the position of stage manager, and begged to remind you of the importance of the post, and of the additional one or two pennies that go with the situation. I suppose that you thought that the great and last wonderful day of your dream had arrived, and you held your head a little higher for a week, and looked down on the vast land which seemed to stretch out before you.

But after then, what was it? Am I not right in saying that it meant an early attendance at the theatre to see after the carpenters, and whether the nails had been ordered, and whether the cards were fixed to the doors of the dressing rooms? Am I not right in saying that you had to descend again to the stage and stand around waiting to see if things were done on time? . . . . whether the scenery was brought in and hung up to time? Did not the costumière come tearfully to you saying that some one had taken a dress from its box and substituted another? Did you not request the costumière to bring the offending party before you? and did you not have to manage these two in some tactful way so as to offend neither of them, and yet so as to get at the truth of the matter? . . . . And did you ever get at the truth of the matter? And did these two go away nursing anything but a loathèd hate towards you? . . . . Put the best case, . . . . one of them liked you, and the other began to intrigue against you the next hour. Did you find yourself still on the stage at about half past ten, and did not the actors arrive at that hour apparently in total ignorance that you had been there already four hours, and with their superb conviction that the doors of the theatre had just that moment been opened because they had arrived? And did not at least six of these actors in the next quarter of an hour come up to you and with an "I say, old chap," or "Look here, old fellow," start asking you to arrange something for them on the stage so as to make their task a little easier? And were not the things which they asked all so opposed one to the other, that to assist any one actor would have been to offend the other five? Having told them that you would do your best, were you not relieved by the sudden appearence of the director of the theatre, . . . . generally the chief actor? And did you not instantly go to him with the different requests which had been made to you, hoping that he, as master, would take the responsibility of arranging all these different matters? And did he not reply to you, "Don't bother me with these details; please do what you think best," and did you not then instantly know in your heart of hearts that the whole thing was a farce, . . . . the title, the position, and all?

And then the rehearsal commenced. The first words are spoken; the first difficulty arrives. The play opens with a conversation between two gentlemen seated at a table. Having gone on for about five minutes, the director interrupts with a gentle question. He asks if he is not correct in saying that at yesterday's rehearsal Mr. Brown rose at this or that line, twisting his chair back with a sudden movement? The actor, a trifle distressed that he has been the cause of the first delay in the day's proceedings, and yet not wishing to take any fault to himself, asks with equal courtesy, "Are these the chairs which we are supposed to use on the night?" The director turns to the stage manager, and asks him, "Are these the chairs we use upon the night?" "No, Sir," replies the stage manager. A momentary look of disapproval, ever so slight, passes from the director, and is reflected upon the faces of the two actors and a little restless wind passes round the theatre. It is the first little hitch. "I think it would be best to use at rehearsal the chairs we are going to use on the night." "Certainly, Sir,!" The stage manager claps his hands. "Isherwood," he cries, . . . A thin, sad looking little man, with a mask which is impenetrable on account of its extreme sadness, comes on to the stage and stands before the judgment seat. He hesitates. "We shall use the chairs at rehearsal which have been ordered for this scene." "No chairs, Sir, have been ordered for this scene." The wind rises. A sharp flash of lightening shows itself on the face of the director, and a sudden frown of thunder hangs upon the brows of the actors. The stage manager asks to see the property list, that is to say, the list of things used in the scene. Isherwood casts his eyes pathetically across the desert of the stage in search of the leading lady. Being the wife of the director, she has seen no reason for arriving in time. When she arrives she will have the look

*17*

upon her face of having been concerned with more important business elsewhere. Isherwood replies, "I had orders, Sir, to put these two chairs in Scene II, as they are chairs with pink and red brocade." Great moment for the director. Thunder clap, . . . . "Who gave you these orders,"? "Miss Jones." (Miss Jones is the daughter of the leading lady who is the wife of the director. Her position is not defined in the theatre, but she may be said to "assist her mother.") Hence the absence of the chairs. . . . Hence the irritation of the entire company . . . . Hence the waste of time in many theatres and certainly in many English Theatres.

This is but one and the first trial of the stage manager, who rather plays the part of the tyre than the axle of the wheel of the stage. The rehearsal continues. The stage manager has to be there all the time with but little control and permitted to have less opinions, and yet held responsible for all errors; and after it is over, while the actors may retire to their luncheon, he must retire to the property room, the scene painting room, the carpenters room, must hear all their grievances, must see everything being delayed and when the company returns to the theatre fresh after a pause of an hour or so he is expected to be as fresh and as good humoured *without* a break of a minute. This would be an easy & pleasant matter if he had the authority of his title; that is to say, if in his contract lay the words "Entire and absolute control of the stage and all that is on the stage."

But it is none the less a good if a strange experience. It teaches the man who assumes these terrible responsibilities how great a need there is for him to study the science of the stage, so that when it comes to his turn to be the director of the theatre, he may dispense with the services of a so-called 'stage manager' by being the veritable stage manager himself.

You will do well, after having remained an actor for five years to assume these difficult responsibilities of stage manager for a year or two, and never forget that it is a position capable of development. About the ideal stage manager I have written in my book "The Art of the Theatre," and I have shown there that the nature of his position should make him the most important figure in the whole world of the theatre. It should therefore be your aim to become such a man, . . . one who is able to take a play and produce it himself, . . . . rehearsing the actors and conveying to them the requirements of each movement, each situation; . . . . designing the scenery and the costumes and explaining to those who are to make them the requirements of these scenes and costumes; . . . . and working with the manipulators of the artificial light, and conveying to them clearly what is required.

Now, if I had nothing better to bring to you than these suggestions, if I had no further ideal, no further truth, to reveal to you about the stage and about your future than this that I have told you of, I should consider that I had nothing to give you whatever and I should urge you to think no more of the theatre. But I told you at the beginning of my letter that I was going to give you all sorts of things to cheer yourself with, so that you should have absolute faith in the greatness of the task which you set out to achieve; and here I remind you of this again lest you should think that this ideal manager of whom I speak is the ultimate achievement possible for you. It is not. Read what I have written about him in the "Art of the Theatre," and let that suffice you for the time being; but rest perfectly sure that I have more, much more to follow, and that your Hope shall be so high, that no other Hope, not even that of the poets or the priests, shall be higher.

To return to the duties of the stage manager. I take it that I have already explained to you, or that you have already experienced, these ordinary difficulties, and that you have learned that great tact is required and no great talent. You have only to take care that in exercising this tact you do not become a little diplomatist, for a little diplomatist is a dangerous thing. Keep fresh your desire to emerge from that position, and your best way to do this is to study how to master the different materials which, later on, you will have to work in when your position is that of the ideal stage manager. You will then possess your own theatre, and what you place upon your stage will all be the work of your brain, much of it the work of your hands, and you must waste no time so as to be ready.

---

## ON SCENE AND MOVEMENT.

---

It is now time to tell you how I believe you may best become a designer of stage scenery and costumes, and how you may learn something about the uses of artificial light; how you may bring the actors who work with you to work in harmony with each other, with the scene, and, most of all, with the ideas of the author. You have been studying, and will go on studying, the works which you wish to present. Let us here limit them to the four great tragedies by Shakespeare. You will know these so well by the time you begin to prepare them for the stage, . . . . and the preparation will take you a year or two for each play . . . you will have no more doubts as to what impression you want to create; your exercise will be to see how best you can create that impression.

Let me tell you then at the commencement that It Is the large and sweeping impression produced by means of scene and the movement of the figures, which is undoubtedly the most valuable means at your disposal. I say this only after very many doubts and after much experience; and you must always bear in mind that it is from my experience that I speak, and that the best I can do is but to offer you that experience. Although you know that I have parted company with the popular belief that the *written* play is of any deep value to the Art of the Theatre, we are not going so far as that here. We are to accept it that the play still retains some value for us and we are not going to waste that; our aim is to increase it. Therefore it is, as I say, the production of general and broad effects appealing to the eye which will add a value to that which has already been made valuable by the great poet.

First and foremost comes the *scene.* It is ideal to talk about the distraction of scenery, because the question here is not how to create some distracting scenery, but rather how to create a place which harmonises with the thoughts of the poet.

Come now, we take "Macbeth." We know the play well. In what kind of place is that play laid? How does it look, first of all to our mind's eye, secondly to our eye?

I see two things. I see a lofty and steep rock, and I see the moist cloud which envelops the head of this rock. That is to say, a place for fierce and warlike men to inhabit, a place for phantoms to nest in. Ultimately this moisture will destroy the rock; ultimately these spirits will destroy the men. Now then, you are quick in your question as to what actually to create for the eye. I answer as swiftly . . . . place there a rock! Let it mount up high. Swiftly I tell you, . . . . convey the idea of a mist which hugs the head of this rock. Now, have I departed at all for one eighth of an inch from the vision which I saw in the mind's eye? But you ask me what form this rock shall take and what colour? What are the lines which are the lofty lines, and which are to be seen in any lofty cliff? . . . Go to them, glance but a moment at them; now quickly set them down on your paper; *the lines and their direction,* never mind the cliff. Do not be afraid to let them go high; they cannot go high enough; . . . . and remember that on a sheet of paper which is but two inches square, you can make a line which seems to tower miles in the air, and you can do the same on your stage for it is all a matter of proportion and nothing to do with actuality.

You ask about the colours? . . . What are the colours that Shakespeare had indicated for us? Do not first look at nature, but look in the play of the poet. Two; one for the rock, the man; one for the mist, the spirit. Now, quickly, take and accept this statement from me. Touch not a single other colour, but only these two colours through your whole progress of designing your scene and your costumes, yet forget not that each colour contains many variations. If you are timid for a moment and mistrust yourself or what I tell, when the scene is finished you will not see with your eye the effect you have seen with your mind's eye, when looking at the picture which Shakespeare has indicated.

It is this lack of courage, lack of faith in the value which lies in limitation and in proportion which is the undoing of all the good ideas which are born in the minds of the scene designers. They wish to make twenty statements at once. They wish to tell us not only of the lofty crag and the mist which clings to it; they wish to tell you of the moss of the Highlands and of the particular rain which descends in the month of August. They cannot resist showing that they know the form of the ferns of Scotland, and that their archeological research has been thorough in all matters relating to the castles of Glamis and Cawdor. And so in their attempt to tell us these many facts, they tell us nothing; all is confusion . . . . "Most sacrilegious murder hath broke ope the Lord's annointed Temple, and stole thence the life of the building."

So, do as I tell you. Practice with the pencil on paper both on a small scale and on a large scale; practice with colour on canvas; so that you may see for yourself that what I say to you is true . . . . and, if you are an Englishman, make haste! for if you do not others who read this in other countries will find in it technical truths and will outstrip you before you are aware of it. But the rock and its cloud of mist is not all that you have to consider. You have to consider that at the base of this rock swarm the clans of strange earthly forces, and that in the mist hover the spirits innumerable; . . . . to speak more technically you have to think of the 60 or 70 actors whose movements have to be made at the base of the scene, and of the other figures which obviously may not be suspended on wires, and yet must be seen to be clearly separate from the human and more material beings. It is obvious then that some curious sense of a dividing line must be created somewhere upon the stage so that the beholder, even if he look but with his corporal eye, shall be convinced that the two things are separate things. I will tell you how to do this. Line and proportion having suggested the material rock-like substance, tone and colour (one colour) will have given the ethereal to the mist-like vacuum. Now then, you bring this tone and colour downwards until it reaches nearly to the level of the floor; but you must be careful to bring this colour and this tone down in some place which is removed from the material rock-like substance.

You ask me to explain technically what I mean. Let your rock possess but half the width of the stage, Let it be the side of a cliff round which many paths twist, and let these paths mingle in one flat space taking up half or perhaps three quarters of the stage. You have room enough there for all your men and women. Now then, open your stage and all other parts. Let there be a void below as well as above, and in this void let your mist fall and fade; and from that bring the figures which you have fashioned and which are to stand for the spirits. I know you are yet not quite comfortable in your mind about this rock and this mist; I know that you have got in the back of your head the recollection that a little later on in the play come several 'interiors' as they are called. But, bless your heart, don't bother about that! call to mind that the interior of a castle is made from the stuff which is taken from the quarries. It is not precisely the same colour to begin with? and do not the blows of the axes which hew out the great stones give a texture to each stone which resembles the texture given it by natural means, as rain, lightening, frost? So you will not have to change your mind or change your impression as you proceed. You will have but to give variations of the same theme, the rock . . . . the brown; the mist . . . the grey; and by these means you will, wonder of wonders, actually have preserved unity. Your success will depend upon your capacity to make variations upon these two themes; but remember never to let go of the main theme of the play when searching for variations in the Scene.

By means of your scene you will be able to mould the movements of the actors, and you must be able to increase the impression of your numbers without actually adding another man to your 40 or 50. You must not therefore waste a single man, nor place him in such a position that an inch of him is lost. Therefore the places on which he walks must be the most carefully studied parts of the whole scene. But in telling you not to waste an inch of him I do not therefore mean to convey that you must *show* every inch of him. It is needless to say more on this point. By means of suggestion you may bring on the stage a sense of all things; the rain, the sun, the wind, the snow, the hail, the intense heat; but you will never bring them there by attempting to wrestle and close with nature, in order so that you may seize some of her treasure and lay it before the eyes of the multitude. By means of suggestion in movement you may translate all the passions and the thoughts of vast numbers of people, or by means the same you can assist your actor to convey the thoughts and the emotions of the particular character he impersonates. Actuality, accuracy of detail, is useless upon the stage.

Do you want further directions as to how to become a designer of scenes and how to make them beautiful, &, let us add for the sake of the cause, practical and inexpensive? I am afraid that if I were to commit my method to writing I should write something down which would prove not so much useless as bad. For it might be very dangerous for many people to imitate my method. It would be a different thing if you could study with me, practising what we speak about for a few years. Your nature would in time learn to reject that which was unsuited to it, and, by a daily and a much slower initiation, only the more important and valuable parts of my teaching would last. But I can give you now some more general ideas of things which you might do with advantage and things which you may leave undone. For instance, to begin with, don't worry;—particularly don't worry your brain, and for Heaven's sake don't think it is important that you have got to do something, especially something clever.

I call to mind the amount of trouble I had when I was a boy of 21 over the struggle to somehow produce designs traditional in character without feeling at all in sympathy with the tradition; and I count it as so much wasted time. I do not hold with others that it was of any value whatever. I remember making designs for scenes for Henry IV. I was working under an actor manager at the time. I was working in a theatre where the chairs and the tables and other matters of detail played important and photographic parts, and, not knowing any better, I had to take all this as a good example. The play of Henry IV therefore consisted to my mind of one excellent part, Prince Hal, and 30 or 40 other characters that trotted round this part. There was the usual table with the chairs round it on the right side. There at the back was the usual door, and I thought it rather unique and daring at the time to place this door a little bit off the straight. There was the window with the latches and the bolts and the curtains ruffled up to look as if they had been used for some time, and outside the glimpses of English landscape. There were the great flagons; and of course, on the curtain rising there was to be a great cluster and fluster of "scurvy knaves" who ran in and out, and a noise of jovial drinkers in the next room. There was the little piece of jovial music to take up the curtain, . . . . that swinging jig tune which we have all grown so familiar with, there were the three girls who pass at the back of the window, laughing. One pops her head in at the window with a laugh and a word to the potman. Then there is the dwindling of the laughter and the sinking to piano of the orchestra as the first speaking character enters, . . . and so on.

My whole work of that time was based on these stupid restless details which I had been led to suppose a production could be made from; and it was only when I banished the whole of this from my thoughts and no longer permitted myself to see with the eyes of the producers of the period of Charles Kean, that I began to find anything fresh which might be of value to the play. And so for me to tell you how to make your scenes is well nigh impossible. It would lead you into terrible blunders. I have seen some of the scenery which is supposed to be produced according to my teaching, and it is utter rubbish.

I let my scenes grow out of not merely the play, but from broad sweeps of thought which the play has conjured up in me, or even other plays by the same author have conjured up. For instance, the relation of Hamlet to Macbeth is quite close, and the one play may influence the other. I have been asked so many times by people eager to make a little swift success or a little money, to explain to them carefully, how I make my scenes; because, said they with sweet simplicity, "then I could make some too," You will hardly believe it, but the strangest of people have said this to me and if I could be of service to them without being treacherous to myself as an artist, and to the art, I would always do so. But you see how vain that would be! To tell them in five minutes or in five hours or even in a day how to do a thing which it has taken me a life time to begin to do would be utterly impossible. And yet when I have been unable to bring myself to tear my knowledge up into little shreds and give it to these people they have been most indignant, at times malignant.

And so you see it is not that I am unwilling to explain to you the size and shape of my back-cloths, the colour which is put upon them, the pieces of wood that are not to be attached to them, the way they are to be handled, the lights that are to be thrown upon them, and how and why I do everything else; it is only that if I were to tell you, though it might be of some service to you for the next two or three years, and you could produce several plays with enough effects therein to satisfy the curiosity of quite a number of people, . . . . though you would benefit to this extent you would lose to a far greater extent, and the Art would have in me its most treacherous minister. We are not concerned with short cuts. We are not concerned with what is to be effective and what is to pay. We are concerned with the heart [of] this thing, and with loving and understanding it. Therefore approach it from all sides, surround it, and do not let yourself be attracted away by the idea of scene as an end in itself, of costume as an end in itself, or of stage management or any of these things, and never lose hold of your determination to win through to the secret . . . . the secret which lies in the creation of another beauty and then all will be well.

In preparing a play, while your mind is thinking of scene, let it instantly leap around and consider the acting, movement and voice. Decide nothing yet, . . . instantly leap back to another thought about another part of this unit. Consider the movement robbed of all scene, all costume, merely as movement. Somehow mix the movement of the person with the movement which you see in your mind's eye in the scene. Now pour all your colour upon this. Now wash away all the colour. Now begin over again. Consider only the words. Wind them in and out of some vast and impossible picture, and now make that picture possible through the words. Do you see at all what I mean? Look at the thing from every standpoint and through every medium, and do not hasten to begin your work until one medium forces you to commence. You can far sooner trust other influences to move your will and even your hand than you can trust your own little human brain. This may not be the methodical teaching of the schools. The results they achieve are on record, . . . . and the record is nothing to boast about. Hard, matter of fact, mechanical teaching may be very good for a class, but it is not much good for the individual; and when I come to teach a class I shall not teach them so much by words as by practical demonstration.

By the way, I may tell you one or two things that you will find good not to do. For instance, do not trouble about the costume books. When in a great difficulty refer to one in order to see how little it will help you out of your difficulty, but your best plan is never to let yourself become complicated with these things. Remain clear and fresh. If you study how to draw a figure, how to put on it a jacket, coverings for the legs, covering for the head, and try to vary these coverings in all kinds of interesting, amusing, or beautiful ways, you will get much further than if you feast your eyes and confound your brain with Racinet, Planchet, Hottenroth and the others. The coloured costumes are the worst, and you must take great care with these and be utterly independent when you come to think about what you have been looking at. Doubt and mistrust them thoroughly. If you find afterwards that they contain many good things you will not be so far wrong; but if you accept them straight away your whole thought and sense for designing a costume will be lost; and you will be able to design a Racinet costume or a Planchet costume, and you will lean far too much on these historically accurate men who are at the same time historically untrue.

Better than these that I have mentioned is Viollet le Duc. He has much love for the little truths which underlie costume, and is very faithful in his attitude; but even his is more a book for the historical novelist, and one has yet to be written about imaginative costume. Keep continually designing such imaginative costumes. For example, many a barbaric costume; and a barbaric costume for a sly man which has nothing about it which can be said to be historical and yet is both sly and barbaric. Now make another design for another barbaric costume, for a man who is bold and tender. Now make a third for one who is ugly and vindictive. It will be an exercise. You will probably make blunders at first for it is no easy thing to do but I promise you if you persevere long enough you will be able to do it. Then go further; attempt to design the clothing for a divine figure and for a demonic figure: These of course will be studies in individual costumes, but the main strength of this branch of the work lies in the costume as mass. It is the mistake of all theatrical producers that they consider the costumes of the mass individually.

It is the same when they come to consider movements, the movements of masses on the stage. You must be careful not to follow the custom. We often hear it said that each member of the Meiningen Company composing the great crowd in Julius Caesar was acting a special part of his own. This may be very exciting as a curiosity, and attractive to a rather foolish audience, who would naturally say, "Oh, how interesting to go and look at one particular man in a corner who is acting a little part of his own! How wonderful! It is exactly like life!", . . . . And if that is the standard and if that is our aim, well and good.

But we know that it is not. Masses must be treated as masses, as Rembrandt treats a mass, as Bach, as Beethoven treats a mass, and detail has nothing to do with the mass. Detail is very well in itself and in its place. You do not make an impression of mass by crowding a quantity of details together. Detail is made to form mass only by those people who love the elaborate, and it is a much easier thing to crowd a quantity of details together, than it is to create a mass which shall possess beauty and interest. On the stage they instantly turn to the natural when they wish to create this elaborate structure. . . . A hundred men to compose a crowd, or, let us say, all Rome, as in Julius Caesar; a hundred men, and each is told to act his little part. Each acts himself, giving vent to his own cries; each a different cry, . . . . though many of them copy the most effective ones so that by the end of the first 20 nights they are all giving out the same cry. And each of them has his own action, which after the first twenty nights is exchanged for the most effective and popular action; and by this means a fairly decent crowd of men with waving arms and shouting voices may be composed, and may give some people the impression of a vast crowd. To others it gives the impression of a crush at a railway station.

Avoid all this sort of thing. Avoid the so-called 'naturalistic' in movement as well as in scene and costume. The naturalistic stepped in on the Stage because the artificial had grown finicking, insipid; . . . . but do not forget that there is such a thing as *noble* artificiality. Someone writing about natural movement and gesture says, "Wagner had long put in practice the system of *natural* stage action tried of late years at the Théâtre Libre in Paris by a French comedian; a system which, most happily, tends more & more to be generally adopted." It is to prevent such things being written that you exist.

This tendency towards the natural has nothing to do with art, and is abhorrent when it shows in art, even as artificiality is abhorrent when we meet it in every day life. We must understand that the two things are divided, and we must keep each thing in its place; we cannot expect to rid ourselves in a moment of this tendency to be "natural"; to make "natural" scenes, and speak in a "natural" voice, but we can fight against it best by studying the other arts.

Therefore we have to put the idea of natural or unnatural action out of our heads altogether, and in place of it we have to consider necessary or unnecessary action. The necessary action at a certain moment may be said to be the natural action for that moment; and if that is what is meant by 'natural' well and good. In so far as it is right it is natural, but we must not get into our heads that every haphazard natural action is right. In fact there is hardly any action which is right, there is hardly any which is natural. Action is a way of spoiling something, says Rimbaud.

And to train a company of actors to show upon the stage the actions which are seen in every drawing room, club, public house or garret must seem to everyone nothing less than tomfoolery. That companies are so trained is well known, but it remains almost incredible in its childishness. Just as I told you to invent costume which was significant, so must you invent a series of significant actions, still keeping in mind the great division which exists between action in the mass and action in the individual, and remembering that no action is better than little action.

I have told you to make three costumes based on the idea of a barbaric sense, each particularized by some special individuality. Give action to these figures which you have made. Create for them significant actions, limiting yourself to those three texts that I have given you, the sly, the bold tenderness, the ugly and vindictive. Make studies for these, carry your little book or pieces of paper with you and continually be inventing with your pencil little hints of forms and faces stamped with these three impressions; and when you have collected dozens of them select the most beautiful.

And now for a word on this. I particularly did not say the most 'effective' although I used the word 'beautiful' as the artists use it, not as those of the stage use it.

I cannot be expected to explain to you all that the artist means by the word beautiful; but to him it is something which has the most balance about it, the *justest* thing, that which rings a complete and perfect bell note. Not the pretty, not the smooth, not the superb always, and not always the rich, seldom the 'effective' as we know it in the theatre, although at times that, too, is the beautiful. But Beauty is so vast a thing, and contains nearly all other things; contains even ugliness, which sometimes ceases to be what is held as ugliness, and contains harsh things, but never incomplete things.

Once let the meaning of this word *"Beauty"* begin to be thoroughly felt once more in the theatre, and we may say that the awakening day of the theatre is near. Once let the word *'effective'* be wiped off our lips, and they will be ready to speak this word Beauty. When we speak about the effective, we in the theatre mean something which will reach across the foot lights. The old actor tells the young actor to raise his voice, to "Spit it out"; . . . . "Spit it out, laddie, fling it at the back of the gallery." . . . . Not bad advice either; but to think that this has not been learnt in the last five or six hundred years, and that we have not got *further;* that is what is so distressing about the whole business. Obviously all stage actions and all stage words must first of all be clearly seen, must be clearly heard. Naturally all pointed actions and all pointed speeches must have a clear and distinct form so that they may be clearly understood. We grant all this. It is the same in all art, & as with the other arts it goes without saying; but it is not the one & only essential thing which the elders must be continually drumming into the ears of the younger generation when it steps upon the stage. It teaches the young actor soon to become a master of tricks. He takes the short cut instinctively to these tricks, and this playing of tricks has been the cause of the invention of a word,—"Theatrical," and I can put my finger on the reason why the young actor labours under this disadvantage the moment he begins his stage experience. It is because previous to his experience he has passed no time as student or as apprentice.

I do not know that I am such a great believer in the schools. I believe very much indeed in the general school which the world has to offer us, but there is this great difference between the "world" schooling of the actor and the "world" schooling of the other artists who do not go to the Academies either. A young painter, or a young musician, a young poet, or a young architect, or a young sculptor may never enter an Academy during his life, and may have ten years knocking about in the world learning here, learning there, experimenting and labouring unseen and his experiments unnoticed. The young actor may not enter an Academy either, and he may also knock about in the world, and he too may experiment just the same as the others, but . . . . and here is the vast difference . . . . *all his experiments he must make in front of a public.* Every little atom of his work from the first day of his commencing until the last day of his apprenticeship must be seen, and must come under the fire of criticism. I shall ever be beholden to the higher criticism, and for a man of ten year's experience at any work to come under the fire of criticism will benefit him and his work a thousandfold. He has prepared himself; he has strength; he knows what he is going to face. But for every boy and girl to be subjected to this *the first year that they timidly attempt this enormous task is not only unfair on them but is disastrous to the art of the stage.*

Let us picture ourselves as totally new to this work. We are on fire with the desire to begin our work. Willingly and with an enormous courage we accept some small part. It is eight lines and we appear for ten minutes. We are delighted although almost in a panic. Say it is twenty lines . . . . Do you think we say no? We are to appear six times, . . . do you think we shall run away? We may not be angels but we are certainly not fools for stepping in. It appears to us heaven. On we go. . . . . Next morning . . . . "It is a pity that the manager elected an incompetent young man to fill so important a part."

I am not blaming the critic for writing this; I am not saying that it will kill a great artist or that it will break our heart; I only say that this seems so unfair that it is only natural that *we retaliate by taking an unfair advantage of the very art which we have commenced to love, by becoming "effective"* at all costs. We have received this criticism; we have done our best; the others have received good criticism; we can stand it no longer; we do as they do, . . . . we become *"effective."* It takes most young actors but five years' acute suffering to become effective, to become theatrical. Too early criticism breaks the young actor who would be an artist as far as possible, and causes him to be a traitor to the art which he loves. Beware of this and rather be ineffective. Receive your bad criticism with a good grace and with the knowledge that with patience and with pride you can outlive and outdistance all around you. It is right that the critic should say that you were ineffective at a certain moment, or that you played your part badly, if you have been but three, four or five years on the stage, and if you are but still feeling your way slowly, instead of rushing to tricks for support. It is quite right of them to say that, for they are speaking the entire truth; you should be glad of this; but unconsciously they disclose a still greater truth. It is this; That the better the artist the worse the actor.

So take entire courage. Continue as I have said at the beginning to remain an actor until you can stand it no longer, until you feel you are on the point of giving way; then leap nimbly aside into the position of stage manager. And here as I have pointed out you will be in a better position if not a much better position, for you are approaching the point at which stands, (slumbering, it is true) the artist of the theatre. Your most effective scenes, productions, costumes and the rest, will of course be the most theatrical ones. But here tradition is not so strong, and it is here that you will find something that you can rely on.

The critic is not more lenient towards the producer of plays, but some how or other he is less inclined to use the word 'effective'. He seems to have a wider knowledge of the beauty or the ugliness of these things. It may be that the tradition of his art permits him this; for "production," as it is understood nowadays, is but a more modern development of the theatre, and the critic has more liberty to say what he wishes. At any rate, when you become stage manager, you will no longer have to appear each evening upon the stage in person, and therefore anything which is written about your work you cannot take in a personal way.

I thought to tell you here something about the uses of artificial light; but apply what I have said of scene and costume to this other branch as well. Some of it may apply. To tell you of the instruments which they use, how they use them so as to produce beautiful results, is not quite practical. If you have the wit to invent the scenes and the costumes that I have spoken about, you will soon have the wit to find your own way of using the artificial light we are given in the theatre.

Finally, before we pass out of the theatre on to other more serious matters, let me give you the last advice of all. . . . . When in doubt listen to the advice of a man in a theatre even if he is only a dresser, rather than pay any attention to the amateur. A few painters, a few writers, and a few musicians, have used our theatre as a kind of after-thought.

Take care to pay no attention to what they say or what they do. An ordinary stage hand knows more about our art than these amateurs. The painter has lately been making quite a pretty little raid upon the outskirts of the stage. He is very often a man of much intellectual ability and full of very many excellent theories, the old and beautiful theory of art which each in his own piece of soil knows how to cultivate best; and these theories he has exemplified in his own particular branch of art so well. In the theatre they become sheer affectation. It is reasonable to suppose that a man who has spent fifteen to twenty years of his life painting in oils on a flat surface, etching on copper, or engraving on wood will produce something which is pictorial and has the qualities of the pictorial but nothing else. And so with the musician; he will produce something which is musical. So with the poet; he will produce something which is literary. It will all be very picturesque and pretty, but it will unfortunately be nothing to do with the Art of the Theatre. Beware of such men; . . . . you can do without them. If you have anything to do with them you will end by being an amateur yourself. If one of these should wish to talk with you about the theatre be careful to ask him how long he has actually worked in a theatre before you waste any more time listening to his unpractical theories.

And as the last but one word was about these men so the last word of all shall be about their *work*. Their work is so fine, they have found such good laws and have followed these laws so well, have given up all their worldly hopes in this one great search after beauty, that when nature seems to be too difficult to understand, go straight to these fellows, . . . . I mean to their work . . . . and they will help you out of all the difficulties, for they are the best and the wisest people in the world.

And now I intend to carry you on beyond this stage management about which I have spoken, and unveil to you some greater possibilities which I think are in store for you.

I have come to the end of talking with you about matters as they are, and I hope you will pass through those years as actor, manager, designer and producer without any very great disturbances. To do this successfully, although in your apprenticeship you must hold your own opinion, you must hold it very closely to yourself; and above all things remember that I do not expect you to hold my opinion or to stand up for it publicly. To do that would be to weaken your position and to weaken the value of this preparation time. It is of no value to me that people should be convinced of your belief in the truth of my statements, theories or practises: it is of great value to me that *you* should be so convinced. And so as to let nothing stand in the way of that I would have you run no risks, but keep our convictions to ourselves. Try to win no support for me. Run no risk of being faced with the dismissal from your post with the option of the denial of our mutual beliefs. Besides, there is no need for either of these two alternatives. I have taken so large a share of the rebuffs by loudly proclaiming my beliefs in the cause of the truth of this work, and am always prepared to take more if you will but leap forwards and secure the advantages, using me as the stalking horse. I shall appreciate the fun, . . . . for there is a spice of fun in it all . . . . and that will be my reward. Remember we are attacking a monster; a very powerful & subtle enemy; and when you signal to me let it be by that more secret means even than wireless telegraphy. I shall understand the communication.

When you have finished your apprenticeship, . . . . 6 to 10 years, . . . . there will be no need to use further concealment: you will then be fitted to step out and, in your turn, unfurl your banner, for you will be upon the frontier of your kingdom, . . . . and about this kingdom I will speak now.

I use the word 'Kingdom' instinctively in speaking of the land of the Theatre. It explains best what I mean. May be in the next three or four thousand years the word Kingdom will have disappeared, . . . . Kingdom, . . . . Kingship, . . . . King, . . . but I doubt it; and if it does go something else equally fine will take its place. It will be the same thing in a different dress. You can't invent anything finer than Kingship . . . the idea of the King. It is merely another word for the Individual, the calm shrewd personality; and so long as this world exists the calmest and the shrewdest personality will always be the King. It some rare instances he is called the President, but he is none the less the King. In some instances he is called the Pope, & sometimes the General; . . . . it all comes to the same thing, and it is no good denying it; he is the King. To the artist the thought is very dear. There is the sense of the perfect balancer. The king (to the artist) is that superb part of the scales, which the old workmen made in gold and sometimes touched with beautiful stones; . . . the delicately worked handle without which the scales could not exist and upon which the eye of the measurer must be fixed. Therefore I have taken as the device of our new Art these scales, for our art is based upon the idea of perfect balance, the result of movement.

Here then is the thing which I promised at the beginning to bring to you. Having passed through your apprenticeship without having been merged in the trade, you are fitted to receive this. Without having done so you would not even be able to see it. I have no fear that what I throw to you now will be caught by other hands because it is visible and tangible only to those who have passed through such an apprenticeship. . . . . In the beginning with you it was Impersonation; you passed on to Representation, and now you advance into Revelation. When Impersonating and Representing you made use of those materials which had always been made use of; that is to say, the human figure as exemplified in the actor, speech as exemplified in the poet through the actor, the visible world as shown by means of Scene. You now will reveal by means of movement the Invisible things, . . . those seen through the eye and not with the eye, by the wonderful and divine power of Movement.

There is a thing which man has not yet learned to master, a thing which man dreamed not was waiting for him to approach with love; it was invisible and yet ever present with him . . . . Superb in its attraction and swift to retreat, a thing waiting but for the approach of the right men . . . . prepared to soar with them through all the circles beyond the earth . . . . Movement.

It is somehow a common belief that only by means of words can truths be revealed. Even the wisdom of China has said. "Spiritual truth is deep and wide, of infinite excellence, but difficult of comprehension. . . . . Without words it would be impossible to expound its doctrine; without images its form could not be revealed. Words explain the law of two and six, images delineate the relation of four and eight. Is it not profound, . . . . as infinite as space, . . . . beyond all comparison lovely?"

. . . . But what of that infinite and beautiful thing drawn from space called Movement? From Sound has been drawn that wonder of wonders called Music. Music, . . . . one could speak of it as St Paul speaks of love. It is all love . . . . it is all that he says true love should be. It suffereth all things, & is kind; is not puffed up, doth not behave itself unseemly; believeth all things, hopeth all things, . . . . infinitely vast!

And as like as one sphere to another, so is movement like to music. I like to remember that all things spring from movement, even music; and I like to think that it is to be our supreme honour to be the ministers to the supreme force. . . . Movement. For you see where the theatre (even the poor distracted and desolate theatre) is connected with this service. The theatres of all lands, east and west, have developed (if a degenerate development) from movement . . . . the movement of the human form. We know so much for it is on record: and before the human being assumed the grave responsibility of using his own person as an instrument through which this Beauty should pass, there was another and a wiser race, who used other instruments.

In the earliest days the dancer was a priest or a priestess, . . . . and not a gloomy one by any means; too soon to degenerate into something more like the acrobat, and finally to achieve the distinction of the ballet dancer. By association with the minstrel, the actor appeared. I do not hold, that with the renaissance of the dance comes the renaissance of the ancient art of the theatre, for I do not hold that the ideal dancer is the perfect instrument for the expression of all that is most perfect in movement. The ideal dancer, male or female, is able by the strength or grace of the body to express much of the strength and grace which is in the nature, but it cannot express all, nor a thousandth part of that all. For the same truth applies to the dancer and to all those who use their own person as instrument. Alas, the human body refuses to be an instrument, even to the mind which lodges in that body. The sons of Los rebelled and still rebel against their father. The old divine unity, the divine square, the peerless circle of our nature has been ruthlessly broken by our moods, and no longer can instinct design the square or draw the circle on the grey wall before it. But with a significant gesture we thrill our souls once more to advance without our bodies upon a new road and win it all back again. This is a truth which is not open to argument, and a truth which does not lessen the beauty which exhales from the dearest singer or the dearest dancer of all times.

To me there is ever something more seemly in man when he invents an instrument which is outside his person, and through that instrument translates his message. I have a greater admiration for the organ, for the flute and for the lute than I have for the human voice when used as instrument. I have a greater feeling of admiration and fitness when I see a machine which is made to fly than when I see a man attaching to himself the wings of a bird. For a man through his person can conquer but little, but through his mind he can conceive and invent that which shall conquer all things.

I believe not at all in the personal magic of man, but only in his impersonal magic. It seems to me that we should not forget that we belong to a period after the Fall and not before it, . . . . I can at least extract a certain hint from the old story. And though it may be only a story, I feel that it is just the very story for the artist. In that great period previous to this event we can see in our mind's eye the person of man in so perfect a state that merely to wish to fly was to fly, merely to desire that which we call the impossible was to achieve it. We seem to see man flying into the air or diving into the depths and taking no harm therefrom. We see no foolish clothes, we are aware of no hunger and thirst. But now that we are conscious that this "square deific" has been broken in upon, we must realise that no longer is man to advance and proclaim that his person is the perfect and fitting medium for the expression of the perfect thought.

So we have to banish from our mind all thought of the use of a human form as the instrument which we are to use to translate what we call *Movement*. We shall be all the stronger without it. We shall no longer waste time and courage in a vain hope. The exact name by which this art will be known cannot yet be decided on, but it would be a mistake to return and look for names in China, India or Greece. We have words enough in our English language, and let the English word become familiar to the tongues of all the nations. I have written elsewhere, and shall continue to write, all about this matter as it grows in me, and you from time to time will read what I write. But I shall not remove from you the very difficulty which will be the source of your pleasure; I wish to leave all open and to make no definite rules as to how and by what means these movements are to be shown. This alone let me tell you. I have thought of and begun to make my instrument, and through this instrument I intend soon to venture in my quest of beauty. How do I know whether I can achieve that or not? Therefore how can I tell you definitely what are the first rules which you have to learn? Alone and unaided I can reach no final results. It will need the force of the whole race to discover all the beauties which are in this great source, . . . . this new race of artists to which you belong. When I have constructed my instrument and permitted it to make its first assay I look to others to make like instruments. Slowly, and from the principles which rule all these instruments some better instrument will be made.

I am guided in the making of mine by only the very first and simplest thoughts which I am able to see in movement. The subtleties and the complicated beauties contained in movement as it is seen in nature, these I dare not consider; I do not think I shall ever be able to hope to approach these. Yet that does not discourage me from attempting some of the plainest, barest and simplest movements, . . . . I mean those which seem to me the simplest, those which I seem to understand. And after I have given activity to those I suppose I shall be permitted to continue to give activity to the like of them; but I am entirely conscious that they contain but the simplest of rhythms . . . . the great movements will not yet be captured, . . . . no, not for thousands of years. But when they come, great health comes with them, for we shall be nearer balance than we have ever been before.

I think that movement can be divided into two distinct parts, . . . . the movement of two and four which is the square, the movement of one and three which is the circle. There is ever that which is masculine in the square and ever that which is feminine in the circle. And it seems to me that before the female spirit gives herself up, and with the male goes in quest of this vast treasure, perfect movement will not be discovered; for I believe that as only the male can conceive and can control that which is contained within the square, only the female can discover that which is contained in the circle.

I like to suppose that this art which shall spring from movement will be the first and final Belief of the world; and I like to dream that for the first time in the world men and women will achieve this thing together. How fresh, how beautiful it would be! And as this is a new beginning it lies before men and before women of the next centuries as a vast possibility. In men and women there is a far greater sense of movement than of music. Can it be that this idea which comes to me now will at some future date blossom through help of the woman, or will it be as ever the man's part to master these things alone? The musician is a male, the builder is a male, the painter is a male, and the poet is a male. Come now, here is an opportunity to change all this . . . . But I cannot follow the thoughts any further here, neither will you be able to.

Get on with the thought of the invention of an instrument by which means you can bring movement before our eyes. When you have reached this point in your developments you need have no further fear of hiding your feeling or your opinion, but may step forward and join me in the search. You will not be a revolutionary against the theatre, for you will have risen above the theatre and entered into something beyond it. Maybe you will pursue a scientific method in your search, and that will lead to very valuable results. There must be a hundred roads leading to this point, not merely one, and a scientific demonstration of all that you may discover can in no way harm this thing. Well, do you see any value in the thing I give you? If you do not at first you will bye and bye. I could not expect a hundred or even fifty, . . . no, not ten, to understand. But *one*? It is possible, . . . just possible.

1. See "The Actor & The Über-Marionette," p. 37.

# THE ACTOR AND THE ÜBER-MARIONETTE. *The Mask,*
Volume I, no. 2, April, 1908[1]

*"To save the Theatre, the Theatre must be destroyed, the actors and actresses*
*must all die of the plague. . . . They make art impossible."* —Eleonora Duse.
"Studies in Seven Arts." Arthur Symons. (Constable.)

t has always been a matter for argument whether or no
Acting is an art, and therefore whether the actor is an
Artist, or something quite different. There is little to
show us that this question disturbed the minds of the
leaders of thought at any period, though there is much
evidence to prove that had they chosen to approach
this subject as one for their serious consideration, they would have applied
to it the same method of enquiry as used when considering the arts of
Music and Poetry, or Architecture, Sculpture and Painting.

On the other hand there have been many warm arguments in certain
circles on this topic. Those taking part in it have seldom been actors, very
rarely men of the theatre at all, and all have displayed any amount of
illogical heat, and very little knowledge of the subject. The arguments
against acting being an art, and against the actor being an artist, are
generally so unreasonable and so personal in their detestation of the actor,
that I think it is for this reason the actors have taken no trouble to go into
the matter. So now regularly with each season comes the quarterly attack
on the actor and on his jolly calling; the attack usually ending in the
retirement of the enemy. As a rule it is the literary or private gentlemen
who fill the enemy's rank. On the strength of having gone to see plays all
their lives, or on the strength of never having gone to see a play in their
lives, they attack for some reason best known to themselves. I have followed these regular attacks season by season, and they seem mostly to
spring from irritability, personal enmity or conceit. . . . They are illogical
from beginning to end. . . . There can be no such attack made on the actor
or his calling. My intention here is not to join in any such attempt; I would
merely place before you what seem to me to be the logical facts of a
curious case, and I believe that these admit of no dispute whatever.

Acting is not an art. It is therefore incorrect to speak of the actor as an
artist. For accident is an enemy of the artist. Art is the exact antithesis of

Pandemonium, and Pandemonium is created by the tumbling together of many accidents; Art arrives only by design. Therefore in order to make any work of art it is clear we may only work in those materials with which we can calculate. Man is not one of these materials.

The whole nature of man tends towards freedom; he therefore carries the proof in his own person, that as *material* for the theatre he is useless. In the modern theatre, owing to the use of the bodies of men and women *as their material*, all which is presented there is of an accidental nature. The actions of the actor's body, the expression of his face, the sound of his voice, all are at the mercy of the winds of his emotions; these winds which must blow for ever round the artist, moving without unbalancing him. But with the actor, emotion *possesses* him; it seizes upon his limbs moving them whither it will. He is at its beck and call, he moves as one in a frantic dream or as one distraught, swaying here and there: his head, his arms, his feet, if not utterly beyond control, are so weak to stand against the torrent of his passions, that they are ready to play him false at any moment. It is useless for him to attempt to reason with himself. . . . Hamlet's calm directions (the dreamer's not the logician's directions, by the way) are thrown to the winds. His limbs refuse, and refuse again, to obey his mind the instant emotion warms, while the mind is all the time creating the heat which shall set these emotions afire. As with his movement, so is it with the expression on his face. The mind struggling and succeeding for a moment, in moving the eyes, or the muscles of the face whither it will; . . . the mind bringing the face for a few moments into thorough subjection, is suddenly swept aside by the emotion which has grown hot through the action of the mind. Instantly, like lightening, and before the mind has time to cry out and protest, the hot passion has mastered the actor's expression. It shifts and changes, sways and turns, it is chased by emotion from the actor's forehead between his eyes and down to his mouth; now he is entirely at the mercy of emotion, and crying out to it: "Do with me what you will!" his expression runs a mad riot hither and thither, and lo! "nothing is coming of nothing." It is the same with his voice as it is with his movements. Emotion cracks the voice of the actor. It sways his voice to join in the conspiracy against his mind. Emotion works upon the voice of the actor, and he produces . . . . the impression of discordant emotion. It is of no avail to say that emotion is the spirit of the gods and is precisely what the artist aims to produce; first of all this is not true, and even if it were quite true, every stray emotion, every casual feeling, cannot be of value. Therefore the mind of the actor, we see, is less powerful than his emotion, for emotion is able to win over the mind to assist in the destruction of that which the mind would produce; and as the mind becomes the slave of the emotion it follows that accident upon accident must be continually occurring. So then, we have arrived to this point; . . . . that emotion is the cause which first of all creates, and secondly destroys. Art as we have said, can admit of no accidents. That then which the actor gives us, is not a work of art; it is a series of accidental confessions. In the beginning the human body was not used as material in the art of the theatre. In the beginning the emotions of men and women were not considered as a fit exhibition for the multitude. An elephant and a tiger in an arena suited the taste better, when the desire was to excite. The passionate tussle between the elephant and the tiger gives us all the excitement that we can get from the modern stage, and can give it us unalloyed. Such an exhibition is not more brutal, it is more delicate; it is more humane; for there is nothing more outrageous than that men and women should be let loose on a platform, so that they may expose that which artists refuse to show except veiled, in the form which their minds create. How it was that man was ever persuaded to take the place which until that time animals had held is not difficult to surmise.

The man with the greater learning comes across the man with the greater temperament. He addresses him in something like the following terms: . . . "You have a most superb countenance; what magnificent movements you make! Your voice, it is like the singing of birds; and how your eye flashes! What a noble impression you give! You almost resemble a god! I think all people should have pointed out to them this wonder which is contained in you. I will write a few words which you shall address to the people. You shall stand before them, and you shall speak my lines just as you will. It is sure to be perfectly right."

And the man of temperament replies; "Is that really so? Do I strike you as appearing as a god? It is the very first time I have ever thought of it. And do you think that by appearing in front of the people I could make an impression which might benefit them, and would fill them with enthusiasm? "No, no, no," says the intelligent man; "by no means only by *appearing*; but if you have something to say you will indeed create a great impression." The other answers, "I think I shall have some difficulty in speaking your lines. I could easier just appear, and say, something instinctive, such as 'Salutation to all men'; I feel perhaps that I should be able to be more myself if I acted in that way." "That is an excellent idea," replies the tempter, "that idea of yours, 'Salutation to all men.' On that theme I will compose say one hundred or two hundred lines; you'll be the very man to speak those lines. You have yourself suggested it to me. Salutation! It is agreed then, that you will do this?'' ''If you wish it,'' replies the other, with a good-natured lack of reason, and flattered beyond measure.

And so the comedy of author and actor commences. The young man appears before the multitude and speaks the lines, and the speaking of them is a superb advertisement for the art of literature. After the applause the young man is swiftly forgotten; they even forgive the way he has spoken the lines; but as it was an original and new idea at the time, the author found it profitable, and shortly afterwards other authors found it an excellent thing to use handsome and buoyant men as *instruments*. It mattered nothing to them that the instrument was a human creature. Although they knew not the stops of the instrument, they could play rudely upon him and they found him useful. And so to-day we have the strange picture of a man content to give forth the thoughts of another, which that person has given form to, while at the same time he exhibits his person to the public view. He does it because he is flattered,—and vanity—will not reason. But all the time, and however long the world may last, the nature in man will fight for freedom, and will revolt against being made a slave or medium for the expression of another's thoughts. The whole thing is a very grave matter indeed, and it is no good to push it aside and protest that the actor is not the medium for another's thoughts, and that he invests with Life the dead words of an author; because even if this were true (true it cannot be) and even if the actor was to present none but the ideas which he himself should compose, his nature would still be in servitude; his body would have to become the slave of his mind; and that as I have shown is what the healthy body utterly refuses to do. Therefore the body of man, for the reason which I have given, is *by nature* utterly useless as a material for an art. I am fully aware of the sweeping character of this statement, and as it concerns men and women who are alive and who as a class are ever to be loved, more must be said lest I give unintentional offence. I know perfectly well that what I have said here is not yet going to create an exodus of all the actors from all the theatres in the world, driving them into sad monasteries where they will laugh out the rest of their lives, with the Art of the Theatre as the main topic for amusing conversation. As I have written elsewhere, the theatre will continue its growth and actors will continue for some years to hinder its development. But I see a loop-hole by which in time the actors can escape from the bondage they are in. They must create for themselves a new form of acting, consisting for the main part of symbolical gesture. To-day they *impersonate* and interpret; tomorrow they must *represent* and interpret; and the third day they must create.

By this means style may return. To-day the actor impersonates a certain being. He cries to the audience "Watch me; I am now pretending to be so and so, and I am now pretending to do so and so;" and then he proceeds to *imitate* as exactly as possible, that which he has announced he will *indicate*. For instance, he is Romeo. He tells the audience that he is in love, and he proceeds to show it, by kissing Juliet. This, it is claimed is a work of Art: it is claimed for this that it is an intelligent way of suggesting thought. Why . . . . why, that is just as if a painter were to draw upon the wall a picture of an animal with long ears, and then write under it 'This is a donkey.' The long ears made it plain enough one would think, without the inscription, and any child of ten does as much. The difference between the child of ten and the artist is, that the artist is he who by drawing certain signs and shapes creates the impression of a donkey: and the greater artist is he who creates the impression of the whole genus of donkey, the *spirit* of the thing.

The actor looks upon life as a photo-machine looks upon life; and he attempts to make a picture to rival a photograph. He never dreams of his art as being an art such for instance as music. He tries to reproduce nature; he seldom thinks to invent with the aid of nature, and he never dreams of creating. As I have said, the best he can do when he wants to catch and convey the poetry of a kiss, the heat of a fight, or the calm of death, is to copy slavishly, photographically . . . . he kisses . . . . he fights . . . . he lies back and mimics death . . . . and when you think of it, is not all this dreadfully stupid? Is it not a poor art and a poor cleverness, which cannot convey the spirit and essence of an idea to an audience, but can only show an artless copy, a facsimile of the thing itself. This is to be an Imitator not an Artist. This is to claim kinship with the Ventriloquist.[2]

There is a stage expression of the actor "getting under the skin of the part." A better one would be getting "*out* of the skin of the part altogether." "What then," cries the red-blooded and flashing actor, "is there to be no flesh and blood in this same art of the theatre of yours? . . . No life?" It depends what you call life, signor, when you use the word in relation with the idea of art. The painter means something rather different to actuality when he speaks of Life in his art, and the other artists generally mean something essentially spiritual; it is only the actor the ventriloquist or the animal-stuffer who, when they speak of putting life into their work, mean some actual and lifelike reproduction, something blatant in its appeal, that it is for this reason I say that it would be better if the actor should get out of the skin of the part altogether. If there is any actor who is reading this, is there not some way by which I can make him realise the preposterous absurdity of this delusion of his, this belief that he should aim to make an actual copy, a reproduction? I am going to suppose that such an actor is here with me as I talk; and I invite a musician and a painter to join us. Let them speak. I have had enough of seeming to decry the work of the actor from trivial motives. I have spoken this way because of my love of the theatre, and because of my hopes and belief that before long an extraordinary development is to raise and revive that which is failing in the theatre, and my hope and belief that the actor will bring the force of his courage to assist in this revival. My attitude towards the whole matter is misunderstood by many in the Theatre. It is considered to be *my* attitude, mine alone; a stray quarreller I seem to be in their eyes, a pessimist, grumbling; one who is tired of a thing and who attempts to break it. Therefore let the other artists speak with the actor, and let the actor support his own case as best he may, and let him listen to their opinion on matters of art. We sit here conversing, the actor, the musician, the painter and myself. I who represent an art distinct from all these, shall remain silent.

As we sit here, the talk first turns upon Nature. We are surrounded by beautiful curving hills, trees, vast and towering mountains in the distance covered with snow; around us innumerable delicate sounds of nature stirring . . . Life. "How beautiful," says the painter, "how beautiful the sense of all this!" He is dreaming of the almost impossibility of conveying the full earthly and spiritual value of that which is around him on to his canvas, yet he faces the thing as man generally faces that which is most dangerous. The musician gazes upon the ground. The actor's is an inward and personal gaze at himself. He is unconsciously enjoying the sense of himself, as representing the main and central figure in a really good scene. He strides across the space between us and the view, sweeping in a half circle, and he regards the superb panorama without seeing it, conscious of one thing only, himself and his attitude. Of course an actress would stand there meek in the presence of nature. She is but a little thing, a little picturesque atom; . . . for picturesque we know she is in every movement, in the sigh which, almost unheard by the rest of us, she conveys to her audience and to herself, that she is there *"little me,"* in the presence of the God that made her!! and all the rest of the sentimental nonsense. So we are all collected here, and having taken the attitudes natural to us, we proceed to question each other. And let us imagine that for once we are all really interested in finding out all about the other's interests, and the other's work. (I grant that this is very unusual, and that mind-selfishness, the highest form of stupidity, encloses many a professed artist somewhat tightly in a little square box.) But let us take it for granted that there is a general interest; that the actor and the musician wish to learn something about the art of painting; and that the painter and the musician wish to understand from the actor what his work consists of and whether and why he considers it an art. For here they shall not mince matters, but shall speak that which they believe. As they are looking only for the truth, they have nothing to fear; they are all good fellows, all good friends; not thin skinned, and can give and take blows. "Tell us," asks the painter, "is it true that before you can act a part properly you must feel the emotions of the character you are representing?" "Oh well, yes and no; it depends what you mean," answers the actor. "We have first to be able to feel and sympathise and also criticise the emotions of a character; we look at it from a distance before we close with it: we gather as much as we can from the text and we call to mind all the emotions suitable for this character to exhibit. After having many times rearranged and selected those emotions which we consider of importance we then practice to reproduce them before the audience; and in order to do so we must feel as little as is necessary; in fact the less we feel, the firmer will our hold be upon our facial and bodily expression." With a gesture of genial impatience, the artist rises to his feet and paces to and fro. He had expected his friend to say that it had nothing whatever to do with emotions, and that he could control his face, features, voice and all, just as if his body were an instrument. The musician sinks down deeper into his chair. "But has there never been an actor," asks the artist, "who has so trained his body from head to foot that it would answer to the workings of his mind without permitting the emotions even so much as to awaken? Surely there must have been one actor, say one out of ten million, who has done this?" "No," says the actor emphatically, "never, never; there never has been an actor who reached such a state of mechanical perfection that his body was *absolutely* the slave of his mind. Edmund Kean of England, Salvini of Italy, Rachel, Eleonora Duse, I call them all to mind and I repeat there never was an actor or actress such as you describe." The artist here asks, "Then you admit that it would be a state of perfection?" "Why of course! But it is impossible; will always be impossible," cries the actor; and he rises . . . . almost with a sense of relief. "That is as much as to say, there never was a perfect actor, there has never been an actor who has not spoiled his performance once, twice, ten times, sometimes a hundred times during the evening? There never has been a piece of acting which could be called even almost perfect and there never will be?" For answer the actor asks quickly, "But has there been ever a painting, or a piece of architecture, or a piece of music which may be called perfect?" "Undoubtedly," they reply, "The laws which control our arts make such a thing possible." "A picture for instance," continues the artist, "may consist of four lines, or four hundred lines, placed in certain positions; it may be as simple as possible, but it is possible to make it perfect. That is to say, I can first choose that which is to make the lines; I can choose that on which I am to place the lines: I can consider this as long as I like; I can alter it; then in a state which is both free from excitement, haste, trouble, nervousness, in fact in any state I choose, (and of course I prepare, wait and select that also) I can put these lines together . . . . so . . . . now they are in their place. Having my material nothing except my own will can move or alter these; and as I have said my own will is entirely under my control. The line can be straight or it can wave; it can be round if I choose, and there is no fear that when I wish to make a straight line I shall make a curved one, or that when I wish to make a curved there will be square parts about it. And when it is ready . . . . finished . . . . it undergoes no change but that which Time, who finally destroys it, wills." "That is rather an extraordinary thing," replied the actor. "I wish it was possible in my work." "Yes," replies the artist, *'it is a very extraordinary thing*, and it is that which I hold makes the difference between an intelligent statement and a casual or haphazard statement. The most intelligent statement, that is a work of art. The haphazard statement, that is a work of chance. When the intelligent statement reaches its highest possible form it becomes a work of fine art. And therefore I have always held, though I may be mistaken, that your work has not the nature of an art. That is to say (and you have said it yourself) each statement that you make in your work is subject to *every* conceivable change which emotion chooses to bring about. That which you conceive in your mind, your body is not permitted by nature to complete. In fact, your body, gaining the better of your intelligence, has in many instances on the stage driven out the intelligence altogether. Some actors seem to say, "What value lies in having beautiful ideas. To what end shall my mind conceive a fine idea, a fine thought, for my body which is so entirely beyond my control to spoil? I will throw my mind overboard, let my body pull me and the play through;" and there seems to me to be some wisdom in the standpoint of such an actor. He does not dilly-dally between the two things which are contending in him, the one against the other. He is not a bit afraid of the result. He goes at it like a man, sometimes a trifle too like a centaur; he flings away all science . . . . all caution . . . . all reason and the result is good spirits in the audience, . . . and for that they pay willingly. But we are here talking about other things than excellent spirits, and though we applaud the actor who exhibits such a personality as this, I feel that we must not forget that we are applauding his personality . . . *he* it is we applaud, not what he is doing or how he is doing it; nothing to do with art at all, absolutely nothing to do with art, with calculation, or design.

"You're a nice friendly creature," laughs the actor gaily, "telling me my art's no art! But I believe I *see* what you mean. You mean to say that before I appear on the stage and before my body commences to come into the question, I am an artist." "Well yes, *you* are, you happen to be, because you are a very bad actor; you're abominable on the stage, but you have ideas, you have imagination; you are rather an exception I should say. I have heard you tell me how you would play Richard III; what you would do; what strange atmosphere you would spread over the whole thing; and that which you have told me you have seen in the play, and that which you have invented and added to it, is so remarkable, so consecutive in its thought, so distinct and clear in form, that *if* you could make your body into a machine, or into a dead piece of material such as clay, and *if* it could obey you in every movement for the entire space of time it was before the audience, and *if* you could put aside Shakespeare's poem, you would be able to make a work of art out of that which is in you. For you would not only have dreamt, you would have executed to perfection; and that which you had executed could be repeated time after time without so much difference as between two farthings." "Ah," sighs the actor, "you place a terrible picture before me. You would prove to me that it is impossible for us ever to think of ourselves as artists. You take away our finest dream and you give us nothing in its place." "No, no, that's not for me to give you. That's for you to find. Surely there must be laws at the roots of the Art of the Theatre, just as there are Laws at the roots of all true Arts, which if found and mastered, would bring you all you desire?" "Yes, the search would bring the actors to a wall." "Leap it, then!" "Too high!" "Scale it, then!" "How do we know where it would lead?" "Why, up and over." "Yes, but that's talking wildly, talking in the air." "Well, that's the direction you fellows have to go; . . . fly in the air, live in the air. Something will follow when some of you begin to. I suppose," continued he, "you will get at the root of the matter in time, and then what a splendid future opens before you! In fact I envy you. I am not sure I do not wish that photography had been discovered before painting, so that we of this generation might have had the intense joy of advancing, showing that photography was pretty well in its way, but there was something better!" "Do you hold that our work is on a level with photography?" "No, indeed, it is not half as exact. It is less of an art even than photography. In fact you and I who have been talking all this time while the musician has sat silent, sinking deeper and deeper into his chair, our arts by the side of his art, are jokes, games, absurdities." At which the musician must go and spoil the whole thing by getting up and giving vent to some foolish remark. The actor immediately cries out, "But I don't see that that's such a wonderful remark for a representative of the only art in the world to make," at which they all laughed, the musician in a sort of crest-fallen, conscious manner. "My dear fellow, that is just because he is a musician. He is nothing except in his music. He is, in fact, somewhat unintelligent, except when he speaks in notes, in tones, and in the rest of it. He hardly knows our language, he hardly knows our world, and the greater the musician, the more is this noticeable; indeed it is rather a bad sign when you meet a composer who is intelligent. And as for the intellectual musician, why that means another . . . . ; but we mustn't whisper that name here . . . . he is so popular to-day. What an actor this man would have been, and what a personality he has. I understand that all his life he had yearnings towards being an actor, and I believe he would have been an excellent comedian, whereas he became a musician . . . . or was it a playwright? Anyhow, it all turned out a great success . . . . a success of personality." "Was it not a success of art?" asks the musician. " Well , which art do you mean ? " " Oh , all the arts combined," he replies, blunderingly but placidly. "How can that be? How can all arts combine and make one art? It can only make one joke . . . . one theatre. Things which slowly, by a natural law join together, may have some right in the course of many years or many centuries to ask nature to bestow a new name on their product. Only by this means can a new art be born. I do not believe that the old mother approves of the forcing process; and if she ever winks at it, she soon has her revenge; and so is it with the arts. You cannot co-mingle them and cry out that you have created a new art. *If you can find in nature a new material, one which has never yet been used by man to give form to his thoughts, then you can say that you are on the high road towards creating a new art. For you have found that by which you can create it.* It then only remains for you to begin. The theatre, as I see it, has yet to find that material." And so their conversation ended. For my part I am with the artist's last statement. My pleasure shall not be to compete with the strenuous photographer and I shall ever aim to get something entirely opposed to life as we see it. This flesh and blood life, lovely as it is to us all is for me not a thing made to search into, or to give out again to the world, even conventionalized. I think that my aim shall rather be to catch some far off glimpse of that spirit which we call *death* . . . . to recall beautiful things from the imaginary world; . . . they say they are cold, these dead things, . . . I do not know . . . . they often seem warmer and more living than that which parades as life. Shades . . . . spirits seem to me to be more beautiful, and filled with more vitality than men and women; cities of men and women packed with pettiness, creatures in-human, secret . . . . coldest cold . . . . hardest humanity. For looking too long upon life, may one not find all this to be not the beautiful, nor the mysterious nor the tragic, but the dull, the melodramatic, and the silly: the conspiracy against vitality . . . . against both red heat and white heat; and from such things which lack the sun of life it is not possible to draw inspiration. But from that mysterious, joyous, and superbly complete life which is called Death . . . . that life of shadow and of unknown shapes, where all can not be blackness and fog as is supposed, but vivid colour, vivid light, sharp cut form, and which one finds peopled with strange, fierce and solemn figures, pretty figures and calm figures, and those figures impelled to some wonderous harmony of movement, all this is something more than a mere matter of fact; from this idea of death which seems a kind of spring, a blossoming—from this land and from this idea can come so vast an inspiration, that with unhesitating exultation I leap forward to it and behold, in an instant, I find my arms full of flowers . . . . I advance but a pace or two and again plenty is around me . . . . I pass at ease on a sea of beauty I sail whither the winds take me—there, there is no danger. So much for my own personal wish; . . . but the entire theatre of the world is not represented in me, nor in a hundred artists or actors, but in something far different. Therefore what my personal aim may be is of very little importance. Yet the aim of the theatre as a whole is to restore its art and it should commence by banishing from the theatre this idea of impersonation, this idea of reproducing nature; for while impersonation is in the Theatre, the Theatre can never become free. The performers should train under the influence of an earlier teaching (if the very earliest and finest principles are too stern to commence with) and they will have to avoid that frantic desire to put *"life"* into their work; for three thousand times against one time, it means the bringing of excessive gesture, swift mimicry, speech which bellows and scene which dazzles, on to the stage, in the wild and vain belief that by such means vitality can be conjured there. And in a few instances, to prove the rule, all this partially succeeds. It succeeds partially with the bubbling personalities of the stage. With them it is a case of sheer triumph *in spite* of the rules, in the very teeth of the rules, and we who look on, throw our hats into the air, . . . cheer, and cheer again. *We have to*; we don't want to consider or to question;—we go with the tide through admiration and suggestion . . . . That we are hypnotised, our taste cares not a rap . . . . We are delighted to be so moved, and we literally jump for joy.

47

The great personality has triumphed both over us and the art. But personalities such as these are extremely rare, and if we wish to see a personality assert itself in the theatre and entirely triumph as an actor we must at the same time be quite indifferent about the play, the other actors, and Beauty.

Those who do not think with me in this whole matter are the worshippers, or respectful admirers, of the personalities of the stage. It is intolerable to them that I should assert that the stage must be cleared of all its actors and actresses before it will again revive. How could they agree with me? That would include the removal of their favourites . . . . the two or three beings who transform the stage for them from a vulgar joke into an ideal land. But what should they fear? No danger threatens their favourites—for were it possible to put an act into force to prohibit all men and women from appearing before the public upon the stage of a theatre, this would not in the least affect these favourites—these men and women of personality whom the playgoers crown. Consider any one of these personalities born at a period when the stage was unknown; would it in any way have lessened their power . . . . hindered their expression? Not a whit. Personality invents the means and ways by which it shall express itself; and acting is but one, (the very least) of the means at the commands of a great personality: and these men and women would have been famous at any time, and in any calling. But if there are many to whom it is intolerable that I should propose to clear the stage of ALL the actors and actresses in order to revive the Art of the Theatre, there are others to whom it seems agreeable.

"The artist," says Flaubert, "should be in his work like God in creation, invisible and all-powerful; he should be felt everywhere and seen nowhere. Art should be raised above personal affection and nervous susceptibility. It is time to give it the perfection of the physical sciences by means of a pitiless method." He is thinking mainly of the Art of Literature; but if he feel this so strongly of the writer, one who is never actually seen, but merely stands half revealed behind his work, how totally opposed must he have been to the actual appearance of the actor—personality or no personality.

Charles Lamb says, "To see Lear acted . . . . to see an old man tottering about with a stick, turned out of doors by his daughters on a rainy night, has nothing in it but what is painful and disgusting. We want to take him into shelter, that is all the feeling the acting of Lear ever produced in me. The contemptible machinery by which they mimic the storm which he goes out in, is not more inadequate to represent the horror of the real elements than any actor can be to represent Lear. They might more easily propose to personate the Satan of Milton upon a stage, or one of Michaelangelo's terrible figures . . . . Lear is essentially impossible to be represented on the stage."

"Hamlet himself seems hardly capable of being acted," says William Hazlitt.

Dante in "La Vita Nuova" tells us that in dream Love in the figure of a youth appeared to him. Discoursing on Beatrice, Dante is told by Love "to compose certain things in rhyme, in the which thou shalt set forth how strong a mastership I have obtained over thee, through her. . . . And so write these things that they shall seem rather to be spoken by a third person, and not directly by thee to her, which is scarce fitting." And again "There came upon me a great desire to say somewhat in rhyme: but when I began thinking how I should say it, methought that to speak of her were unseemly, unless I spoke to other ladies in the second person." We see then that to these men it is wrong that the living person should advance into the frame and display himself upon his own canvas. They hold it as "unseemly" . . . . "scarce fitting."

We have here witnesses against the whole business of the modern stage. Collectively they pass the following sentence: . . . That it is bad art, or no art, to make so personal, so emotional an appeal that the beholder forgets the thing itself while swamped by the personality, the emotion, of its maker. And now for the testimony of an actress.

Eleonora Duse has said: "To save the theatre, the theatre must be destroyed, the actors and actresses must all die of the plague. They poison the air, they make art impossible."[3]

We may believe her. She means what Flaubert and Dante mean, even if she words it differently. And there are many more witnesses to testify for me, if this is held to be insufficient evidence. There are the people who never go to theatres, the millions of men against the thousands who do go. Then, we have the support of most of the managers of the theatre of to-day. The modern theatre manager thinks the stage should have its plays gorgeously decorated. He will say that no pains should be spared to bring every assistance towards cheating the audience into a sense of reality; he will never cease telling us how important all these decorations are; he urges all this for several reasons and the following reason is not the least . . . . He scents a grave danger in simple and good work; he sees that there is a body of people who are opposed to these lavish decorations; he knows that there has been a distinct movement, in Europe, against this display, it having been claimed that the great plays gained when represented in front of the plainest background. This movement can be proved to be a power-ful one—it has spread from Krakau to Moscow, from Paris to Rome, from London to Berlin and Vienna. The managers see this danger ahead of them; they see that if once people came to realise this fact, if once the audience tasted of the delight which a sceneless play brings, they would then go further and desire the play which was presented without actors; and finally they would go on and on and on until *they*, and not the managers, had positively reformed the Art.

Napoleon is reported to have said, "In life there is much that is unworthy which in art should be omitted; much of doubt and vacillation; and all should disappear in the representation of the hero. *We should see him as a statue in which the weakness and tremors of the flesh are no longer perceptible.*"[4] And not only Napoleon, but Ben Jonson, Lessing, Edmund Scherer, Hans Christian Andersen, Lamb, Goethe, George Sand, Cole-ridge, Ruskin, Pater and I suppose all the intelligent men and women of Europe (one does not speak of Asia for even the unintelligent in Asia fail to comprehend Photographs while understanding Art as a simple and clear manifestation) have protested against this reproduction of Nature, and with it photographic and weak actuality; they have protested against all this, and the theatrical managers have argued against them energetically, and so we look for the truth to emerge in due time. It is a reasonable conclusion. Do away with the real tree, do away with the reality of delivery, do away with the reality of action, and you tend towards the doing away with the actor. This is what must come to pass in time, and I like to see the managers supporting the idea already. Do away with the actor, and you do away with the means by which a debased stage-realism is produced and flourishes. No longer would there be a living figure to confuse us into connecting actuality and art; no longer a living figure in which the weak-ness and tremors of the flesh were perceptible.

The actor must go, and in his place comes the inanimate figure—the über-marionette we may call him, until he has won for himself a better name. Much has been written about the puppet—or marionette. There are some excellent volumes upon him, and he has also inspired several works of Art. To-day in his least happy period many people have come to regard him as rather a superior doll—and to think he has developed from the doll. This is incorrect. He is a descendant of the stone images of the old Temples—he is to-day a rather degenerate form of a God. Always the close friend of children he still knows how to select and attract his dev-otees.

When anyone designs a puppet on paper, he draws a stiff and comic looking thing. Such a one has not even perceived what is contained in the idea which we now call the Marionette. He mistakes gravity of face and calmness of body for blank stupidity and angular deformity. Yet even Modern Puppets are extraordinary things. The applause may thunder or dribble, their hearts beat no faster, no slower, their signals do not grow hurried or confused; and, though drenched in a torrent of bouquets and love, the face of the leading lady remains as solemn, as beautiful and as remote as ever. There is something more than a flash of genius in the Marionette, and there is something in him more than the flashiness of displayed personality. The Marionette . . . . appears to me to be the last echo of some noble and beautiful art of a past civilization. But as with all art which has passed into fat or vulgar hands, the Puppet has become a reproach. All puppets are now but low comedians.

They imitate the comedians of the larger and fuller blooded stage. They enter only to fall on their back. They drink only to reel, and make love only to raise a laugh. They have forgotten the counsel of their Mother, the Sphinx. Their bodies have lost their grave grace, they have become stiff. Their eyes have lost that infinite subtlety of seeming to see; now they only stare. They display and jingle their wires and are cocksure in their wooden wisdom. They have failed to remember that their art should carry on it the same stamp of reserve that we see at times on the work of other artists, and that the highest art is that which conceals the craft and forgets the craftsman. Am I mistaken, or is it not the old Greek Traveller of 800 B.C. who, describing a visit to the Temple-Theatre in Thebes, tells us that he was won to their beauty by their "noble artificiality." "Coming into the House of Visions I saw afar off the fair brown Queen seated upon her throne . . . . her tomb . . . . for both it seemed to me. I sank back upon my couch and watched her symbolic movements. With so much ease did her rhythms alter as with her movements they passed from limb to limb; with such a show of calm did she unloose for us the thoughts of her breast; so gravely and so beautifully did she linger on the statement of her sorrow, that with us it seemed as if no sorrow could harm her; no distortion of body or feature allowed us to dream that she was conquered; the passion and the pain were continually being caught by her hands, held gently, and viewed calmly. Her arms and hands seemed at one moment like a thin warm fountain of water which rose, then broke and fell with all those sweet pale fingers like spray into her lap. It would have been as a revelation of art to us had I not already seen that the same spirit dwelt in the other examples of the art of these Egyptians. This 'Art of Showing and Veiling' as they call it, is so great a spiritual force in the land that it plays the larger part in their religion. We may learn from it somewhat of the power and the grace of courage, for it is impossible to witness a performance without a sense of physical and spiritual refreshment." This in 800 B.C. And who knows whether the Puppet shall not once again become the faithful medium for the beautiful thoughts of the artist. May we not look forward with hope to that day which shall bring back to us once more the figure, or symbolic creature, made also by the cunning of the artist, so that we can regain once more the "noble artificiality" which the old writer speaks of. Then shall we no longer be under the cruel influence of the emotional confessions of weakness which are nightly witnessed by the people and which in their turn create in the beholders the very weaknesses which are exhibited. To that end we must study to remake these images—no longer content with a puppet, we must create an über-marionette. The über-marionette will not compete with Life—but will rather go beyond it. Its ideal will not be the flesh and blood but rather the body in Trance—it will aim to clothe itself with a death-like Beauty while exhaling a living spirit. Several times in the course of this essay has a word or two about Death found its way on to the paper . . . . called there by the incessant clamouring of "Life! Life! Life!" which the Realists keep up. And this might be easily mistaken for an affectation especially by those who have no sympathy or delight in the power and the mysterious joyousness which is in all passionless works of art. If the famous Rubens and the celebrated Raphael made none but passionate and exuberant statements, there were many artists before them and since to whom moderation in their art was the most precious of all their aims, and these more than all others exhibit the true masculine manner. The other flamboyant or drooping artists whose works and names catch the eye of to-day do not so much speak like men as bawl like animals, or lisp like women.

The wise, the moderate masters, strong because of the laws to which they swore to remain ever faithful . . . . their names unknown for the most part . . . . a fine family . . . . the creators of the great and tiny gods of the East and the West, the guardians of those larger times, . . . these all bent their thoughts forward towards the unknown, searching for sights and sounds in that peaceful and joyous country, that they might raise a figure of stone or sing a verse, investing it with that same peace and joy seen from afar, so as to balance all the grief and turmoil here.

In America we can picture these brothers of that family of masters, living in their superb ancient cities, colossal cities which I ever think of as able to be moved in a single day; cities of spacious tents of silk and canopies of gold under which dwelt their gods; dwellings which contained all the re-

quirements of the most fastidious; those moving cities which, as they trav-
elled from height to plain, over rivers and down valleys, seemed like some
vast advancing army of peace. And in each city not one or two men called
"artists" whom the rest of the city looked upon as ne'er do well idlers, but
many men chosen by the community because of their higher powers of
perception . . . . artists; for that is what the title of artist means, one who
perceives more than his fellows, and who records more than he has seen.
And not the least among those artists was the artist of the ceremonies, the
creator of the visions, the minister whose duty it was to celebrate their
guiding spirit . . . . the spirit of Motion.

In Asia, too, the forgotten masters of the temples and all that those
temples contained, have permeated every thought, every mark in their
work with this sense of calm motion resembling death . . . . glorifying and
greeting it. In Africa, (which some of us think we are but now to civilize) this
spirit dwelt, . . . the essence of the perfect civilization. There too dwelt the
great masters, not individuals obsessed with the idea of each asserting his
personality as if it was a valuable and mighty thing, but content because of
a kind of holy patience to move their brains and their fingers only in that
direction permitted by the law—in the service of the simple truths.

How stern the law was, and how little the artist of that day permitted
himself to make an exhibition of his personal feelings can be discovered by
looking at any example of Egyptian art. Look at any limb ever carved by
the Egyptians, search into all those carved eyes, they will deny you until
the crack of doom. Their attitude is so silent that it is death like. Yet
tenderness is there, and charm is there; prettiness is even there side by side
with the force; and love bathes each single work; but gush, emotion,
swaggering personality of the artist? . . . not one single breath of it. Fierce
doubts or hopes? . . . not one hint of such a thing. Strenuous determination? . . . not a sign of it has escaped the artist; none of these confessions
. . . . stupidities. Nor pride, nor fear, nor the comic, nor any indication that
the artist's mind or hand was for the thousandth part of a moment out of
the command of the laws which ruled him. How superb! This it is to be a
great artist; and the amount of emotional outpourings of to-day and of
yesterday are no signs of supreme intelligence, . . . that is to say, are no
signs of supreme art. To Europe came this spirit, hovered over Greece,
could hardly be driven out of Italy, but finally fled, leaving a little stream of
tears, . . . pearls . . . . before us. And we, having crushed most of them,
munching them along with the acorns of our food, have gone further and
fared worse and have prostrated ourselves before the so-called "great
masters," and have worshipped these dangerous and flamboyant per-

sonalities. On an evil day we thought in our ignorance that it was us they were sent to draw, that it was our thoughts they were sent to express; that it was something to do with us that they were putting into their architecture, their music, and so it was we came to demand that we should be able to recognize ourselves in all that they put hand to; that is to say, in their architecture, in their sculpture, in their music, in their painting, and in their poetry we were to figure . . . and we also reminded them to invite us with the familiar words "come as you are."

The artists after many centuries have given in, that which we asked them for they have supplied. And so it came about that when this ignorance had driven off the fair spirit which once controlled the mind and hand of the artist, a dark spirit took its place; the happy-go-lucky Hooligan in the seat of the Law, that is to say, a stupid spirit reigning; and everybody began to shout about Renaissance! while all the time the painters, musicians, sculptors, architects, vied one with the other to supply the demand . . . . that all these things should be so made that all people could recognize them as having something to do with themselves.

Up sprang portraits with flushed faces, eyes which bulged, mouths which leered, fingers itching to come out of their frame, wrists which exposed the pulse; all the colours higgledy piggledy; all the lines in hub-bub, like the ravings of lunacy. Form breaks into panic; the calm and cool whisper of life in trance which once had breathed out such an ineffable hope is heated, fired into a blaze and destroyed, and in its place . . . . *realism*, the blunt statement of Life, something everybody misunderstands while recognizing. And all far from the purpose of art. For its purpose is not to reflect the actual facts of this life, because it is not the custom of the artist to walk behind things, having won it as his privilege to walk in front of them—to lead. Rather should life reflect the likeness of the spirit, for it was the spirit which first chose the artist to chronicle its Beauty.[5] And in that picture, if the form be that of the living, on account of its beauty and tenderness, the colour for it must be sought from that unknown land of the imagination, . . . and what is that but the land where dwells that which we call Death. So it is not lightly and flippantly that I speak of Puppets and their power to retain the beautiful and remote expressions in form and face even when subjected to a patter of praise, a torrent of applause. There are persons who have made a jest of these Puppets. "Puppet" is a term of contempt, though there still remain some who find beauty in these little figures, degenerate though they have become.

To speak of a Puppet with most men and women is to cause them to giggle. They think at once of the wires; they think of the stiff hands and the jerky movements; they tell me it is "a funny little doll." But let me tell them a few things about these Puppets. Let me again repeat that they are the descendants of a great and noble family of Images, Images which were made in the likeness of God; and that many centuries ago these figures had a rhythmical movement and not a jerky one; had no need for wires to support them, nor did they speak through the nose of the hidden manipulator. (Poor Punch, I mean no slight to you! You stand alone, dignified in your despair, as you look back across the centuries with painted tears still wet upon your ancient cheeks, and you seem to cry out appealingly to your dog, "Sister Anne, sister Anne, is *nobody* coming?" And then with that superb bravado of yours, you turn the force of our laughter (and my tears) upon yourself with the heartrending shriek of "Oh my nose! Oh, my nose! Oh my nose!) Did you think, ladies and gentlemen, that these puppets were always little things of but a foot high?

Indeed, no! The Puppet had once a more generous form than yourselves.

Do you think that he kicked his feet about on a little platform six foot square, made to resemble a little old fashioned theatre; so that his head almost touched the top of the proscenium; and do you think that he always lived in a little house where the door and windows were as small as a doll's house, with painted window blinds parted in the centre, and where the flowers of his little garden had courageous petals as big as his head? Try and dispel this idea altogether from your minds, and let me tell you something of his habitation.

In Asia lay his first Kingdom. On the banks of the Ganges they built him his home, . . . a vast palace springing from column to column into the air and pouring from column to column down again into the water. Surrounded by gardens spread warm and rich with flowers and cooled by fountains; gardens into which no sounds entered, in which hardly anything stirred. Only in the cool and private chambers of this palace the swift minds of his attendants stirred incessantly. Something they were making which should become him, something to honour the spirit which had given him birth. And then, one day, the ceremony. In this ceremony he took part; a celebration once more in praise of the Creation; the old thanksgiving, the hurrah for existence, and with it the sterner hurrah for the privilege of the existence to come, which is veiled by the word Death. And during this ceremony there appeared before the eyes of the brown worshippers the symbols of all things on earth and in Nirvana. The symbol of the beautiful tree, the symbol of the hills, the symbols of those rich ores which the hills contained; the symbol of the cloud, of the wind, and of all swift moving

55

things; the symbol of the quickest of moving things, of Thought, of Re-membrance; the symbol of the Animal, the symbol of Buddha and of Man . . . . and here he comes, the figure, the Puppet at whom you all laugh so much. You laugh at him to-day because none but his weaknesses are left to him. He reflects these from you; but you would not have laughed had you seen him in his prime, in that age when he was called upon to be the symbol of man in the great ceremony, and stepping forward, was the beautiful figure of our heart's delight. If we should laugh at and insult the memory of the Puppet, we should be laughing at the fall that we have brought about in ourselves . . . . laughing at the Beliefs and Images we have broken. A few centuries later, and we find his home a little the worse for wear. From a temple it has become, I will not say a theatre, but something between a temple and a theatre, and he is losing his health in it. Something is in the air; his doctors tell him he must be careful. "And what am I to fear the most?" he asks them. They answer him; "Fear most the vanity of men." He thinks, "But that is what I myself have always taught; that we who celebrated in joy this our existence, should have this one great fear. Is it possible that I, one who has ever revealed this truth, should be one to lose sight of it and should myself be one of the first to fall? Clearly some subtle attack is to be made on me. I will keep my eyes upon the Heavens." And he dismisses his doctors and ponders upon it.

And now let me tell you who it was that came to disturb the calm air which surrounded this curiously perfect thing. It is on record that some-what later he took up his abode on the far Eastern Coast, and there came two women to look upon him. And at the ceremony to which they came he glowed with such earthly splendour and yet such unearthly simplicity, that though he proved an inspiration to the thousand nine hundred and ninety eight souls who participated in the festival, an inspiration which cleared the mind even as it intoxicated, yet to these two women it proved an intoxication only. He did not see them, his eyes were fixed on the heavens: but he charged them full of a desire too great to be quenched; the desire to stand as the direct symbol of the Divinity in Man. No sooner thought than done; and arraying themselves as best they could in gar-ments ("like his," they thought) moving with gestures ("like his" they said) and being able to cause wonderment in the minds of the beholders ("even as he does," they cried) they built themselves a temple ("like his" "like his"), and supplied the demand of the vulgar, . . . the whole thing a poor parody. This is on record. It is the first record in the East of the actor . . . . The actor springs from the foolish vanity of two women who are not strong enough to look upon the symbol of godhead without desiring to tamper

56

with it; and the parody proved profitable. In fifty or a hundred years, places for such parodies were to be found in all parts of the land. Weeds, they say, grow quickly, and that wilderness of weeds, the modern theatre, soon sprang up. The figure of the Divine Puppet, attracted fewer and fewer lovers, and the women were quite the latest thing. With the fading of the Puppet and the advance of these women who exhibited themselves on the stage in his place, came that darker spirit which is called Chaos, and in its wake the triumph of the riotous Personality. Do you see then, what has made me love and learn to value that which to-day we call the puppet and to detest that which we call life in art? I pray earnestly for the return of the Image . . . . the über-marionette, to the Theatre; and when he comes again and is but seen, he will be loved so well that once more will it be possible for the people to return to their ancient joy in ceremonies . . . . once more will Creation be celebrated . . . . homage rendered to existence . . . . and divine and happy intercession made to Death.

1. [Reprinted in *On The Art of The Theatre.* (Heinemann and Theatre Arts Books.)]
2. "And therefore when any one of these pantomimic gentlemen, who are so clever that they can imitate anything comes to us, and makes a proposal to exhibit himself and his poetry, we will fall down and worship him as a sweet and holy and wonderful being; but we must also inform him that in our State such as he are not permitted to exist; the law will not allow them. And so, when we have annointed him with myrrh, and set a garland of wool upon his head, we shall lead him away to another city. For we mean to employ for our soul's health the rougher and severer poet or story-teller, who will imitate the style of the virtuous only, and will follow those models which we prescribed at first when we began the education of our soldiers." Plato, (The whole passage being too long to print here, we refer the reader to *The Republic*, Book III p. 395).
3. *Studies in Seven Arts.* Arthur Symons. (Constable.)
4. Of sculpture Pater writes:
   "Its white light, purged from the angry, bloodlike stains of action and passion, reveals, not what is accidental in man, but the god in him, as opposed to man's restless movement."
   Again, "The base of all artistic genius is the power of conceiving humanity in a new striking rejoicing way, of putting a happy world of its own construction in place of the meaner world of common days, of generating around itself an atmosphere with a novel power of refraction, selecting, transforming, recombining the images it transmits, according to the choice of the imaginative intellect."
   And again; "All that is accidental, all that distracts the simple effect upon us of the supreme types of humanity, all traces in them of the commonness of the world, it gradually purges away."
5. "All forms are perfect in the poet's mind: But these are not abstracted or compounded from nature; they are from imagination." William Blake.

## MOTION. BEING THE PREFACE TO THE PORTFOLIO OF ETCHINGS. *The Mask,* Volume I, no. 10, December, 1908.[1]

he Beginning. . . . the Birth. . . .

We are in Darkness . . . . all is still.

We hear no sound. . . . we feel no movement . . . . we see nothing.

And from this Nothing shall emerge a spirit . . . . Life . . . . a perfect and balancing life . . . . to be called Beauty . . . . The Immortal Beauty of Change Eternal.

Even now as we wait watching, in the very centre of the void a single atom seems to stir . . . . it spreads . . . .

It is the faint trembling of the first false dawn.

Around us spreads a mist motionless and colourless.

The silence commands.

Some Spirit seems to work there in the gloom as in a little buoyant wind . . . . a breeze which blows upon the veiled spaces and stirs them into life.

At last the Dawn, ineffably hushed . . . . beyond Silence, silent.

The light ascends, spreading ceaselessly . . . . Day arrives and passing turns to night . . . . The fainting Light . . . the passing and the renewal of the promise . . . . Divisible and Indivisible.

Onward! The profound spirit throbs incessantly at its sweet task.

A form simple and austere ascends with prolonged patience like the awakening of a thought in dream.

A second and a third form seem to follow . . . . Always a double birth repeating . . . . a fourth, a fifth, a seventh, and yet as we look we seem to see but four . . . . that first form which gave birth has passed; those two forms to which it gave birth have passed.

Four shapes remain.

Ah, birth of my love, already you have multiplied fourfold! . . . . Cease not until you will . . . . continue to increase!

But no eyes away from what is happening.

Look there to the East! Something seems to unfold, something to fold.

Slowly quick'ning without haste, fold after fold loosens itself and clasps another till that which was void has become shapely. And now from East to West, one chain of life moves like a sea before us, while slowly breaking from units into pairs, shapes continue to appear in endless procession while still the folds fold and unfold . . . .

Some rising, others falling . . . . passing and repassing one another.

Lingering . . . . responding to an approach . . . . shrinking at a repulse . . . . blindly towering . . . . fainting . . . . parting . . . . meeting.

And then a pause . . . . a perfect balanced thought is poised before us, and all is still . . . . All is accomplished. Silence. All rests . . . . and only is it left now for the tender liquid light to feel its way across this form.

Like freezing water it descends a little with ever-increasing delay, and like a dew it settles.

No more . . . .

Enough . . . .

And may this love beginning have no end.

*     *     *

For the fulfilment of this most superb dream must first come the union of the three Arts . . . . The Arts of Architecture, Music and Motion.

These three Arts bring to the Religion of Truth three vital needs.

The First brings the Place . . . . The Second the Voice . . . . The Third reveals the Event . . . . The Temple . . . . The Hymn . . . . The Balance.

Without Architecture we should have no Divine Place in which to praise.

Without Music no Divine Voice with which to praise.

Without Motion no Divine Act to perform.

Architecture . . . . Music . . . . Motion . . . .

These are the great Impersonal Arts of the Earth . . . . and together form the mysterious link between Now and the Hereafter.

For the fulfilment of our most superb Life, these three must be again united from one end of the Earth unto the other.

1. [Originally published as a four-page folder, Nizza-Firenze, 1907.]

## A NOTE ON MARIONETTES by Adolf Furst. *The Mask*, Volume II, nos. 4-6, October, 1909.

*"We are such stuff as dreams are made of and our little life is rounded by a sleep."*

f only this were really the truth of men and women! Yet it may be believed of the Marionettes. They are made of such ideal stuff, far more than we are, and is not their little life one perfect round of sleep?

The race of these dream folk is a small one; but, whether of rag or gold, rich or poor, king or peasant the marionette is always distinguished, and it is curious to note that he only loses his distinction when allied with a human being. For come across him when he is suspended in his quiet chamber of rest and you will be awed by his distinguished manner, but let a human being but touch him and he will act in the most outrageous manner. For these humans even make him copy the actors; they make him behave like a man in the street, whereas if left to himself he will do nothing wrong . . . . doing nothing.

And it is this doing nothing, this saying nothing, this meaning nothing which raises him to an altitude that is limitless. Not many people have seen these little beings, and very few have seen them doing nothing. Those people who have been persuaded for one reason or another to enter the small theatres where the marionettes are obliged to fret their hour on the stage, have seen them under great disadvantages for they have seen them as slaves of men who are ignorant of the existence of the Holy Ghost. But of course there are some who are able to tell us of strange sights they have seen, of strange pleasures that they have tasted through Marionettes inspired by artists . . . . men of spiritual power.

These are the travellers who have visited China, Java and India, and even visitors to Paris, Vienna and Naples have also had something good to see at one time or another, while in England the vision of Punch and Judy[1] whispers to us of something "once upon a time." But it is those who travel furthest who see more than the rest. It is they who travel in the imagination and who realise the unlimited possibilities of that Holy Land.

In the olden days a marionette performance was called a 'Motion,' and this 'Motion,' took place in silence.[2]

The 'unspoken meanings of the earth' are not to be explained by speech, for as there is always that part of nature which can be stated perfectly by words, there must ever remain some mysteries of nature which can only be expressed by movement. We may take it that the Motion is the just and best means of expression for that which lies outside beyond the province of words.

Dumb show by pantomimists (especially the modern dumb show) is but a negative kind of expression. When you have a voice, to refrain from making good use of it is niggardly and for twelve people to be wandering about on a stage continually clapping their hands, pointing, waving, struggling to express what we see could be quite simply expressed if they would but open their mouths, is foolish and no art. You have a mouth; use it. You have a voice; speak. Are you still a child . . . . have you no voice? . . . . then move . . . . play.

The marionette has no voice, though a degenerate public has at times begged that he shall be made to speak. His power and his expression lies in movement. By movement he can tell us of the very things that Shakespeare, with all his words, cannot tell us; and so to manufacture for him a voice is foolish and extravagant.

And now a word or two about his construction, for he is, after all, in his private life just a little machine.

Sometimes he is made of wood and suspended by wires from above. These wires are attached to a short stick which some human machine holds from above: . . . . two machines, you see, the one human, the other, when constructed with art-Divine. Some marionettes are supported from beneath by a rod held by a human manipulator underneath the stage which is generally a narrow platform. Punch is one of these. In his case the arm of the manipulator plays the part of the rod and the fingers move his arms and head. Some marionettes are flat like a piece of cardboard and cut in silhouette. Some have a little more complicated mechanism as in the case of the Chinese figures. We must realise that the whole thing is a little matter of a very little mechanism. Pull a string, an arm goes up; another string and it bends, another string, and it comes round. Nowadays a man controls all this but might it not perhaps be possible that at a later date we may have these little figures brought to so great a mechanical perfection that they may not need the assistance of that human machine, man?

Bernardino Baldi, Abbot of Guastalla, who was both poet and geometrician and who wrote of Marionettes in 1589, declares a knowledge of mathematics to be essential to their construction, and the value of such knowledge to both the constructor and the manipulator is easy to understand.

We are told that in Greece a life sized figure was once made by an artist mechanic in such a way that without assistance it could move its legs and arms and advance upon the beholders to whom it gave a blessing. This movement was caused by the mercury with which it was filled, the inward construction of the figure setting the mercury in motion and this, in its turn, setting in motion the figure; while mention is made of such a figure by Aristotle, who admits that it was the mercury which she contained which gave movement to the famous wooden Venus attributed to Daedalus.

Another means of causing the figures to move was by the power of a magnet, of which we have an example in the inscription given by Diodore of the ceremonies which took place in the temple of Heliopolis. — "When the god wished to deliver his oracle" he tells us, "the statue, which was of gold, moved of itself; if the priests delayed to raise it on their shoulders it struggled and moved again. When they had taken it and placed it on a litter it led them and obliged them to make several turns. At last the high priest presented himself before the statue of the god and put to him the questions on which it was wished to consult him. If Apollon disapproved of the enterprise the statue drew back; if he approved of it it pushed its bearers forward as if drawing them with reins. "And," he adds in conclusion, "the priests having taken the statue on their shoulders it left them on the ground and raised itself quite alone towards the vault of the temple."

Now there seems no reason why my keen, clever and energetic countrymen, especially those who dwell in Berlin, should not soon master these matters of mercury and magnet and produce some figures capable of exquisite, if mechanical, movement. Though even then the difficulty would not be ended, for it is one thing to make a piece of mechanism and another to set it to its right use, and after the mechanism of these figures is made perhaps we shall have to go to France or England to find those who shall know how to extract and conjure some beauty from it all.

For what artists the young Englishmen are beside the Americans, in so many traits akin to us! By the side of these how an Englishman shines! Indeed, young England possesses probably more artists with a more virile and distinguished sense of beauty, nay, with more brains, than any other western state.

But to glance again most briefly at the history of the Marionette.

Very far back across the centuries may we trace the procession of this silent race to their remote origin in the figure of the gods in Egypt. For the little figures which it has become the custom to treat as something trivial, perhaps even rather contemptible, a diversion for children only, have a most noble ancestry. To quote Mr. Ernest Maindron, "They come from far away. They have been the joy of the unnumbered generations which preceded our own; they have gained, with our direct ancesters, many and brilliant successes; they have made them laugh but they have also made them think; they have had eminent protectors; for them celebrated authors have written. At all periods they have enjoyed a liberty of manners and language which has rendered them dear to the people for whom they were made.

Always they have touched on everything, they have directed their shafts at everything; art, poetry, politics and religions. More courageous than men, they have often attacked the powerful and have sometimes put them to confusion."

As to their true origin theories may vary. Mr. Charles Nodier finds it in "the first doll put into the hands of a child." "It is impossible," he asserts, "not to recognise the type of them in that cosmopolitan toy which we call a doll." But I would rather incline to the theory put forward by Mr. Magnin, in support of which he cites Heroditus and other ancient writers, that the marionettes are descended from those jointed statuettes which, in celebration of the feast of Bacchus, the Egyptian women bore from village to village; and in the figure of Jupiter Ammon which, carried in procession on the shoulders of eighty priests, indicated the route it wished to follow by a movement of the head.

That the Egyptians used these moving figures as means of amusement in what we today call a theatre we have no evidence, nor does it seem probable. It is true that in miniature they were used as toys for children, but their real place was in the religious ceremonies, and it was just in these ceremonies, these silent rites and movements, and not, as was once upon a time asserted, in the words of the poets, that the theatre had its birth, being born of motion, not of sound.

Both in Egypt and Greece many little jointed figures have been found, in wood, ivory and terra cotta, the heads set upon a pivot which permitted movement; the limbs jointed that they might be moved by means of a string.

In Greece they had evidently been early adopted as a means of entertainment, since Xenophon relates, in connection with a famous banquet, that among the diversions provided by the host was a Syracusian player of marionettes.

The author of the treatise, "de Mundo" treating of these little figures, writes as follows: "The Sovereign master of the universe has not need of numerous ministers nor of complicated means, to direct all the parts of his immense empire; one act of his will suffice him, just as those who control the marionettes have only need to put in motion the head or hand of these little beings, then their shoulders, their eyes, and sometimes all the parts of their bodies, which at once obey with grace and rhythm." And, as Mr. Gordon Craig points out, it is just this passivity, obedience and responsiveness which renders the marionettes such valuable material for the artist of the theatre, which would make possible that which with the living material of the living actor's body remains impossible, . . . the creation of a work of art. In a performance in which the actors are living persons it is impossible, however well disciplined they be, that they subdue entirely their own will and personality to the will of their director, and thus the unity, the expression of but one will which is a necessary quality of a work of art, is unattainable. With the marionettes, however, those who direct the movement and the gestures of the little figures of men made of wood have, as Apulée wrote in the second century, A. D. "only to draw the string destined to move such and such a limb; immediately one sees the neck bend, the head bow, the eyes take vivacity of expression, the hands lend themselves for all the offices required; in short, the whole person shows itself graceful and as if alive."

In regard to the performances given at Athens in the Theatre of Dionysus we are told by some authorities that, since the ancient theatres were ill adapted for such a use, a kind of second little stage composed of a four sided draped scaffolding was arranged upon the thymele or orchestra, so constructed as to allow the spectators to see the little actors but not the hands which manipulated them, the piece being given without words while the story was narrated by one who stood in front. One distinguished authority, however, referring to the celebrated performances given in this theatre by Pothein, opposes the idea that the figures were small ones and puts forward another theory. "I think," he writes, "that Pothein presented life-size figures or even larger than life, each of which contained a manipulator, and my reason for holding this view is that I do not find the Greeks lacking in a sense of proportion . . . ." Not so unlike Mr. Craig's über-marionette, this.

Passing on to the middle ages we find the moving figures have again reverted to their original religious character and dwell once more in the churches in the form of Madonnas and crucifixes, with eyes that turn and limbs that move, and as the actors of the sacred dramas which it was customary to perform at the great festivals of the church. The introduction of those moving statues into the ceremonies met, however, with vigorous though unsuccessful opposition on the part of the prelates, and in 1086 we learn that Abbot Hugues of Cluny, "refused to ordain a monk who was a mechanician, that is to say, a conjurer and necromancer."

Of the construction of the figures at this period we can find but little information, but a manuscript of the 12th century which formerly existed in the Strasbourg Library and of which miniatures were later reproduced by Ch. Marice Engelhard under the title "Hortus deliciarum" were represented two little warriors in full armour, which were caused to fight and move by two manipulators by means of a string crossed in the centre and of which each manipulator holds an end, the action thus being horizontal instead of, as is usual, perpendicular.

In England, as elsewhere, we find the moveable statuettes playing their parts in the churches, in those dramas and sacred pageants which have ever been the delight of the Catholic Church. Even today the white pigeon which in olden days, coming through an opening in the vault, represented on Whitsunday the descent of the Holy Ghost, has its counterpart in Florence in the mechanical dove which on Easter Saturday carries the Easter fire from the altar of the cathedral to the "carro" set before the wide-open western door.

But when the storm of the Reformation swept over England, and Henry VIII in his fight against the Pope despoiled the churches, the "miraculous" crucifixes, the little figures which had performed the Nativity and Passion plays, were destroyed and the new religion cast out as idols what the old religion had sheltered as saints.

Turned out from their altars we find the moving statuettes reappearing in more secular guise as marionettes upon the ordinary stage.

Many names have been given to this silent race in different ages and countries . . . . for a silent people we must remember that they are, their grave eyes and immobile lips having nothing in common with the squeaky tones which a more trivial age than that which saw their birth has insisted on attributing to them.

The title of puppet is perhaps the most ancient in derivation; coming through the French *poupée* from the Latin *pupa*. *Maumet* or *mammet* as we find them called in France has, Mr. Maindron tells us, "as in our ancient word of *marmouset* in its origin the sense of an idol" but the modern name marionette comes from Marion the man who first during the reign of Charles IX introduced them into France; while the Italian title of Burattini comes from Burattino, a famous manipulator living in 1622.

The performances in which they appeared in England seem to have been generally known by the name of *"motions"* which, signifying "a movement" came to be applied to a show of puppets, either automatic or moved by strings; but in Shakespeare's time we often find the word "drollery" used; meaning a farce played by wooden actors.

It is a curious fact worthy of notice that in the bills passed by the Puritans in 1642 and 1647, the first for the suspension, the second for the abolition, of theatres, no mention was made of marionettes and no measures taken against them, which seems to afford a good proof that what the reformers objected to was the exposure of the human body on the stage rather than the mere representation of a drama, a reason which was probably at the root, even if unconsciously, of much of the pious horror of the stage which even to-day is felt, though in a modified degree, by many.

The original performances by the marionettes in England and France seem to have been in "miracles" and "mysteries" which were held under the direction of the clergy and confraternities in celebration of the church feasts; but in the middle of the fifteenth century we find the figures of the simple old Bible narratives and the legends of the saints beginning to give place to the more theological and allegorical personifications of vices and virtues such as Vanity, Gluttony, False Doctrine, and that most celebrated personage, Old Vice, or Old Iniquity, the inseparable companion of the devil of whom two centuries later, under the rule of the house of Orange, Punch was born; and about the same time the marionette theatres began to rise to a better social standing, to afford more luxuries and to offer for the first time seats at varied prices. Indeed, the end of the 17th century seems to have seen the English puppet theatre at the height both of its popularity and its success.

In those days, Mr. Magnin tells us, "all the limbs of these little figures were jointed, and from the top of their heads came out a metal stalk which united all the strings in the hand of the manipulator," so that it was evidently not until later that Punch and his companions took the form under which we now see them, being worked, not from above, but from beneath.

In the British Museum is to be found the original of a curious advertisement dating back to the days of Queen Anne and announcing Punch as an actor together with John Spendall, an ancient and popular performer of moralities. This document runs as follows:[3] "At Crawley's Booth, over against the Crown Tavern in Smithfield, during the time of Bartholemew Fair, will be presented a little opera, called the Old Creation of the World; yet newly revived; with the addition of Noah's Flood; also veral fountains playing water during the time of the play. The last scene does present Noah and his family coming out of the Ark, with all the beasts two and two,

66

and all the fowls of the air seen in a prospect sitting upon trees; likewise over the ark is seen the Sun rising in a most glorious manner; moreover a multitude of Angels will be seen in a double rank; which presents a double prospect, one for the sun, another for a palace, where will be seen six Angels ringing of bells. Likewise Machines descend from above, double and treble; with Dives rising out of Hell; and Lazarus seen in Abraham's bosom; besides several figures dancing jigs, sarabands, and country dances; to the admiration of the spectators; with the merry conceits of squire Punch and Sir John Spendall."

This curious medley was, we are told, "completed by an Entertainment of singing and dancing with several naked swords, performed by a Child of eight years of age."

A famous English puppet showman was Martin Powell, who began to distinguish himself about this time and continued under the succeeding reigns of George I, George II, George III, and we find in him something of those powers which we look for today in the Artist of the Theatre, since he was not only the author of the pieces which he put on this tiny stage, but also the maker of the puppets, (we hear of his devoting especial care to Punch, whom he endowed with a moveable jaw) the costumier and the controller of every action, and gesture.

The subject of Punch and his fellows is, however, so wide and interesting a one as to call for a special and separate study, and the same must be said of that wonderful company of marionettes which have their homes in the East, in Java, China, Burmah and Japan.

To speak of the marionettes once more, therefore, in conclusion, in the general sense.

Two of the most salient characteristics which chiefly impress us in them are their simplicity and their calm. The gestures which seem so varied, so complicated as to necessitate the most elaborate mechanism are produced by means amazingly simple, while a marionette "greenroom" between the performances is, . . . and in this it forms a welcome contrast to the real theatre, . . . as tranquil a spot as can be found. Each little figure, strangely human in its repose, hangs upon its nail in the dim light, gazing before it with eyes as inscrutable as those which yet meet ours from under the quiet brows of the gods of Egypt and Etruria. It is their silence, their passionless gaze, their profound indifference which give so supreme a dignity to the frail little bodies tricked out in gauze and tinsel. As in the fallen descendant of a great family some one trait may yet remain to recall a noble origin, so does that impassive gaze, that air of seeing *beyond* all the transitory and the accidental, still proclaim for the marionette his kinship with the grave stone images of the ancient eastern world. And when, in more than his former dignity and dowered with more than his former gifts, the puppet returns to our stage in the form of that Über-Marionette whom Mr. Gordon Craig has created, bringing with him his supreme quality, that of perfect obedience to the hand and mind of the master whom he serves as material, with him will come that Renaissance of the Art of the Theatre of which the first hints are even now beginning to appear.

1. The derivation of these personages from the Pontius Pilate and Judas Iscariot of miracle plays is the merest philological whimsy, Punch is doubtless the Pulcinella, who makes his appearance about 1600 as a stock figure in the impromptu comedy of Naples. Under other names his traditions may, for all one knows, go back far beyond the miracle plays to the "Fabulae Atelanae." But the particular drama in which alone he now takes the stage, although certainly not a miracle play, follows closely upon the traditional lines of the moralities. E. K. Chambers. *The Mediaeval Stage*, Vol. 2. 159-160.
2. The term "Motion" is not however, confined to puppet-plays; Bacon, Essay XXXVII, uses it of the dumb shows of masquers, and Jonson, "Tale of a Tub," v. 1, of Shadow-plays. *Ibid.*, 158, note.
3. "Sports and Pastimes." Strutt.

---

# ANIMADVERSIONS ON DANCERS. *The Observer*, May 29, 1932.[1]

---

 was looking at a book on costume and armour, and it led me to reflect about actors and dancers and singers—and if you will believe me that I have no particular conviction that these thoughts are very original, I will write some of them down here and now.

This is what occurred to me as I thought about European dancers. I remembered how I had, once in my life, seen an actor dancing in a ballet, and how curious it had seemed to me, and interesting; and I had thought to myself: "By Jove, this is a man!" Why that should have impressed me so much, I did not discover at the time—but ever since, when watching the performance of a ballet, I have been sorry to feel that "By jingo, these are not men!"

They are men, of course—very manly young fellows become dancers, and in the last twenty-five years or so, Europe has had several famous young dancers: and though none except Nijinsky may be quite so famous as was young Vestris, many, I daresay, are as good dancers as the best of the eighteenth century.

I have no recollection of having seen Dolin or Massine dance, but I have seen many whose names, unfortunately, I forget.

These dancers interpreted all sorts of things besides men—in fact they rarely, if ever, transformed themselves into men ... but gods, slaves, savages, roses, swans, or Harlequin or Pierrot; and it was strange to note that they, one and all, would always seem to be making efforts to fly.

I came, in time, to look for this bird-like expression in every ballet, and I never failed to find it.

Then I began to look at the dancers' costumes, and saw that there was not the same regular attempt made by the dancers to dress themselves like birds; but one and all seemed agreed upon dressing up in something resembling bathing-dresses. I had an impression of leaping, shivering figures, costumed in something tight and elastic—not masked, but wearing rather pained expressions even when smiling—and they seldom failed to smile. Bad dancers, you will say . . . not at all—they were some of the best dancers of the day—and all of them gave us pleasure.

Up they leapt—and down they came, ever so lightly—thud! Undismayed, they went at it again—up they went and down they came, even more lightly—pat! And now thoroughly encouraged, they went up and up again—but ever descended, later . . . always gracefully, sometimes exquisitely, but down they came—ping!

They all seemed to favour a descent fairly near the footlights. They would then trip off to the back of the stage, as near to the backcloth as possible, and once again make a rapid bee-line for the footlights—jumping—twiddling with the feet—bouncing and plunging—and, it seemed, thoroughly enjoying themselves in their futile attempts to fly. The muscular arms, spread out very much as wings, emphasized the suggestion of flying.

Looking at a book of costumes[2] and armour, I began to think of actors and dancers; and I recalled all this leaping and twiddling of the latter—and a number of questions came leaping and twiddling into my head. "Why all that bounding into the air?—why that failure to fly?—and I wonder why they reveal quite so much bone and muscle," I thought, pausing a long time over this, in the hope of discovering some real, sound reason. . . . "And why are they all in such a hurry?—and why those bathing-dresses?"

Was it that some trainer or producer had told them they must leap—must try to fly—must wear what they wore—and must positively reveal all the bones and muscles possible? Or can it be that these are among the unwritten laws?

The questions left me no rest, and I could find no answer to them—and still I do not know whose fault it is—for to me these things seem to be defects which surely could be put right.

What might a man do who would dance, and how might he be dressed?

"Well," I reasoned, "if he must try to fly—but that's all nonsense . . . to dance cannot mean to do something else—or rather, to fail to do it. To dance means to dance—*ballare*. A ball bounces, or it rolls—but a dancer is not a ball, and never was a ball; so banish the notion of rolling and bouncing. Dance is something else. I fancy I know what it is, but for the moment perhaps it would be more helpful not to develop a theory, but to suggest what a dancer should *not* do and *not* wear." So I jotted some of these things down.

The dancer should not everlastingly look happy about nothing . . . nor grave, neither; he should not let us see him assume the "first position," the moment he is about to begin to bounce or spin. He must not keep on repeating himself; he must not seem to struggle over his work.

And what should he wear? Messrs. Kelly and Schwabe gave me a very definite suggestion. First, he might wear a kind of light armour, in which to practise; and secondly, by this practice, he might in time come to wear his muscles, bones, limbs and carry his head and move his feet more easily—dancing with his mind and using his face . . . not grimacing—using his face; and then it would matter less what he wore on his limbs.

Let us look into this question of light armour as stuff to train in, so as to cure this growing tendency to hop and leap and bounce.

I have seen young men training, in the schools, to be dancers, and I have noticed that they remove almost all clothing, so as not to be encumbered. Why, you ask, should I want to put them in even the lightest of armour?

I would like to do something to make *superfluous* movement more difficult than it is at present. Armour, as worn by knights in battle in the Middle Ages, would make movement impossible to dancers; but I mean something else: we should be able, I believe, to contrive some other, more reasonable costume, heavy enough here and there to curb, automatically, unessential movement . . . for it is this unessential movement which is the death of the dance.

Do not laugh at my suggestion, but remember how Demosthenes put pebbles into his mouth, in order to teach himself how to speak . . . what an obstruction these pebbles must have been! Think a while about that. Ask a man who can write, paint, play on instruments, engrave on wood or metal, or practise any of the crafts, whether the craftsman is encouraged to free himself of all restrictions, or whether he welcomes obstructions; and ask him to explain how it is that the enforced limitations of his material do not baffle him and render him desperate. He will tell you that he welcomes the assistance of these constraints.

I suggest that you obstruct movement, and then see if all the unnecessary flim-flam of motion does not begin to disappear.

The whole race of European dancers seems to have been able, far too easily, to acquire graces, to reproduce gestures and to dance in a way which begins to tire the public. Why should it not master something different—overcome a few more difficult things—and so advance a step, this century?

1. [Reprinted in *Essays of the Year. 1931-32*, compiled by F. J. Harvey Darton. (London: The Argonaut Press.) 1932.]
2. *A Short History of Costume and Armour.* By F. M. Kelly and Randolph Schwabe. (Batsford.)

# PART II.

## GORDON CRAIG ON THE CLASSIC DANCE

## ETERNITY AND SOAP BUBBLES by J. Van Holt. *The Mask*, Volume IV, no. 1, July, 1911.

adame Ida Rubinstein is ambitious. She seems to have the ambition to become eternal through blowing soap-bubbles. It is decidedly original.

Madame Rubinstein having by some great magic, (probably that magic of personality about which we hear so much), procured large sums of money, goes to Paris, takes a quantity of D'Annunzio, mixes it with some Debussy, Bakst and Hahn, and begins blowing the bubbles. The first bursts in Paris, the second in London.

In the first bubble, which was called "The Martyrdom of Saint Sebastian" but was really a chapter from the martyrdom of Art, Madame Rubinstein figured as a saint. In the second, called "The Blue God" Madame Rubinstein figured as a goddess. Blue being too ordinary a pigment, the lady had herself gilded. One has heard of gilding the pill before now.

The *Daily Mail* has provided most of the air for the bubble experiments and some of this is very refined.

Concerning "The Blue God" Mr. Hahn said, "our ballet is to be of the Impressionist school. We want to show London what can be done away from the senseless traditions of the ballet skirt with its antiquated poses and gesture."

(Mr. Hahn here strikes one as a little late, for the senseless traditions were done away with quite five or six years ago. Possibly Mr. Hahn doesn't know of this. Ecco! the comic side of the bubble!)

"Some quite extraordinary experiments," he goes on, "are to be tried with regard to the principle characters. Madame Rubinstein, who is to represent a Hindu goddess, will probably be entirely gilded. M. Nijinsky the great solo dancer will dye his face, hands and legs bright blue. The feature of the ballet will be when Madame Rubinstein, wearing her diamonds over the gilding, emerges from a huge lotus flower, etc, etc, etc."

These certainly are very extraordinary experiments, but why not make them and keep them in the bathroom? Or if Madame Rubinstein, in gilt and diamonds, went out to tea to the Countess of Winkleboro and M. Nijinsky, dyed blue, could be persuaded to take black coffee at the Reform Club, might not nearly as great a sensation be produced?

Why drag in the Theatre? The answer is all too easy: . . . because the theatre is sufficiently low to oblige willingly when such a proposal is made to it and a cheque offered. The theatre is indeed becoming what the manager in Zola's "Nana" held it to be. The theatre is so low that it cannot protect itself. Any vulgar woman or man can make it serve their sensational purpose.

Again and again I give praise that the Censor rules over the London stage preventing further vulgarities in the name of Art. My only regret is that he is not ten times as strict as he is: that he passes these exhibitions of the nude on the stage; that he lets much that is vulgar pass on the Music Hall stage.

We all know perfectly well that eccentric comedians can keep the house in a roar of laughter without resorting to vulgarities. Dan Leno was the most successful English comedian of his day, and avoided all vulgarity. We also know that perfect dancing is possible without a display of naked or semi-naked limbs. Sada Yacco was perhaps the most perfect dancer of her day, and she avoided all such display.

All these liberties taken upon the stage are ruining the stage. Let the Censor act twice as stringently as before. Let his office be invested with new powers, and let the modern theatre-music-hall have a chance to develop its strength.

If the Censor postpones action any longer the matter will be out of his hands, and the public will have to step in . . . . Then look out for disturbances! For there is a very large section of the public which realizes that such licence as is allowed today in the music hall is dangerous to the nation.

The Church knows this only too well and deplores the matter.

The Archbishop of Paris protested, and rightly, against the production of "Saint Sebastian." Others have supported that protest. They have been keen-witted enough to perceive the vast gulf which separates this confused, decadent and hysterical spectacle from those grave and sincere "Mysteries" of the middle ages whose title it presumes to adopt.

They feel the impropriety, the bad taste, of the person of the saint being played by an actress; they resent the lowering of moral standards, the lessening of reverence towards fine traditions, which such licence encourages.

The function of a church is to protect and strengthen the noblest ideals of a people, and these ideals are perpetually outraged, belittled and ridiculed in the theatre; thus moral sense becomes confused.

The church does well to condemn the evil; but it should not stop there. It should not only protest, and far more strongly, against the evil in the theatre but it should cooperate strongly and vigorously in the efforts being made for the reform of that evil. It should give its warmest support to those artists and workers who are endeavouring to drive out of the theatre that which is harmful to the nation and to introduce in its place that which shall be for the nation's moral welfare.

---

LADY DIANA GOES TO THE BALLET. *The English Review*, Volume IX, August, 1911.[1]

---

 he Lady Diana, who was a very grand person in Society, looked up the meaning of the word "choreography," and took a party to the Russian Ballet.

"It's a new thing," she said, "choreography they call it; but personally I think this *Cleopatra* ballet rather tiresome, don't you — too long?" And her friends mostly agreed.

But there was one occupant of her box who boldly dissented.

He said simply, "I think *Cleopatra* is the most beautiful spectacle I ever saw."

"Really! I suppose, being a man, you think so because of its *décolletage*."

"No," he retorted, "it is just a superb artistic design, carried out as no stage performance ever is in England, the whole idea and execution being in the hands of artists, directly towards one end — unity."

"So is the grand scene in the pantomime at the Lane, isn't it?" interposed the lady who had come in "just for half an hour."

"If you like, yes, but the difference is essential. It is the difference between the amateur and the professional — say, that of a work by Augustus

John and a conventional portrait of a worthy R.A. The one is traditional, commercial; the Russian Ballet is creative."

"I see; but tell me what it is you see that is so beautiful in this *Cleopatra*."

The man, who wore a beard, muttered something inaudible.

"The details," he said, "the harmony, the music, the whole. Take, now, the best things we do on our stage—the musical comedies. Now there are plenty of pretty girls, but they cannot dance. Most of them have had no stage-training at all. Take the music; it is not quite serious, is it? There is some difference between Glazounov's *Bacchanale* and that popular dirge 'Yip-i-addy,' you must admit. Or look at the grouping, the stage arrangements. In *Cleopatra* it is all controlled by an artist. There is a single eye and hand over it all. And then it is a splendid historical illustration, a presentation of Egyptian life in the time of Cleopatra more vivid than a hundred written descriptions, real as the wonderful scene between Cleopatra and the messenger of Shakespeare. Look at these Grecian-Egyptian dances. Think of the processional entry. And that spot of black at the end against the gold silence of the temple. Why, the thing is pulsating with life. All the barbaric splendour of that age is conjured up in that Nilotic pageantry of love. You think it dull. I think it superb, inspiring, absolutely beautiful. You see the best dancing the world can produce. You see a living picture designed by real artists. You have delicious music, delicious colour—rhythm. As for the Censor, the man who deems *Cleopatra* immoral had better go down on his knees and pray for a cleaner spirit."

"I don't quite understand," and the Lady Diana turned upon him her famous Luini smile.

"I know. That's it. You think this is a Russian discovery, don't you? You see this house chock-full of people applauding what they consider to be some Muscovite revelation. In part it is. The dancing is Russian, the music is Russian, the splendid unity of design is Russian. But that beautiful blue hanging in *Carnaval,* the lighting and colour scheme of the stage that you liked so much in *Pavillon d'Armide*, in *Igor*, in *Spectre de la Rose*, where do you think the idea of that came from? From Paris? From St. Petersburg? You loved *Sumurun*, I know. Well, *Sumurun* was taken from these Russian choreographic ballets—from *Cleopatra, Antar, Scheherazade*, etc. But where do you imagine the Russians got theirs from? Let me tell you. Ten years ago the Russian ballet had no such thing. It is a new art, and, strange as it may seem to you, it came from England."

The lady who came in late began to think of escape. She had three parties to go on to, and was in no mood for such talk.

"Oh, Bernard Shaw, I suppose," she said; and her remark made the placid man smile all over his face.

"No, not quite," he answered. "The man I am thinking of is the son of indubitably the greatest English actress of our generation, Ellen Terry."

"Really! Now, I never even heard of him," said the Lady Diana.

"Quite so. That is why I am protesting. We don't use our true artists. We seem to have lost the art of seeing art. I repeat, the whole choreographic idea emanated from this artistically ignorant, right-little, tight-little island, and if we had been more perceptive and less insular we should have shown Europe this new stage art instead of obtaining it back second-hand, like a receiver of stolen goods. And yet he revealed it to us. He opened his shop, presented his wares, invited us all, sciolist, patron, critic, and professional, into his sanctuary. We laughed, just as we laughed at Wagner, and still laugh at Ibsen. Our *tartine* standard of art feared and mocked the new idea, and there is nothing the bread-and-butter miss fears more than ideas. We shut down the scuppers and drove the man out of the country. That is what we did."

"Oh, do go on! I simply must know his name."

"You shall, dear Lady Diana," said the man. "You have seen the new choreographic art. It has conquered Russia, Berlin, Paris, and it is now conquering London. The man who gave that beautiful new stage art to Europe is, as I have said, an Englishman, and his name is Gordon Craig."

1. [Reprinted in *Dance Index*, Volume II, no. 8, August, 1943. There is no clear indication that this piece was written by Craig; it is entirely possible that the author was the editor of *The English Review*, a periodical no longer in existence. The current owner of the title writes that files and records for *The English Review* of this date are not in his possession nor can he locate them.]

## KLEPTOMANIA, OR THE RUSSIAN BALLET by John Balance. *The Mask*, Volume IV, no. 2, October, 1911.

here is so much Russian art being let loose into the theatres of Europe lately that it may be as well to study some specimens of it and see what has made the thing so popular and whether there is sufficient ground for so much sudden and insincere enthusiasm.

One finds upon enquiry that some queer and commonplace points arrest attention and dispose of the idea which has somehow gained credence that this art differs from other theatrical work or that it is in any way remarkable.

Mr. Gordon Craig has told us that the Moscow Art Theatre is the first in Europe, but I have noticed that when writing of that theatre he has invariably treated of it as an organization and made no mention of its art. He has been very particular upon this point and his discrimination is significant.

With that side of the story, however, I am not here concerned. What I am interested in are the results. Mr. Craig tells us that the Russians are excellent workers and I do not question his statement; I merely observe that the results obtained by that work of theirs are essentially commonplace.

I do not intend to write here of the Moscow Art Theatre; that is a subject into which I hope to go in my next article, when I shall point out that their work, admirable as it is in execution, is very much the same as that which any other theatre in Europe has to offer us. I hope to consider the Russian Theatre in general under its three aspects of Drama, Ballet and Opera, but here and now shall confine myself to the consideration of the Ballet, which is visiting the European capitals and which is called Russian.

## THE RUSSIAN BALLET.

And first what is this Russian Ballet which has lately caught the fancy of the impressionable Frenchman?

Well, to begin with, it is nothing new. It is the old French ballet warmed up; it is a charming absurdity which has survived the centuries. The French

Ballet is the most deliciously artificial impertinence that ever turned up its nose at Nature.

Nature, so tolerant, has never objected to man making a fool of himself ("no, nor woman neither though by your smiling. . ."). Nature loves a century or two of idiots, and if she can wreck a world on the score of its stupidity, then she is in her seventh heaven, and we fools of Nature, desiring nothing but a little notice to make us intoxicated, often lose our lives by playing thus into the hands of our savage and inexorable mother. But she is our mother, and when we forget that we forget an essential truth.

The Russians have forgotten it. They have borrowed an artificiality from a blasé people and have elaborated it: . . . and France is charmed. They transplanted the French Ballet to St Petersberg, and with the assistance of the cane they persuaded their young dancers into leaping higher than ever. St Petersberg enjoyed the fun for years, but they never sent any troupe into France until quite lately. What has encouraged them to do so now?

Indeed, there seems to be no exquisite reason. Perhaps the Japanese war had something to do with it. This seems to me as good an excuse as any other, for, as I have said, they bring nothing new.

There are equally good dancers already in the Ballet at the Paris Opera House, and there are ballet masters and mistresses who are most certainly quite as talented in this old-fashioned artifice; and the Paris scene-painters and costumiers are as capable as any of these new arrivals.

But the Russians have done one clever thing: they have increased the value of their French Ballet by adding to it a few tricks stolen from other lands and other arts. This was clever of them, . . . . and highly reprehensible.

They invited painters of taste to assist them. They knew that some painters who are not very great as painters are only too delighted to air their knowledge of colour and decoration in the more refined atmosphere of the footlights. It gives them a chance.

So when the painters were secured they dressed up their old Ballet afresh and gave it a new coat of paint.

While doing this they stole an idea or two from the only original dancer of the age, the American, and another idea or two from the most advanced scene designers of Europe and superimposed all these upon the wirey artificial framework of the old French Ballet.

Such is the modern Russian Ballet which Paris has today taken into its dear feeble old arms. The whole spectacle is not a little farcical. Let us now look at the work of M. Bakst who, once an intelligent if successful painter, has become a scene and costume designer to the troupe and who shares the laurels with the dancers Nijinsky and Karsavina.

M. Bakst has a pretty knack of drawing coloured supplements and covers for the illustrated papers. Although the designs are ugly they are only ugly enough to shock Parisians. (This has become a very easy feat of late years). The ugliness of Bakst's designs is not due to any stern qualities in his work; it is never terrible like Daumier, nor has it the irony of Beardsley's demon. Bakst is ugly on account of his clumsy sense of the sensual. All his women, (and he is never tired of putting them before the public,) are drugged and in a kind of sofa orgy. They seem to hate ecstacy and they adore a good wriggle.

The costumes he puts them into are mute; they want to speak and cannot; they are the old refurbished wardrobe of the old Racinet and of Sarah Bernhardt, save that these two spoiled us often with stockings, underwear and sleeves, vests and pinafores.

Bakst has a passion for beads, and his evidently sincere devotion to thick lips and flat noses enables him to indulge in a ring or two now and again. When he is at a loss how to get away from Racinet he fills in the gap, he covers his confusion, with a bead.

The women he draws protrude; therefore when he attempts to suggest something Indian or Chinese (and Russian Ballets are wedded to the East), he gets curiously confused. Indians and Chinese hate that which bulges. Bakst adores bulge; . . . it helps his beads so much. In short Bakst is vulgar. He is like a decorator of the French match boxes; on seeing these maidens of the French match box one is reminded of Bakst.

On paper his vulgarity beams with a kind of blue glow which is not without charm and he has fingers which can draw in delicate outlines his gross visions.

On the stage Bakst is not vulgar, he is simply lost.

His designs for "La Peri" and "Narcisse" are charming in the magazines; in actuality they are non-existent. No one has seen them on the stage. This is an oversight on his part for which he can hardly be held responsible for he has the misfortune to be an amateur, and in amateur theatricals these accidents always happen.

Many of his designs for costumes have lately been published, but to his eternal undoing photographs of these same costumes have been published at the same time. These photographs give M. Bakst away, for the designs and the photographs are unlike each other, and the stage with which he has merely flirted opens its artifical arms for a last embrace. M. Bakst is dead.

The stage does not like philanderers, . . . and M. Bakst was a philanderer. R. I. P.

M. Benois is even worse than M. Bakst. He is a serious old rake. He is another painter who without caution rushed in. The stage is killing him too, but he still manages to totter along pleased to death with himself.

When the two were together they suggested nothing so much as our old friends Pantalone and Il Dottore, such a skit did they seem upon the uselessness of impotence.

If I am incorrect, . . . . if these old gentlemen have really created something, really been of some benefit to the European Theatre; if their scenes and costumes are anything but the old vulgarity warmed up again; if they are artists and not merely blunderers, then let them bring evidence to prove it.

They are blunderers because they draw their designs on paper and then attempt to translate them into the language of the stage. They cannot think in the language of stage land . . . . or let us say, in the material of the stage, because, as the only serious master of theatrical art has said,[1] there is no material; "you cannot comingle the arts and cry out that you have created a new art. If you can find in nature a new material,[2] one which has never yet been used by man to give form to his thoughts, then you can say that you are on the high road to creating a new art. For you have found that by which you can create it, it then only remains for you to begin. The theatre, as I see it, has yet to find that material."

---

## THE DANCERS.

---

The Russian Dancers have always been most agile. Until quite lately in fact only since Miss Isadora Duncan's visit to St Petersberg in, I think, 1904, they have not understood the value of the curve. The last seven years they have been studying the charm of the weak and tender line won by non-resistence. The great American was the first to demonstrate this in Europe.

The two most perfect Russian dancers are Pavlowa and Nijinsky. These two have been the most successful in acquiring the grace taught them by the American, and every performance of theirs becomes less and less the old French thing and more and more American. As with M. Bakst and his scenes and costumes so it is with their Dancing. It is not original; it is something learned and then made. They create nothing.

In order to create anything a fierce belief is essential. The Artificial is that which is made by hands, and any sceptic can make it. A work of art is that which is created in distinction to that which is made. All modern dancing is manufactured and the Russian dancers are merely a copy of this made thing.

It is pretence, fascinating and daring pretence, just as their scenery is pretentious. All great Art is very simple and direct. The Russians are sly about their work, oh, very very sly. There is no trusting it, and it is very elaborate like most sly things are.

And this elaboration and these winks are very comforting to the wornout Parisian society and to a certain weary group of Londoners who ask for nothing better than artifice to keep them awake.

As a work of Art then the Russian Ballet is a myth; as a work of originality it is a fraud. The dancers, painters and wig-makers of the troupe are all charming will o' the wisps and their light is certainly not to be trusted.

We await the time when Dancing shall move onward and upwards into a quite different plane before we can accept it as a fine art.

1. Gordon Craig in "The Actor and the Über-Marionette." See p. 37.
2. When that material has been discovered and tested it will be time enough to take M. Bakst and M. Benois seriously.

## THE RUSSIAN BALLET. 1911 by A. C. [Allen Carric.] *The Mask*, Volume IV, no. 3, January, 1912.

hy has the Russian Ballet appealed with such force to modern Paris? Has Paris become a lover of the prudish? And what has taken London by storm? Is it the prudery and "the court-like coldness" of the whole exhibition?

For the dancers and painters have given us no new creation . . . . no new life has been created: an old and dusty wardrobe has been brought up from the cellars of the Paris Opera House and the Russian collectors of curios have indulged their mania for the old-fashioned and have dressed up living dolls with the cast off clothes of a dead age . . . . an age which was dead at the time of its birth.

And that is exactly what the discerning Publics of Europe will very soon be saying.

## THE RUSSIAN BALLET, a letter from George Calderon and Mr. John Balance's Reply. *The Mask*, Volume IV, no. 3, January, 1912.

Sir,

In your article on the Russian Ballet, among many stupid things, there is one so overwhelmingly stupid that the rest don't matter: and that is the use of the words "stealing," "fraud," and "kleptomania" in speaking of the lessons which the Russian dancers have learnt from Isadora Duncan. When the Russians saw that she danced better than themselves, what on earth did you expect them to do? To go on dancing badly, and not try to improve by the methods she showed them? Is that what is done in other arts? Is it "stealing" if a painter or an author pursues a road opened up by his predecessor? In that case all Schools of artists (the history of painting and literature is founded on the assumption of continuous influence) are merely dens of thieves; Millais or Holman Hunt or somebody was the only Pre-Raphaelite; the rest were thieves. Gauguin or Matisse or somebody was the only Post-impressionist; the rest were thieves. Craig is a thief, because he has cribbed his lighting from the barn-theatre, where they hang stable-lanterns on hooks; and all his intending pupils had better go and give themselves up to the police at once.

This John Balance seems to be a most unbalanced person. (It is plain from his article, by the bye, that he has never been to Covent Garden at all to see the "weary group of Londoners" propping their jaded eyelids open to peer at the dismal old doings on the stage.) Does he allege that the Russians have mastered the principles of Isadora Duncan's dancing, or does he allege that they have merely pinched a wheeze or two? In one sentence he says that they have taken "a few tricks"; in another he says that for seven years, since she first danced in St Petersburg, they have been studying "the weak and tender line won by non-resistance" (whatever that may mean) which "the great American" was the first to demonstrate. A trick or two after seven years was poor stealing!

But, gracious Nature! (our Mother, as John Balance says), has Isadora Duncan a copyright in "weak and tender" lines? Has she appropriated a whole sphere of attitudes and gestures for her very own? And must they perish when she dies, on pain of hue and cry? or will she leave them to someone in her will?

The Ballet has *all* human movements for its sphere, Duncan or no Duncan, and the first man who jumped in the air or stood on his head is not going to call 'Police!' out of his grave. There never was and never can be 'theft' in gesture. I have never seen Isadora Duncan dance, but I'll wager that her range of gesture does not cover one-twentieth part of the range of the Russian ballet. What have any of those Egyptian dances to do with her? Carnaval? Scheherazade? Prince Igor? what would she make of Harlequin, or Pierrot, or a Polovtsian warrior? If she sees the Article, I think she will write herself to say how stupid it is.

Heathfield Lodge,                                    Yours faithfully
    Hampstead Heath, N. W.                        George Calderon.

---

## MR. JOHN BALANCE'S REPLY

---

Mr. George Calderon is an Englishman; hence his enthusiasm for the Russian-Tartar-French dancers who have invaded London lately. He is not content with saying that these ladies and gentlemen are magnificent and that the English speaking race are better dancers; he goes crazy with delight rather than enquire. Note what he says; "I have never seen Isadora Duncan dance," and then with blind Russophobia he "wagers" that she can't dance.

What can be said in reply to so charming, so childish a being? Merely this: that he is almost as rash and prejudiced as some of our friends on the staff of *The Mask*, . . . . but that he really need not be careless.

For instance when he asks "what would Miss Duncan make of Harlequin, Pierrot or a Polovtsian warrior we have no reply to make: we can only make a speechless if somewhat tickled appeal to those who are students of the greatest dancing and we know that their reply will be an equally silent one.

I wonder if Mr. Calderon always goes about bumping into people who are seriously at work and excusing himself on the ground of his ignorance? I cannot think that that kind of thing leads anywhere, for there is so much to learn for the great artists of today and if some resistance from the enquirer is healthy, a great deal too much of it may easily be mistaken for ignorance and boorishness.

John Balance.

Editorial Note. THE RUSSIANS by John Semar. *The Mask*, Volume IV, no. 3, January, 1912.

he visit of the Russian Ballet to Covent Garden has proved a grand failure. Over three hundred pounds sterling was lost each week.

It would be curious to know when Englishmen will be willing to achieve one such grand defeat rather than survive the many ignominious successes they always manage to manipulate.

Foreign Note. London. THE RUSSIAN BALLET by R. S. [Rudolf Schmerz.] *The Mask,* Volume V, no. 1, July, 1912.

 t becomes more and more amazing to some of us how it is that the Russian Ballet was ever let into London at all. We used to be so strict in London and still are so strict about some things and they are some of those things which are very closely connected with the Russian Ballet.

Still, the ladies are very fascinating and quite the nicest part of the whole show.

I suppose it is a little late to advise England about such matters, for did not Wilde say, "It is always a silly thing to give advice but to give good advice is absolutely fatal."

Foreign Note. New York. CANNIBALISM, COSTUME AND A COAT OF PAINT by P. G. [Giulio Piero.] *The Mask,* Volume V, no. 3, January, 1913.

 he Germans and Professor Reinhardt practically exhausted the Turkish theme in "Sumurun" and in their other assumptions, . . . (for "Oedipus," "A Venetian Night," "The Miracle" and the rest are Turkish in temperature in spite of their Greek and German source).

Owing to this the Russians and Léon Bakst have been driven to Cannibalism, which after all is a kind of off-shoot of Post Impressionism.

The Cannibalist paints on flesh. To M. Bakst the credit of being the first of this new school must be given. He has been painting the legs of the ballet dancers of New York.

This is a practical as well as a most distinguished idea. Why buy tights when a coat of paint will do, with here and there a stripe or a star?

There are some people who will cry out at this revolution which a Parisian Dancer has declared is Sacrilege. "Paint my beautiful legs!" she cried; "Never!".

We agree with her; . . . but the idea is very distinguished; we are all bound to admit that much, . . . . what?

So "Cannibalism" has arrived, and M. Bakst has said farewell to his last bead. It was a versatile bead; it served every purpose of costume. But its possibilities were limited by the side of this coat of paint.

The Russian Ballet has solved the problem of costume and managements need send no longer to Damascus for silks, but only to Aspinalls for a few pots of their sixpenny enamel.

---

THE RUSSIAN BALLET. NIJINSKI'S ACKNOWLEDGEMENT
by J. S. [John Semar.] *The Mask,* Volume V, no. 3, January, 1913.

---

ast year, when London went mad over the Russian Ballet, and every critic in London, professional or otherwise, was losing his head and utterly failing to discern what the Russian Ballet was *exactly* composed of, when all these people were writing and speaking of the Russians as if they had created a new form of dancing, Mr. John Balance pointed out in *The Mask*, that Miss Isadora Duncan had lent her aid, to its creation.

What Mr. Balance wrote, readers of *The Mask* will remember, but critics seem to be ignorant of the fact. Critics, unfortunately for England, seem always ignorant of facts, and think that *every* new production in art, whether it be an opera, a ballet, a painting or a drama, is the happy inspiration of the particular person who at that moment is seen to produce it. He *always* forgets, he never fails to forget, he would die sooner than not forget, that art is the creation of a very few individuals on earth and that all the others are more or less imitators. He fails to note that even certain nations are purely imitative and never produce creative artists and that there are some few nations that do produce creative artists, and he forgets a lot of other things as well. But in this particular case, he forgot completely that which was so obvious, . . . . the debt which Mr. Fokine and Russians owed to Miss Duncan.

When it was pointed out in *The Mask* that she had influenced St. Petersburg, one or two people exclaimed against this, among others, Mr. George Calderon. He grew very cross with Mr. John Balance, and laughed the idea to scorn that Nijinsky, Pavlova and the others had learnt anything from the great American.

It is very agreeable to us that we are able to publish a signed article by Nijinski, the first dancer in Russia, and the head of the Russian Ballet. This is what he says: . . . .

"Isadora Duncan is a great artist. Her influence in modern choreography has been very important. Before being produced with the success that one knows, choreography was to a certain extent restrained by an exacting technique. Isadora dared to give liberty to movement, enlarged the boundaries in which the artist may evolve, and abolished the frontiers established by custom. She has opened the door of their cell to the prisoners. Fokine, the great Fokine, has followed in her footsteps, and attained the summit. Before then, in one word, the fantasy and temperament of the dancer were limited." Nijinsky.

It is not often that the right thing happens, and we little dreamed that Nijinsky would come forward so soon and speak like a true disciple. Would it be too much to ask London to awaken its discernment and rouse its perception so that it too shall understand the difference of THIS and THAT, and realise that the north is precisely the opposite to the south, and the right hand different from the left, and such-like simple things; for by discernment, instead of a kind of fat contentedness to muddle, the whole nation would regain its youth again. As it is, England praises Tom, Dick and Harry and Salvini and praises all alike as though all were of equal value . . . .

We ask for better informed critics.

# VOLUME SIX. PRELUDE. *The Mask*, Volume VI, no. 1, July, 1913.

*We have asked Mr. Gordon Craig, the Founder of "The Mask," and, from the outset, its good friend, to initiate the sixth volume by editing its first number, and this he has consented to do. J.S. [John Semar]*

 am down to write the Preface to this number, indeed, to a new volume, and nothing could give me greater happiness. Not because I want to say how well everyone in *The Mask* has done his or her task since the work began, though I could say a good word on that; but because having escaped from the Daemon who accompanies me . . . . from a really most untheatrical figure who keeps me to my task in my working hours . . . . that is to say, having escaped from the Spirit of the Theatre, I can revel in a holiday, and in this Prelude reveal my personal pleasures of the moment and my personal fancies for the day.

I note among the contributions for this year . . . . and it is even to be in this number . . . . an article which I myself have written at the dictation of the said Spirit of the Theatre, and which, were it not already in the Press, I, as the writer of this Prelude and as temporary Editor of this Journal, should cut through with Pencil blue and refuse to print.

I should refuse it on personal grounds whereas an Editor must be impersonal.

I very much object to myself having written an article which gives anything but the most overwhelming praise to my friend Nijinsky. I object on personal grounds; for I not only admire that amazing genius, having a considerable appreciation of his personal qualities, but besides this feel nothing but good fellowship towards him. To chat with him in six languages over a cigar is one of the most delightful experiences life has to offer.

What then can permit me to allow such an article as this number contains to pass?

My friend Djagelief too. What of him? He will be awfully offended at what I have said of his charming group of dancers, for I do not know a more genial man on the face of this earth; and if he believes that the body produces finer works than the soul produces . . . . why shouldn't he believe it? I at this moment and in this Prelude, not as Editor of this Journal, but as a friend of his and free once more, can find no earthly[1] reason why he should not believe it.

I do not know whether I have mentioned Mademoiselle Karsavina in the article. I shall not look at the wretched thing again . . . . that impertinent article! In fact, I have a very good mind to take serious action against the writer . . . . except that action is, according to Rimbaud, "only a way of spoiling something."

But I suppose Mlle. Karsavina will easily believe me when I tell her that I have sat entranced to see her blowing a trumpet round the stage . . . . a trumpet which she does not blow, but which is blown for her by a gentleman in evening dress. I should like to see her blowing the trumpet whenever I remember that passage of the charming music of that amazing "genius" for "theatrical" music, Stravinsky, and would have given anything to meet her . . . . as they say . . . . to have talked with her for half an hour . . . . , an hour . . . . , two hours, three, four, five, or ten hours on the difficulties she has to encounter in her work, the defeats she has encountered, and the hopes and fears with which she looks forward to the future. Anything . . . . everything . . . . to show that I am a human being and that my only thought is of human beings as human beings.

But, oh, you good people all of you, especially you dear Russians both of St Petersberg and Moscow, . . . . when the devil are we all going to wake up in the Theatre? No, seriously . . . . WHEN ARE WE GOING TO WAKE UP?

That tin trumpet of Stravinsky, even when a Karsavina pretends to blow upon it, will not even wake up a cat.

You have done marvels, . . . we all know it, . . . most of all do I know it; the most marvellous tricks that can be done. But when is the whole family going to wake up and together create one little thing in a moment of inspiration, . . . a thing of inspiration, pure and inspired? A little Law to guide an Art.

This, this most difficult of all things we have forgotten to attend to: We are afraid! That is the reason. We are afraid of time . . . . it would take us years of experiment and lives of thought and oceans of feeling, and we find we are poor in thought and feeling . . . . oh, oh, oh!

We are all geniuses; we know that we are all wonderful beings, . . . that goes without saying. But what is not yet evident is, . . . what have we found that we can place by the side of the Pyramid, . . . that will compare with one of its steps?

What we lack, says Flaubert, is *Conscience*! I know we have in our possession as great a secret as lies hidden in the Pyramids. Well then, my dears, let us whisper over that secret together.

All the boys and girls who shall spring from us must be united together and know that secret. There is not another moment to lose if it is to be clear to them twenty years from today. I shall eat, drink and be merry meantime, . . . and I hope you will eat as much, drink much more and try to be as merry. But I swear I will drop a seed of that secret before I am finished, and I wish that each of you would drop one too. Then we should have GROWTH.

This is a beautiful City, this Florence; . . . . you cannot tell how beautiful it is. Would it not be a nice thing if we should all meet here from time to time? . . . a month in your lives is not so long.

This City has such a curious flavour of ease and merriment. Here is the excitement of great Architecture . . . . Did you ever taste *that*? The City is rich, not gaudy; familiar, not vulgar; it grapples its tried friends to its soul with hoops of steel; . . . to us there is no City as fair. What its architects have said we take for our Law; there is no grief, no misery here, for the towers stand up straight and announce the triumph of tenderness and strength.

Oh! don't fear! . . . It's a real earth-town made by human beings. Every inch of our city breathes a friendliness that is human, and yet over it all there broods something more, . . . something indescribable, . . . and something that if you could describe you wouldn't . . . for who would describe a mystery which has been revealed after long obscurity and is now but part of the obvious?

Not being able to describe it, it impels you towards a condition necessary to the creation of that which we call Art. For only in terms of Art can this mystery which is so obvious be rightly translated for those who could never bear to experience it.

The City is a high experience. What a cradle it would be for the Art which we call the Art of the Theatre! . . . . for the Art of Movement! That movement which all dancers are forced to make after effort and with feet glued to the ground, but which a butterfly makes with ease and by nature!

Every bell in the town breaks out ringing at the moment I write. A hundred . . . . two hundred . . . . three hundred perhaps. It is a wave of sound moving in great circles . . . .

This place is a place of ecstacy.

To all those working in the Theatre who love the Theatre I say . . . do not keep away from me too long.

Come quickly, and come here! Do not consider how you come . . . .

why you come. Would it be so unnatural to come because somebody calls you?

So begins the sixth volume of the best book ever dedicated to the service of our beloved Theatre.

1. This is a slang phrase which in England is only used among artists and by the lower classes. I suppose it is to show the good terms they are on with the earth. Got you there, Pedant of the "New" School which we now know is the "Old" School!

## THE RUSSIAN BALLET. *The Mask*, Volume VI, no. 1, July, 1913.[1]

*We leave ourselves at home when we go to the Theatre; we there renounce the right to our own tongue and choice, to our taste, and even to our courage as we possess it and practise it within our own four walls in relation to God and man. No one takes his finest taste in art into the theatre with him, not even the artist who works for the theatre; there one is people, public, herd, woman, Pharisee, voting animal, democrat, neighbour, and fellow-creature; there even the most personal conscience succumbs to the levelling charm of the "great multitude"; there stupidity operates as wantonness and contagion; there the neighbour rules, there one becomes a neighbour.*

*"The Joyful Wisdom." Nietzsche.*

### OF ART AND ITS CREATOR.

n Art there must be created no feeling of disharmony between the Body and the Soul, yet in creating Art the body must be obedient, true, faithful to the Soul.

It is the Soul must speak, but the lips must not be seen to move, and the throat must be as ivory.

While it is the time of Revelation we ask the Body for silent and invisible service . . . it is the Soul which moves . . . minister to its movements.

I put no query here, nor have I any doubts myself as to the value of the Body or the value of the Soul.

I would not undervalue either.

But in the creating of some things it is certain the Soul must be subservient to the Body; in the creation of others the Body must as certainly be subservient to the Soul. What an alliance when each can obey the other, keeping its place . . . . holding its peace . . . . in time and in tune to the force of the other . . . the Beloved.

There is no such thing as union which excludes *command* or *obedience.* Each honours the other.

I will take the first six examples of great works of art. See the Pyramid . . . . the head of Amenemhat III . . . . or the painting of the Buddha and the Thirty three Bosatsous made by the priest Esshin. Look at the bronze statue of Dai-Butsu at Kamakura; or upon the towers of Tuscany and of Ireland, or at the needlework of a mother on the socks of a child; and I swear to you that these things were made when the soul was working released from the tyranny of the body . . . a body which knows it may claim the right in due time to command the soul.

These truths are just what unreasonable people wish to deny. They will not accept the simplest natural truths. The great hum going round the earth today about uniting the Body and the Soul in smug relationship leads to the building of abominable houses, wretched palaces and meaningless churches; produces the foolish paintings, the trembling books, and the awful music.

Both Soul and Body are helpless to create Art nowadays, for they have been joined, tied, rivetted together by a lie, and equal liberties allowed to each, equal powers and qualities assigned to each.

Hence all works of Art which are the creation of the Soul and nothing but the Soul are looked upon as "queer" and "quaint," . . . those are the words which people use today towards works of Art which show us signs that the Soul made them.

"Glorious," "wonderful," "brilliant," these are the words used towards the works of Art made by the Body today.

By these words the mob excuses its own ignorance and comforts its cowardice . . . for the mob, fearing the individual, stands as much for the Body today as it has always done: the mob, . . . that which is everlastingly fickle and detests the Soul, . . . the inspirer . . . that which alone remains unconquerable through faith.

And so through its blind hatred of its master the mob today comes to find the workings of the Soul incomprehensible, whereas it recognises in the workings of the Body an experience of yesterday.

If Art, the voice of Revelation, were concerned solely with recording what has been, perhaps there would be nothing to be said. But Art is most of all concerned with Tomorrow and the Horizon.

The Pyramids were not only records; they were and still are always pointing towards the Future. The Soul of Man runs easily up the great stairs and in the topmost silence is aware of Truth.

It will be asked why some of the works of Art may not be created by the Body? Why should there not be a great deal of comfortable work so as to make the world more "gemüthlich," with here and there a nice blaze of sensuous stuff too? Why not? . . . why not?

But what a ridiculous thing to call for . . . . what a ridiculous thing to be always calling for and to get excited about when it comes!

For that comfortable and sensuous type of work is all over the place.

It pours out of the Theatre in streams. The novels are soaked with it. Painting bubbles with it. The music which it makes smokes and steams. There is no question but that there will always be sufficient of this. Hence it is needful that we look for the other, and call for the other until we get it.

So much as Prelude to my Note on the Russian Ballet. The Russian Ballet is essentially the "Art" which is created by the Body. Its perfection is physical. Its appeal is to our senses, not through them.[2]

Having excited them it has done its task. It makes no further effort. It is sensuous art and not spiritual, and is just as far removed from Architecture and Music as the Body is from the Soul, and I wish, and millions of people wish, to see the Theatre give birth to an art as spiritual as music or architecture.

---

## OF ART AND ITS DESTROYER.

---

I wonder if any of you will have read the "Life and Works of Chevalier Noverre." I wonder if any of you even know who this famous man was and what he did. You, who have gone to the Russian Ballet every night and speak in the same terms of what you witnessed there as you do when speaking of the works of Aschylus, of Dante, of Donatello or of Bach, have you ever heard of Chevalier Noverre?

It is a hundred to one that he and his work are unknown to you. Noverre was a maître à danser . . . . a Ballet master, the most celebrated of the 18th

Century, and the times and values then were very little different in regard to art from those of today, and people exaggerated the importance of the dashing personality of the charming maître and confounded it with his work, even as they exaggerate and confuse the persons with the work of the modern Ballet masters.

When we discover a dashing personality we conclude that we have discovered a great artist and we speak of him in place of his art: or we are blinded by that personality and take it to *be* his art: . . . for we have taught ourselves some tricky phrase about personality in art and are unable to get free from our conception.

It can't be doubted for a moment that the Chevalier Noverre was a very charming and excellent person. His little way of haggling over money with Garrick and others is a mere nothing, and his delightful conceit in associating his name at every possible turn with those of Haydn, Mozart or Gluck is very natural . . . . but alas! he is comparatively forgotten.

Yet Noverre will live by those of his works which have come down to us, and they show us pretty clearly that he was not an artist, if a maître à danser . . . . that he was a charlatan in so far as art is concerned; and they should warn us to be a little careful before we explode with too much enthusiasm about the nearest things to Noverre's "art" which we can witness now . . . . the Russian Ballet.

I am a great admirer of the Russian Ballet. I find that it is often the best dressed company of ladies and gentlemen who ever assumed a little sock and less buskin.

When I say that I am an admirer of the Russian Ballet, I mean that all the Dancers and their Maître à danser charm me in spite of a few things that I frankly don't like. For, as those of you will know who have read my book written some years before this Ballet left St Petersburg, nay, before it was formed as we see it today, I have reason for being opposed to the entrance of the studio painter into the Theatre; just as many of you would dislike to see a stage painter decorating your churches. The Theatre has its own great scene-painters and needs no others.

I am not a believer in the fluttering, bubbling personality of the stage "Stars"; . . . I am against the emphasis which is laid on the Body in the Theatre, because I am one of those few who love the Stage as a father loves his son, . . . as a son his father.

The dancers of the Russian Ballet and their maître à danser are charming people; Nijinsky a marvel of technique, best when under M. Fokine's control; and all his brother and sister dancers . . . charming; and M.

Fokine, chief master of the dance, quite extraordinary. But if you ask me to look upon their work as a work of art, or to speak of them as great artists, I must refuse, and I hope that some of the visitors to Covent Garden will be with me here.

Noverre once entered the lists against Aeschylus and attempted to interpret anew the story of Agamemnon and Orestes. Noverre was a great maître à danser, but he was no artist. Had he been artist he would have done less . . . succeeded less . . . . but brought the art of dancing a step nearer to the condition of a fine art.

Here is his conception of the mighty works of the Trilogy: . . .

AGAMEMNON REVENGED
A Tragic Ballet
by
Jean Georges Noverre.
Scene I.
Part of the Gardens of Mycene.

Egysthus and Clytemnestra enter, felicitating each on their mutual happiness, and anxious only for the pleasing moment when they shall make public the sentiments which unite their hearts. The distance and uncertainty, however, of that desired period fill Clytemnestra with *the most distressing disquietude*,[3] which is heightened by the alarming presages of a very frightful dream. Egysthus, not less troubled on this account than the queen, throws himself at her feet, and swearing love and everlasting fidelity, promises that his arm shall soon deliver her from the obstacles that seem to threaten an interruption to their mutual bliss.

Scene II.

At the instant of his making these protestations a sound of drums, trumpets, and other war-like instruments is heard, *which throws Egysthus and Clytemnestra into the greatest consternation*[4] *and affright.* He springs from the feet of the queen with equal precipitation and fear. The noise affects their astonished souls like a peal of wrathful thunder . . . they shrink with *confusion.*

Scene III.

A herald from Agamemnon enters with a letter to the queen from that Prince, which he delivers to her on his knees. Clytemnestra *with a trembling hand*[5] receives the letter and makes a motion to the herald to withdraw; he retires to the furthest part of the stage. Terror and affright seize the heart of Clytemnestra; a deathlike paleness over-spreads her countenance; nor can she by any means resolve to read the unwelcome letter. Desirous, however, to conceal her anxiety, she orders the herald to leave her, *assuming at the same time a look of satisfaction and giving him to understand* that his message puts an end to all her griefs and misfortunes.

*Scene IV.*

Clytemnestra and Egysthus draw near to each other with visible emotions of fear. Clytemnestra, sighing, shows him the fatal billet. *She hesitates, but at last opens it with a hastiness*[6] *that displays the agitation and tumult of her disordered mind.* By degrees they assume boldness enough to examine the contents; *every line, every sentence, increases their apprehension and distress;* but the intelligence that the king is immediately following in the steps of his messenger carries the severest stroke to the heart of Clytemnestra. Egysthus feels the same sensations: *both seem annihilated under the pressure of their misfortunes, and they recover from their situation only to sink into the most poignant despair.* Egysthus proposes to murder Agamemnon. *Clytemnestra shudders at the thought,* and rejects the project. He threatens to leave her and destroy himself. *Trembling the queen endeavors* to appease his rage and soothe his transports, and to induce him to stay. She seems at one moment to yield to his horrid proposal, but the next her heart rebels against the thought; she reproaches herself with her barbarity, and becomes *sensibly shocked* at the enormity of such a crime. Egysthus, who is conscious of having no resource but flight or treason, breaks out into passion and menaces. His arm, accustomed to murder, only seeks new victims for his fury. The unhappy queen, not knowing how to resolve, in a fatal moment yields to and joins in the black designs of Egysthus. They go off *in all the agitation which fury, anguish and despair* can excite in the human breast[7] or characterize in the expressions of mind and body.

This is poor Noverre's idea of Tragedy and of Art.

I really can't take up space in reprinting more of the nonsense . . . . but it is enough to show you the amazing *cheapness* of the mind of Noverre . . . . the greatest Ballet Master of his time. I will admit that some of the movements of the dancers may have been quite "splendid," I grant it ever so willingly . . . . all I refuse to let myself tell people is that this could possibly have been *a work of art.*

A splendid line or two in a badly conceived and badly written poem will not make a work of art . . . . and there is something seriously wrong with us if our critical faculty is able to be carried away to such an extent that we apply the same terms of praise to the ballets of Noverre or Fokine as we do to the solemn and lovely works of art by Aechylus, or John Sebastian Bach.

There is another short line or two from Noverre's "Agamemnon Revenged" that I must quote. Upon Agamemnon telling Clytemnestra the name of his young captive Cassandra he recommends her to "the generous protection of the Queen."

*"Clytemnestra then embraces her, and takes off her chains, but in performing this benevolent action seems to swear implacable hatred against the young princess.* At every instant when unobserved, the queen and Egysthus express the fury and impatience with which they burn to satiate their vengeance and to sacrifice every object that seems to oppose their wishes."[8]

Now this even if it be pure ballet, and purely "theatrical" in the silly sense of the word, does not belong to a work of art. As performed by a great dancer it here and there might become noble and tragic .... but only here and there as it were *by accident.*

Art is not at all a matter of accident: it is all a matter of design even as Nature is a matter of design. And so deliberate a misreading of Nature as Noverre is guilty of, is exactly what the Russian Ballet is guilty of.

M. Nijinsky's "Après midi d'un Faun" does not improve matters. Thought out with the all-too-clever twists of the Russian brains, it is daring and nothing else. I am told that M. Rodin was enthusiastic. What of that? Shall a sculptor decide all things? If this be allowed will it also be permitted that we of the Theatre shall be the judges to pronounce of Sculpture, . . . and be listened to? Take care lest we pronounce in favour of our property man who makes our Giant's Head or Blondin donkeys!

Nature is not at all like a charming Carnival, or that ridiculous interpretation of Chopin in muslin skirts .... where the dancers could not even interpret correctly.

For Nature has a Rhythm. The Russian Ballet knows nothing of that Rhythm. It is charming . . . perfectly, deliciously, intoxicatingly charming but its charm is artificial; and Art's great claim to distinction is that it approaches nearer to Nature than anything else can do. And we insult all the masters of old, and those who today are striving to learn a few of the myriad secrets of Nature, when we rave frantically over what the Russian Ballet has to offer us.

I have written this after long deliberation, and because I believe that someone who holds all the Arts in the deepest respect must say a word to stem the tide of gush and error which threatens our development.

I wish our Russian visitors all the *"success"* in the world . . . may they come back to England again and again, and may a rain of bouquets be showered upon the lovely ladies who pass before us so tenderly and so temptingly on the stage of Covent Garden. May Nijinsky leap as loftily as ever and even more lightly, and may our admiration for his surprising technical powers still express themselves in thunders of applause.

As for M. Fokine, let him be crowned King of all the Ballets!

But let us not act towards Art as foolish traitors do who sell the noblest for the silver pieces. We can all of us fall under the spell of these dancers for a moment, but let us not love and reverence them as though they had reached to the high achievement of masters of art.

The Theatre is in this century about to make a new effort to become a fine art . . . . it is preparing to ascend . . . . to approach a very difficult and dangerous incline. Do not thoughtlessly hamper its ascent by ill-advised enthusiasm whenever it stumbles in the ascent.

The Russian Ballet is held to be the finest achievement of the New Theatre. The Russian Ballet belongs to the Theatre of Yesterday.

When our Theatre is re-formed my knowledge of my theatrical brothers forces me to be quite certain that we shall *"reform it altogether."*

The Russian Ballet is one of the modern Theatre's charming accidents. For the sake of the future of the Art of the Theatre, do not in your enthusiasm mistake every taking [sic] Ballet or "Production" for one of its noblest efforts.

1. [Partially reprinted in *Dance Index*, Volume I, no. 7, July, 1942, and Volume II, no. 8, August, 1943.]
2. This life's five windows of the soul / Distort the heavens from pole to pole / And leads you to believe a lie, / When you see with, not through the eye. William Blake. "The Everlasting Gospel."
3. Notice how this Tragic Ballet opens in anxious jerks and distressing spasms, . . . the very opposite way to that in which one expects a tragedy to begin.
4. Consternation and confusion are out of place at the commencement of a great tragic drama. In fact they militate against the tragedy. Consternation and confusion are two states of being which should neither be represented nor stirred up in the spectators. All great art combats consternation and confusion.
5. Is it not preposterous? . . . . Clytemnestra!! . . . . ?

6. No, no, it is exactly what she does not do. Clytemnestra opens it with a hastiness that displays all the agitation and tumult of a ballet-dancer's 'mind.' Aeschlylus opened it differently.
7. Of a Ballet-master.
8. Can't one see it! All stage emotion . . . . stage proportions.

---

## Book Review. THE RUSSIAN BALLET by Ellen Terry. Unsigned. *The Mask*, Volume VI, no. 1, July, 1913.

---

 charming book on the Russian Ballet. Printed on fine paper. With drawings by Miss Pamela Coleman Smith from photos or from other drawings.

---

## Editorial Note. THE RUSSIAN BALLET. *The Mask*, Volume VI, no. 1, July, 1913.

---

 y the bye, about four months ago I saw in the papers that I was to produce a Ballet for you. It was not I that made the announcement.

It seems that I was to have Dr. Vaughan Williams as collaborator.

Of course the idea is cheering, but is it practical? And now is it not far less practical than it was before? . . And have you not already in your hearts given me notice?

For NO amount of Ballets which I might produce would ever be announced by me as Works of Art, and I should, as I have ever done, protest against their being so considered. Well then . . . . where are we?

Editorial Note. M. LEON BAKST, 1913. Unsigned. *The Mask*,
Volume VI, no. 3, January, 1914.

 his talented painter has been speaking to a representa-
tive of "The Daily News and Leader" and the status of
that journal is of course sufficient guarantee that what
he said was carefully and exactly reported. Here are
some of M. Bakst's statements:

"The Theatre of the Future means the triumph of
painting and its gradual abolition of the spoken word."

M. Bakst has evidently had a quarrel with Signor D'Annunzio.

Readers of *The Mask* from 1908 will be quite surprised to hear that
"The Triumph of Painting" is to be celebrated in the future in the Theatre,
for they know that painting is valueless in a theatre.

They have also learnt that true painters prefer to work anywhere rather
than in a theatre.

As for the "abolition of the spoken word," something touching this
subject was broached by Mr. Gordon Craig in 1908 or even earlier. It was
the outcome of a long apprenticeship in the Theatre. M. Bakst, having
gone in for Theatricals only quite lately, dashes in with a charming innocence and echoes Mr. Craig's words, . . . . without having quite grasped
their significance.

M. Bakst is ignorant, . . . he speaks of "Dr. Meyerhold's proscenium"
as being of no use and as ending in failure.

Now M. Bakst must know quite well that the work of Dr. Meyerhold is
not adequately represented by a proscenium, he knows quite well that Dr.
Meyerhold is a regisseur or stage manager of a high order.

M. Bakst should try to speak with respect of those leading men whom he
found at work in the theatre when he casually entered one day into the
scenic room of a theatre.

M. Bakst also talks of Mr. Craig's "art of cubes." What this can mean
none of us can say. We know of no "art of cubes."

M. Bakst continues:

"I have done much to abolish the old spectacle, and I have proved that
people no longer listen to the author."

To abolish is good sometimes, and to prove is always good. But M.
Bakst has done neither the one nor the other. He has made a sensation,

and that is quite an achievement. And now he threatens to become notorious, . . . . and that is quite a different matter.

His scenic and costume effects, allied as they were to the old fashioned Theatre, were brilliant and unique. He now joins the Futurists, and becomes one of a crowd.

Listen to the following: . . . is it not almost the voice of Signor Marinetti? "The triumphant success attained by the music-halls and the cinematographs leads one to conclude that the spectacle of the future will be of a kaleidoscopic nature . . . something like a ride in a motor car or an aeroplane, or a walk amidst a crowd hurrying along with feverish haste. The emotions produced among the spectators at the cinema are a proof of the defeat of the spoken word by the picture. There is no need for it."

And again, "Another form of intelligence is destined to reign upon the stage. Formerly intelligence was of a cerebral nature. In future it will be of a plastic nature. Great truths, great duties, follow no beaten track. The theatre will arrive at great duties, great truths, by plastic spectacles without the collaboration of the man of letters, which is only irritating now."

Something like this we have also heard before: it did not originate with M. Bakst.

In fact M. Bakst appears to have transformed himself from a skillful stringer of beads into a phonograph for repeating the words and ideas of other men, . . . only unfortunately he garbles or weakens these by a mere parrot-like repetition; and in his mouth the serious and significant words by which men of long practical experience and study express their convictions become the mere catch words, the empty shibboleths of a shallow enthusiasm and a volatile taste.

UPON SEVERAL THINGS. SOME NOTES by John Balance.
*The Mask*, Volume VII, no. 1, July, 1914.

## THE RUSSIAN BALLET. M. DIAGHILEW.
## THE DANCER NIJINSKY.
## DESERTERS IN THE ARMY.

### *THE RUSSIAN BALLET.*

he travelling company which we know of by the name of the Russian Ballet is, more correctly speaking, a branch of the Russian Ballet, which has been in existence for more years than any of our readers have seen.

It is a State organization; its pocket money over a million roubles, . . . that is to say, over one hundred thousand pounds a years.

Its founders and supporters are not impelled by a great love of the nobility of art, but they wisely recognise that a great state governed by men instead of by mice and women needs a great Ballet, a great Opera House, a great Theatre.

Neither are these founders of this Ballet concerned about the intellectual, spiritual or moral qualities of those who are to be put upon their stage. A pretty girl? . . . put her on, . . . train her . . . make her dance; . . . she can't? then turn her out: . . . Finished!

If she does well, . . . . retains her looks, her temper, her charm, . . . keep her: . . . . send her flowers, send her jewels, put her in a comfortable house: give her all she wants, . . . . Finished!

No more waste of time or speech.

This is how a state governed by a masculine race acts.

Hence the Russian Ballet, which few of you have seen.

### *M. DIAGHILEW.*

A passionate lover of what is beautiful and thus of that which is most beautiful of music, M. Diaghilew indulges his fancy for organizing.

While he loves music, he knows men and women; and music is the voice which finds for him excuses for their ingratitude, folly and conceit.

He is a very kind man whose very kindness is his chief fault.

He understands men and women, and he imagined that dancers and other performers were men and women.

He reckoned that performers were capable of loyalty.

One by one they broke away from him, their vanity, conceit and cupidity being greater than their devotion to the cause he had at heart.

M. Diaghilew can find plenty of dancers to fill the gaps made in his ranks, . . . he will create new talent, . . . . if he wants to.

These will always break away from him, . . . to their discredit.

But M. Diaghilew helps them to be discreditable, for he has not learned that performers must first learn loyalty to a cause before they are strong enough to bear the strain of the temptations they must encounter and which either make them heroes when victorious or cravens and deserters when they fail.

---

## THE DANCER NIJINSKI.

---

This young gentleman is not a Russian. He is a Pole.

He has lately been tempted to leave the company known as "The Russian Ballet" and he left it.

He was doing well in 1911; then by some means he got hold of a bottle of old wine from the cellar of Mr. Raymond Duncan, and has since been in a state of intoxication.

He lately exhibited himself to London in this condition.

This particular wine is from Mr. Duncan's own vineyard and is quite dangerous to drink, . . . unless you be invited to do so by the master of the house, who knows how much a guest can be entrusted with.

Since drinking this heady draught M. Nijinsky has been carrying on in a way calculated to appal some, ravish others, and somewhat disturb those whose attention should be given strictly to watching and guarding the development of the people and their education in such matters.

If a man reels along Piccadilly in a state of intoxication he is arrested, not because he is drunk, (for he is permitted to be drunk in the privacy of his own home), but because he annoys us with a display of drunkenness, and we know that if he is not put into a strong room Piccadilly will soon be packed with such people.

But then we know the signs and the effects of the intoxication which comes from too much liquor. But the signs and effects of theatrical intoxication seem hidden from most people.

For instance, upon first catching sight of Nijinsky's "L'Après-midi, d'un Faune" the critics should have one and all put it aside with a label, "Imitation Duncan" and laughed the Public out of the way as the Police do in a crush.

But then they none of them seem to have known of or seen the original; they were uninformed . . . . A bad thing in professional criticism and journalism.

Again one can but repeat, "Let more opportunity be given to the critics and journalists to travel and find out *original sources*. Perhaps then we shall in time see rivers instead of barrels of water . . . . slightly muddied in transport."

---

## DESERTION IN THE ARMY.

---

The State realising, (never having forgotten since earliest times) that the Army is a serious institution established for serious work, allows no trifling in its members.

They have to be obedient to discipline, loyal to their country and cause. Should they be disloyal, desert the ranks or show insubordination certain punishments await them.

These men are not children, yet certain punishments await them. . . . Why?

Because discipline and loyalty where serious issues are at stake must sometimes be enforced by examples being made of the disloyal and evil natures.

For desertion in time of war a man if caught is shot. So much for the Army.

And in the Theatre?

No discipline, no punishment for offending and disloyal members or for deserters.

The Theatre, you must realise, is a serious menace to the State unless well and seriously governed.

The managers do their very best, . . . but their very best is very bad.

They have never yet realised the *seriousness* of the institution which is ours and over which chance has placed them for the moment in a kind of power.

When they realise this seriousness, and how grave are the issues involved in the manner in which they discharge their office of government, we shall see the members of the theatre becoming amenable to discipline and growing into loyalty. And when Loyalty and Discipline come into a place there is little of good which cannot follow them.

---

Book Review. THE ART OF NIJINSKY by Geoffrey Whitworth. Unsigned. *The Mask*, Volume VII, no. 1, July, 1914.

---

 nice little book with carefully made pictures by Miss Mullock. But the art of Nijinsky is no art, so the book was not necessary.

He is technically a vivid dancer, rather too clever at times, . . . as the monkey is clever.

Nijinsky is all that is falsest in art, all that is cleverest in Dancer's tricks, all this is most easily realised at the instant and disliked upon remembrance. Dancing must become different before it can be spoken of seriously.

# FRANCESCO CLERICO, A NOTE ON A PORTRAIT by Allen Carric. *The Mask*, Volume IX, 1923.

rancesco Clerico was one of the foremost Italian ballet masters of the 18th century. And this image of him is one of the most spirited things of its kind that I know of.

It was engraved in 1795 and is by some artist unknown to me.

When Clerico was born or where I do not know. I am hoping that some one in one of the museums may know the facts of his existence and will let me know them.

He produced several ballets: In Padova in 1789; in Bologna in 1795; in

*Francesco Clerico, Ballet-Master. 1795. From* The Mask, *1923. Vol. IX.*

Venice and Parma in 1797; and in Milano at the "Scala" in 1790 and 1823.

I am not an engraver, but I am eager to find out who it was put in the sweeping straggling eyebrow in this plate. The nose, mouth and eye seem to me as well done as it is possible to do them.

The whole thing is alive, and I hear a voice coming from the image which begins to say, "Signore, my father the Conte di Bozzola was one of the proudest men, but he was also very human and I loved him dearly. When I was fourteen years of age he took me around the lagoons in his gondola and I shall never forget when he landed, leaving me in the boat which pushed off and returned to Murano.

"Come again soon" he called: but when I came I could not find him — and I was told 'He is dead.' Signore, when I dance I remember these two days: the happy day between his knees in the gondola and the day I could not find him. The tragedy and comedy of my dances which you are kind enough to say pleases you springs from these two days. When I was eighteen I was on my way to Ancona . . . ." — but I hear no more; — a short circuit. I have probably erred in the name of the town, . . . taken the wrong turning, and the voice dies away . . . .

Perhaps he said Ascona.

---

Editorial Note. A CRITICISM CRITICIZED. Unsigned. *The Mask*, Volume X, no. 1, January, 1924.

---

 London journal says that when Pavlova danced last season at Covent Garden she was "the wonder she every was," and that when "she repeated her two most famous poems in movement of the old days — the Saint Saëns "Swan" and the "Autumn Bacchanal" of Glazunov — the most jealous eye could not see any falling away."

That is all as it should be. But why no word about any advance?

Have any of our readers ever asked a dancer whether she feels she has made any progress in her art or not? We recall hearing the Great Dancer speak of the progress she was making in 1920, and already she has outstripped everyone by immeasurable distances. (Is it necessary to say we refer to Isadora Duncan . . . . )

Just to start a ball rolling may we suggest that "wonder" is a rare word and one that we should not use too often.

As when folk cry 'Oh' at a piece of silk, and 'isn't it wonderful!;' — or at a lady one admires and she with but little that is at all to wonder at; . . . or exclaim at any verse of poetry and at every drawing "oh wonderful," — "the most wonderful man," using this word fifty times a week of fifty men, women or things.

There be a few wonderful men and women assuredly, but everyone will not every day see a wonder though it pass under the nose and all comprehension.

---

## DESIGN FROM LAMBRANZI "BALLI TEATRALI" 1716 by the Editor [John Semar.] *The Mask,* Volume IX, 1923.

---

his same Lambranzi, who was he? Seldom has a Dancer Writer (which was he?) eluded us as this one.

We have searched for some word about him but no one seems to know anything of him or his work. His book appeared in 1716. Its title is, "Nuova e curiosa scuola di balli teatrali," and there is a portrait of the author in it.

Can any reader give us the further information we require: — When he was born? . . . died? . . . what he did? . . . where he went, whether he wrote any other books besides this one?

*Buffoon, from Lambranzi's* Balli Teatrali, *1716. From* The Mask, *1923. Vol. IX.*

GIUSEPPA CORTESI by Giovanni Mezzogiorno. *The Mask*, Volume X, no. 3, July, 1924.

f we are asked to name the great European dancers of the past, although never having seen them dance, we come out pat with Fanny Ellsler or La Guimard, La Barbarina or Taglioni. Allow me to come out as pat with La Cortesi, not having seen her either.

She was born sometime about the year 1780, and Bernardino Mezzanotte speaks of her name as destined to be eternal: yet it is today forgotten by all but a rare few, and, (so far as my search of two and a half years goes) has not been heard of out of Italy.

But listen to Mezzanotte: —

I SERTI NOBILI / CHE SON QUI'APPESI / IL NOME ETERNINO / DELLA CORTESI;

and this he prints as I have done in capital letters in his ANACREONTICA made to her in 1804 and printed that year in Perugia, on that well-remembered summer's day when she came to dance at the Teatro Civico del Verzaro in that city "con applauso universale" as PRIMA BALLERINA ASSOLUTA.

Then it was that the great Oldani was prevailed on to engrave the celebrated portrait which is reproduced here, which reproduction, alas, merely gives her head, but in no way shows us that Divine Pepa who inspired Mezzanotte to pen his *Anacreontica:*

Vegeti l'Edera / Cresca il virgulto / Bambino abbraccilo / Lo stringa adulto.

Venga col TEVERE / Il TRASIMENO / Fecondi l'Arbore / D'Arcadia in seno

Il Nome celebre / Sù questa Riva / di PEPPA amabile / Mai sempre viva —

The name of Il Mezzanotte is almost as eternal as that of La Cortesi, yet he too awaits his Biographer. He must not be confounded with A. Mezzanotte the author of "La Disposizione della Croce," etc., Perugia 1818.

The evidence of La Cortesi's immense powers to enchant the Italian nation will be given to "The Mask" readers in due time: "daughter of Terpsichore" she was called, even as La Guimard, Taglioni and La Barbarina; for her the sun arose, the birds sang, in the middle of the night. I

*Giuseppa Cortesi, from a portrait engraved by Oldani. In the history of the stage La Cortesi figures as a dancer of incomparable merit. From* The Mask, *1924. Vol. X.*

should be much surprised if even the great Mlle. Virginie[1], a name hardly less *celebre*, be proved to have won more hearts, gained greater applause, or made more money.

Giuseppa Cortesi seems to have been married to Antonio Cortesi some time about the year 1802.

1. In 1773 Mlle. Virginie made over 60,000 livres in six months in the city of Lyons, says the historian of Mlle. Raucourt.

---

# THE PRETTY THEATRE [in five parts] by X. Y. Z. *The Mask*, Volume X, no. 4, October, 1924; Volume XI, no. 1, January, 1925; Volume XI, no. 4, October, 1925; Volume XII, no. 4, October, 1926; Volume XIV, no. 2, April-May-June, 1928.

---

*The Profession of an actor was infamous among the Romans and honourable among the Greeks. How is it with us? We think of them as the Romans did, and live with them as the Greeks.*

*"Morals and Manners of the 17th century." La Bruyère, 1688.*

---

## OVERTURE.

---

 have been speaking with the Editor of "The Mask" about his policy, (if that be what the steps, hopeful slips or fatal stumblings of any Editor be called), and I fear I may have put him into a rage by my impertinence in imagining that an Editor is human and can slip and stumble as do Statesmen, Divines, or ordinary wood-cutters.

"You are," I began, "a very remarkable man, my dear Semar" . . . . he did not interrupt me . . . . "and you are evidently self-taught" I went on.

Here he shifted in his chair, uncertain whether this meant what he hoped or what he feared.

"Like every great Editor who has preceeded you" (you could have heard a pin drop) you are obstinate."[1]

"And," I went on, "when you are obstinate you are blind to a hundred

114

enchanting trivialities in the world of the Theatre which complete that world and make it what it is."

"Name one" said Semar.

"Prettiness" I said.

"Prettiness!" he cried, and I could see his mind rapidly searching the ten volumes of "The Mask" for proof that I was wrong.

"I do not think "The Mask" has failed to publish essays and illustrations which exhibit prettiness" said he rising and taking down volume I. "Look at this to begin with" . . . . and he pointed to a full page drawing of Miss Isadora Duncan.

Semar is a terrible man; he is always able to find the needle in the bundle of hay, and immediately. I had to admit that this indeed was pretty, though I refused to argue that it was more than that, for I knew that Semar's deft finger had come across the sole needle in the pack. "Yes, that *is* pretty" I admitted; "show me something else."

And here Semar's obstinacy rose to the occasion. With a daring I have seldom encountered in anyone before, he had the firm audacity to turn leaf after leaf of "The Mask" with a "this" to that page and a "there" to another.

The fight was over before it began, and yet he stood his ground. He pointed to the fifteenth century wood-engravings out of the "Sacre Rappresentazioni" and called these "pretty": he turned to Volume IV, Page 97, and said the "Geishas dancing" were pretty: he overlooked the colour-plate by Albert Rutherston on page 80 which has prettiness, and I began to breathe again; but he wanted to take me through volume after volume, so I protested I had had enough.

"You admit then that "The Mask" is packed with pretty things" he said: and he was triumphant in the quiet way of the obstinate.

"Charming in a queer, eccentric or grotesque way" I said; "delightful to those who study the Theatre seriously as you do: but to the world—the large world—as dead as a door-nail: dry stuff from the archives."

"These dead and dry things" he said reproachfully "you helped me to pick out as of the utmost interest to our readers."

He had me there. It was true. He followed it up with, "and when I suggested that some photographs of leading actors and actresses would be attractive you were not too polite about it."

The rest of our conversation I will not print.

It carried on for a day or two. In the end I was utterly routed: although the full force of my very-much-admired Editor had been unable in ten years to bring more than a touch of the really pretty into the pages of "The Mask," he persuaded me that all his life he had known of its existence, and had always very greatly longed to bring numerous examples before the readers of this magazine.

\*  \*  \*  \*  \*

So I perceive that it is my fault for having, as an enthusiastic assistant, even, may I say, as a collaborator, counselled against any intrusion of the pretty into these pages.

\*  \*  \*  \*  \*

I would like to make up for this by coming to Miss Hetty Hecuba right away.

---

## THE SWEETLY PRETTY.

---

What is the Pretty,—how born—why preserved—what its philosophy and its aim, . . . . all this and more besides I must leave to wiser men to set forth. If they have already done so it has been well done, for there is more to be said about this trifle than we ever suspect.

But my only intention is to make a note or two upon the prettiness which exhales from the Theatre.

If in Music and in Architecture, and their handmaids Painting and Sculpture, prettiness be a rather cheap thing, . . . . as I heard many in 1890 saying . . . . I have come to learn that in the Theatre prettiness *has* a place and we should see that it be kept.

It is in the artifice of the Theatre that we must look to find what is often very pretty. If there was, as we have been told, a "noble artificiality" which belonged to the old times and which now and again we may even catch a glimpse of today, it is not of this I wish to write, but only of the sweetly pretty.

Nowhere perhaps is the sweetly pretty quite in its right place except on the stage. It must be admitted that we find some of it in painting, . . . . even Watteau is sweet and pretty. He is something a good deal more than that, but he is pretty too. In Literature we find it; Voltaire's 'Candide' for some of us sparkles with prettiness.

It is only a little thing, this sweet prettiness; yet this little thing has at times annexed a large share of our attention, we who have used our Theatres as pleasant places in which to divert our thoughts in times of stress from duller and more weighty matters.

And so it has been a good thing for many thousands of people for many a century.

And that "The Mask" should have forgotten all this, should have found nothing to say about the Pretty side of the Theatre, either proves that everyone in "The Mask" was blind to it, . . . . or blinded by it. We were dull indeed not to have shown by means of the engravings of those prettier times, or even (to echo my Editor) perhaps by a few photographs of our still daintier days, how large a part the sweet has played in the Theatre at all times.

There is a certain prejudice against the pretty . . . . there has often been a revolt against it amongst the artists—thank goodness not always or we should not have this miracle of prettiness by Moreau and Patas "La Loge à l'opéra" to look and wonder at. It is this design I pick out of many to show off the Pretty of those times at its best.

Within these few inches vibrates the essence of the lighter theatre of the eighteenth century.

There sits the Duc d'Orléans, or do I dream? if not, there too is Mademoiselle Duthé standing in spreadeagle poise about to swoop:— behind her the mighty Madam Montansier advising, encouraging: a nonentity sits in the chair facing Mons. le Duc. In the balcony with their mouths agape sit Miss Fanny and Miss Hetty Burney but recently come to Paris. Mr. Young the farmer is close to them, and dear old Dr. Burney listens to the singers hidden to us, silent to us. Nothing pretty back there:—all the prettiness is in this *Loge*.

Let our imagination toga the figures and we shall get the same theatre of the first century . . . just as pretty: we must some day see if we cannot find almost as graceful a thing in each century to reprint in "The Mask," for it must not be said any longer that we forget the pretty.

How often when I was living in London in 1890 did I hear artists saying hard things about this same prettiness in art . . . as though ugliness, the austere, the superb, and even the noble which abounds everywhere, had always been the sole food of the gods, and consequently to be your sole food.

As it was in the eighteenth century that prettiness came to be valued again at its full worth . . . . and a little more, it is an eighteenth century engraving of a pretty *loge*, in a pretty theatre, of the pretty town of Paris, that I bring you in my hand and lay before us as I speak.

I could have brought a far more ancient document proving how the

pretty was thought well of in Pompeii or Thebes many centuries earlier
. . . . or some strange drawing on silk from China, or a curious little Indian
painting.

But we know our Paris a little better than our Pompeii, or their Poonab
or Poowang and we see what our Paris has become today. We are living in
rather an ugly age and 1777 is not too far off for us still to catch a glance of
it before it fades, and to note how pretty and how real were the puppets as
they stood dallying in those days.

"It is the journalist's business" writes La Bruyère, "to inform us that a
certain book is published, and by whom; to describe it and its style and
character and say where it can be bought. It is foolishness in him to make
any criticism of it."

So I shall come to the eighteenth century Theatre as an ordinary journalist, retelling myself something about the prettiness of the Opera and
Theatre, of Les Filles, of the spectators, actresses, scenes, and the tinkling
music: showing by engravings here and there just how 'jolie' was Mlle. Du
Thé, how 'ravisante' Mlle. Virginie, Mlle. Laguerre and Mlle. Bourgoin and
how sweet the background against which they were placed: how pretty the
gallant gentlemen of their times found everything on the stage (when they
troubled to look at it) from their private *loges* in their private theatres or
from afar.

Beginning not at the beginning but with the first thing to hand, with
Monsieur J. M. Moreau le Jeune and his "La Loge à l'opéra" engraved by
Patas, I shall not be too particular about my progress; it must be the rake's I
fear—I shall go zig-zag, on this broad path, here and now in Paris, perhaps
tomorrow towards Rouen and back, who knows, in the direction of London the next morning.

I shall not moralize . . . . nor take what is charming to be beautiful; but I
want to do justice in "The Mask" to what has been slighted. So I cannot do
better than reprint a number of facts about the pretty theatre and a number
of engravings which show us how pretty it has been.

And in doing so it will be impossible to avoid drawing attention once
more to those fascinating people the actresses, dancers, singers and lady-
spectators who once practically ruled the stage. And amongst these will
figure a few remarkable if less pretty women who are inseparable from the
others: . . . . Madame Montansier, Mlle. Raucourt, (both of them di-
rectresses); Sophie Arnould, La Guimard, and even Emma Hart. Isabella
Andreini, Fragonard and Moreau; the chandeliers in the theatres of Rome,
and the Private theatres in several lands.

All these things certainly did conspire towards prettiness, and all seemed fitting.

You may like prettiness or you may not: you may wear yours with a difference: . . . . one thing which strikes me is that while it was and is not always as unnecessary as too many an artist today pretends to think, it was once or twice perhaps rather out of place in the particular spot where it chose to nestle.

But I will leave it to you to decide where and when it was out of place. I shall merely make a few records.

---

## PART TWO.

---

As I said in my opening notes on this theme, I do not intend to be critical. My purpose is more that of the print-collector than of the writer.

Have you not seen this print-collector in some old shop, in Rue de la Seine or Rue des Beaux Arts, as he sits by the hour turning over hundreds of prints of all subjects and of all centuries . . . . silent . . . . pausing to look at some, turning over others without more than a glance, picking out with deliberation, but without a word said, one here, one there; laying them in a heap. Then, after a good three hours' search, silently paying for these, . . . . going home . . . . undoing his package . . . . going more slowly over each print . . . . saying nothing.

My purpose is his: he thinks a devil of a lot, may be; but whatever he thinks it is his delight in the print as a print, including subject, condition of the print, name of engraver, date, quality of the work and price.

And so is it here with me. If some are censorious, when they hear of Mlle. Guimard, Sophie Arnould and Madame Montansier, to select three of the most remarkable names from a big bouquet, . . . . if some find the private theatres of the first two ladies mere hot-beds of vice and the many public theatres ruled over by the third dens of infamy, I have come to look on them as the old print collector looks upon his treasures. They have cost me very little, and have given me great pleasure: I have read so much about them, seen the houses they made and seen them recorded again; I have seen them die: even come to forget them in the centuries which followed: remembered them again while contemplating subsequent centuries: see them again now. I for one cannot pick one of them out for censure.

But I muse at times: La Guimard is worth the threepence I gave for her: Sophie at a golden guinea was not dear: Madame Montansier . . . . I would any day give again the shilling I was asked for her and without a murmur.

If the price is sometimes low, what of that: I gave what the print-seller asked. For a song by Mozart there is no price, . . . . so rare that few can hear it, so cheap that anyone may have it: for a glance at the Palazzo Ducale in Genova nothing is asked; you may even pass it for nothing and not see it. So that it seems that the price of a thing is nothing by which to guage the value: "nothing for nothing and dam little for sixpence" sounds pretty so far as it goes, but the sound is its principal asset. There is not truth there. You sometimes can get all for nothing and sometimes for a thousand pounds nothing.

The pretty is often held to be so cheap that it is not worth any notice at all; and assuredly a little of it can be afforded by any of us and is useful to all. It is useless to deny that. Whether in certain centuries it was worth quite so much as the price put on it is another matter. I cannot tell; . . . . I leave it to the Duc d'Orléans and the Prince d'Henin to settle that between them . . . . if they ever meet nowadays.

The pretty, spite of it being so cheap, possibly cost the Theatre of Europe and its Drama a pretty penny. What of that? . . . . are we not here today to pay the mortgage?

I have the utmost sympathy with those who feel they are too poor to do more than add to this debt, for the next century will have to pay. Possibly that is one of the reasons why so many well-to do actors nowadays warn their sons against taking up the profession.

But let us return to my print shop.

The last time I was in Zenabella I discovered a book in my print shop. It was a hovel of a place, and there lay Zola's "Nana." I bought it; I took it home and I read it.

---

## NANA.

---

*"All Paris will visit your Theatre." "Say, my brothel, answered the Manager."*

---

I suppose that there are very few people living today who are reading Emile Zola's novel "Nana" for the first time: yet I have but just finished reading it and for the first time, although I began it some thirty years ago and came to a full stop at the passage in Chapter One where a manager of a Theatre asks a habituée of his playhouse to drop the word *"theatre"* and substitute the word "brothel."[2]

Knowing dozens of theatres which were serious places, (serious as churches, banks, or ships) I drew the line at any further interest for a book, whose author, I saw, promised to keep up the fantastic old delusion of the outsider.

That the theatre this Zola was to write of, was no theatre at all, settled it for me that I should not be interested. I put the book down.

*         *         *

That I was probably prejudiced only occurs to me now. For have not there been writers who made novels out of Banks full of Thieves, Churches full of Knaves? The world is full of men and women, and men and women full of pranks, passions, vices and virtues.

Are we to read only about virtues and the virtuous? They exist and are often hidden, and so to reveal them with what we call "art" is to do a trick not without beauty. But no virtue is quite valuable surrounded by a sea of virtues; how mark a poor single virtue, how illumine it, if no vices are there to set off its brilliance? Too much virtue may be as vile as too much vice.

*         *         *

So three days ago when I was in need of a book to read . . . . a novel above all else . . . . I happened to pick up a copy of "Nana" on a bookstall. For three francs I bought it, and in three days I have read it.

And it is a w e f u l l.

It deals with the life of a woman who goes on to the stage without any qualifications, without genius or talent, unable to act, but possessed of an astounding personality . . . . of the personality which attracts . . . . of animal magnetism.

This personality is not the personality of a Rachel, who also attracted besides having a genius as a tragic actress; it is not a brilliant personality, it is just a weak one; she is amiable, a hundred times amiable, loveable, and all over the place.

By means of this personality displayed on the stage she brings all Paris to her feet. She lives every kind of life, . . . . in poor quarters, in gaudy well-to-do ones, in neat ones, in sumptuous ones, and finally dies of the smallpox, her face eaten away.

To the end, and even beyond it, she still continues to attract.

This is not repulsive although it does not sound exactly attractive. But there is an under current which is interesting, more attractive, stranger, for those of us who work in Theatres and want to see the Theatre of the world taking on a new lease of life. It is a theme which recurs and recurs, and each time it does so it reminds us of paragraphs we read today in the newspapers, or of photographs we have seen only yesterday in the shop windows. It is the theme of the Impresario and the hangers-on to Theatres, . . . . let it be instantly added the tenth-rate ones, these flashy gentlemen with their big press agencies and their paragraphed expressions of heartfelt desire to uplift the drama, even to make it sacred, . . . . even if they have to sweeten the pill for the public by serving up the moral with something that tastes good; in short, the most beautiful women that can be found in Europe and America.

We hear of these funny fellows every day. In "Nana" we have their portraits.

## II.

When some suave theatrical impresario or director wrote to Nana, . . . . was she at that time in Berlin or Prague? . . . saying he wanted to see her really a success, that it was his way to work for love, . . . . could not dream of business where she was concerned, . . . . that her immense talents were being hidden, that he felt it was part of his life's work to bring her to Paris (or was it New York?), she naturally ran off to Paris or New York as quickly as possible. Yes, it was to Paris she ran. And became a great success; had some twenty lovers immediately, . . . . yes, instantly . . . . ; took up with a twenty-first, a man of wealth and left the twenty for a month; then after a few weeks more took the twenty back with the twenty first. Then threw them all over; disappeared with a hideous looking actor; stayed with him a few months in more or less poverty in Montmartre; then sank to worse poverty and haunted the café of some old woman who was always eager to see new faces; appeared on the stage for two nights, and in those two nights managed to win another protector, who lavished on her millions of francs; . . . . all this was quite natural. The impresario and the manager, looking holy, were photographed with the lady between them; all Paris was impressed, . . . . just like today.

And our 1924 Theatre is where it was in 1870: it is where these impresarios and managers, with their clever manipulation of women, would have it.

It is devilish clever to be sure. The world gets bitten by a longing to see a sacred play, . . . . having heard that the Oberammergau Passion Play is *not* to be seen unless the world will travel all the way to Oberammergau, and then only once in every ten years. So the impresario and the manager resolve to make up a substitute to console a fretful world. It *shall* have its sacred play, . . . . but it won't *really* be so sacred as all that, because we are prudent gentlemen from the East, and know that the Western world (which, by the way, we despise) only wants to have the shadow of sacred things; if there must be any substance let it be as fleshy as possible.

And Nana is again caught in the net . . . . and landed ever so gently; put on the market; praised by the modern press agent month by month for her dramatic virtues, then each week, then each day; cables are sent round the world of her amazing talents (and she with but one, and that the old magnetism possessed by myriads of women); photographs fill the back pages of daily papers; and a rich man, also from the East, is found to act nobly by supporting the immense expense, . . . . so great is his love for art . . . . and religion, especially the Christian religion. In short the whole thing almost causes the impresario to break down with emotion so noble he is, she is, they all are.

Every day and in every land this is being done in Theatres, on a small scale and on a large scale.

If not a "religious" play it's a Revue, or a Historical play; any old theme serves, . . . . it's the woman is the goods.

Do you want any examples pointed out to you? There's no need, they are so evident.

The small town of Zenabella, in which, I write this, has given me the details which I have here related.

Perhaps in *New York* or in *Paris* or in *London* today there are no ludicrous jokes of this sacred art business being perpetrated. I leave you to decide that.

But here in Zenabella a dark-skinned fellow of the name of Moses Bethany came and bamboozled the entire province (and the town itself) with his productions of a thing he called "*A Miraculous Play*," in which there was nothing sacred at all. But *how* he fooled them!!!

So do read "Nana"; it tells you how it is done so much better than I can.

A strange and sad point made by Zola is the amazing infidelity of his

Heroine: he is always returning and returning to this. Of her amours I do not speak; I refer to the infidelity of her mind. And she and most of her fellow-actresses are adepts at abusing everyone with their tongues. Yet Madame Berton's pretty book had not then appeared.[3]

There is hardly one, favoured or not favoured, whom these ladies do not abuse like pickpockets. It is a curious point: . . . . is it true to life?

Have actresses such utterly unfaithful minds, so little control over their tongues? Do they really slander to the extent Zola makes out? If so, is it due to the constant changing of their very nature each night, due to their profession which forces them to this capacious versatility? Is it due to this profession that they come to behave like nothing real, and see all real life and living beings as false life and false beings, as they open a door on the stage and go on into an unreal existence? I think it is; and so possibly they may be exempt from the blame due to others, for they have no sense left of realities.

If this be true, then, if they lied they would lie like truth, making "the very truth seem falsehood to it": this goes without saying. One is not an actress, I suppose, for nothing. And yet so many of these great ladies in the Paris story are dancers, singers, chorus-girls; all blended together, as in life, I suppose; journalists, singers, bankers, painters and girls; an odd crew . . . . and all so real.

One wonders, is the whole book a libel, or is it true? . . . or is it *mezzo e mezzo*.

### III.

Now it begins to look as though these few notes on the Pretty Theatre were soon to develope into the Ugly Theatre.

But 'tis no such thing. The prettiness is there, and under it what is under all else.

We shall soon come to pretty Mlle. Guimard, her mother, Mr. Leger and the Marquis de Soubise. And Fragonard will step into the room . . . . or rather into that little private Theatre of hers; and Fragonard is a guarantee for the perfection of prettiness.

A few measurements of her theatre, a few dates as to when the place was put up . . . . and put up for auction . . . . cannot detract greatly from the charm; dates are in any case valuable as a basis for Terpsichore to pirouette on . . . . and even to die on, . . . forgotten.

Poor Terpsichore, one of "le ballerine" who dominated not only the realms of the stage but also those of "la Galanterie."

# PART THREE.

## A LETTER FROM MLLE. GUIMARD TO M. DE LE FERTÉ INTENDANT DES MENUS-PLAISIRS.

Londres 26 may 1786 or 1787.[4]

On ne fait pas toujours ce que l'on désire, mon cher petit bon ami, et j'en ay bien la preuve, puisque malgré celui que j'avois de vous écrire, dès mon arrivée à Londres, je n'en ay pu trouver le moment. Mais l'amitié est indulgente, et je compte trop sur la vôtre pour ne pas être convaincue qu'elle ne vous permettra pas d'être injuste envers moi en vous laissant prendre pour négligence une impossibilité réelle.

Depuis que je suis en cette ville on ne m'a pas encore laissé un seul instant de libre, comblée des bontés de toutes les plus grandes dames, et principalement de M$^{me}$ la duchesse de Devonshire. Je passe chez elle tout temps, où je ne suis pas employée au théâtre. En vérité, mon cher petit bon ami, la manière dont on me reçoit partout est si flatteuse qu'elle pourroit bien faire tourner une tête moins sensée que celle de votre petite bonne amie, mais elle est d'une trop rare bonté pour n'être pas à l'abri de toute épreuve. Vous allez en juger par les sages réflexions que ses nouveaus succès lui ont fait faire, et dont elle va vous faire part.

J'ai pensé que je ne pouvois profiter d'une circonstance plus favorable pour terminer brillamment ma carrière theâtrale, et je vous crois trop mon ami pour ne pas approuver la résolution que je prends de quitter l'Opéra. Vous n'ignorez pas, que depuis quelque temps, il est devenu le centre des cabales, par conséquent du mauvais goût, les perruquiers, les laquais, sont devenus les juges des talents, les miens n'ont jamais dû leurs succès qu'à la bonne compagnie, et je ne veux pas risquer de devenir la pâture de celle dont on remplit presentement le parterre. Il me seroit trop dur, après ving-cinq ans de suffrages bien soutenus, de finir par eprouver des désagréments, et parmi *mes chers comarades*, j'en connois qui sont remplis de bonnes volontés sur le chapitre. Or, comme dans tous les temps je n'ai jamais cherché qu'à faire plaisir, je vais mettre le comble à mes procédés pour eux en donnant ma démission. Disposès de ma place mon ami, mais si vous voulès écouter les conseils de l'amitié, ne la donnes qu'au talent et non à la protection ni au charlatanisme. Je vous le répète, il est très dangereux de donner légèrement des premières places, attendu que l'on n'est plus maître de les öter aux sujets que l'on a rendus possesseurs quand on finit par voir clairement qu'ils ne sont en état de les remplir. Il faut encourager les jeunes sujets en les récompensant bien. Soyez libéral en argent, mais avare des premières places, si vous volez ne pas fermer la porte de l'Opéra aux vrais talents qui pourroient les mériter. Excusez, mon ami, si je vous donne des conseils, mais c'est mon amitié pour vous qui me les dicte, ainsy que le désir que j'ay de ne pas voir détruire entièrement la belle danse que j'ai vu exister à l'Opéra.

On m'a mandé que vous aviez suspendu l'arrêt du conseil qui rétablissoit les feux, j'en suis vraiment fâchée; vous savez que je vous ai toujours dit qu'il n'y avoit que ce moyen de retablir le bon ordre dans le service de l'Opéra. On est bien plus empressé à remplir son devoir quand l'intérêt y est attaché, et la certitude de toucher son argent, tous les mois, sans nulle espèce de conventions, rend bien des sujets infiniment paresseux. Je tiens toujours aux feux, sans eux cela ira toujours mal. J'ai encore une grâce à solliciter de votre amitié, mon ami, c'est de permettre à Nivelon de rester à Londres jusqu'à la fin du mois prochain. Indépendamment du service qui vous me rendrez en me laissant ce danseur, vous lui en rendrez aussi un bien grand, car il a paru un libelle à Paris, et il est accusé d'y être pour quelques chose. On m'a mandé ainsi qu'à lui qu'il etoit attendu à Paris par plusieurs mauvaises têtes de la cour et qu'on vouloit le rosser. Ce seroit une chose très fâcheuse pour lui, qui (j'en suis persuadée) ne le mérite pas. Vous seul, mon ami, pouvés le soustraire à cette mauvaise affaire, en lui permettant de passer encore cinq semaines à Londres. Dans cet intervalle, lé têtes se calmeront et à son retour on ne pensera plus au libelle. Accordès-moi cette grâce, mon ami, j'en conserverai une bien vive reconnaissance, attendu qu'elle m'arrangera aussi parfaitement puisque je viens de contracter, pour ces cinq dernières semaines, un engagement de 650 guinées qui, joints aux 950 que j'ai faites à mon bénéfice, me forment une très jolie somme à rapporter à Paris. Ce voyage n'a pas ete si bête, hein! qu'en pensès-vous? Dame, ce n'est pas ma faute. Ils m'aiment à la folie, ces bons Anglais! Voilà ce que c'est que le mérite!

Ah! ça, monsieur mon cher petit bon ami, aimès-moi toujours bien, et autant que je vous aime, entendes-vous? Ecrivés-moi, je vous en prie, et dites-moi que vous me laissés Nivelon. Vous nous rendrez service à tous les deux, et vous êtes trop obligeant pour refuser à votre petite bonne amie, qui vous embrasse de tout coeur.

—GUIMARD.

Mes respects je vous prie à M<sup>me</sup> de la Ferté ainsi qu'à M<sup>me</sup> Desentelles, sans m'oublier auprès de son chaste époux.

M<sup>lle</sup> Saunière vous portera les commissions dont M<sup>lle</sup> de la Bourdonnais m'avait chargée pour vous remettre.

Pall Mall No. 10.

---

You remember this letter which is quoted by M. Edmond de Goncourt in the 62nd paragraph of his delightful book on the famous dancer.

It is a distinguished neatly written[5] example of the usual theatric communications of all time which say "I am a great success because I am sought after for my art by great persons" and which add "I have made a great deal of money."

Sometimes it is less studied as in the case of the fortunate dancer Mlle. Boubon, when she writes from London to the Hairdresser Albert of the Rue des Petits Champs saying "Send me two more boxes of the Powder you keep for the Princess Lamballe, for I am going to take tea on the 1st of next month with the highest personage in British Navy; one writes it so: *Mr. Midshipman* and he has promised me the most sumptuous banquet of fish—they call them *les shrimps*. I must not fail to appear *à l'Albert* and I pray you not to forget, by the 1st of the month."

Mlle. Guimard as we see from her letter was not left alone for an instant by the great ladies—in fact the Duchess of Devonshire keeps her close to her all the time she is not in the Theatre. Fortunate Duchess to be able to afford it—for Mlle. Guimard's time will cost the Duchess, or anybody else, money.

That is what is so admirable about La Guimard: she really did know how to make the Pretty Theatre pay. Only one woman ever surpassed her in this .... the immense Mlle. Montansier; but then Mlle. Montansier surpassed every theatrical one in every theatrical thing, and for this became the head and front of the Pretty Theatre: there was none like her, none. And some wretches even added "Thank God."

But La Guimard ran her close—was less of an agent and more or less of a free lance.

She seems to have managed to raise all her funds without bothering about any chorus, that chorus on which la Montansier counted so greatly.

And in 1772 to assist her to raise funds, she persuaded one or more wealthy gentlemen to build her a *maison*. This Maison de Mlle. Guimard she sold in 1786: she sold it by lottery. 2500 tickets at 120 livres (so they say; others say 5 livres) a-piece were issued, signed by Mlle. Guimard and viséd by M. Chavet the notary of Rue St. Martin. The lucky person to get the house for 120 livres (or for 5) for she bought but one ticket, was the Comtesse du Langin who resold the place for 500,000 francs to the banker Perregaux.

This house contained a little private Theatre from the designs of Architect Le Doux: a jewel of a Theatre: a casket: able to hold 500 spectators. The ceiling was painted by Taraval, the panels by Fragonard, the skirting board by the great David. To the performances given here came every admirer of La Guimard and The Pretty Theatre. The repertoire has been collected under the title "Théâtre d'Amour."

Assisting her would be Mlle. Dervieux, Mlle. Duthé and other talented persons. La Guimard could hardly be described as pretty, but, like Ophelia when mad, she, when sane, turned things to favour and to prettiness.

---

# PART FOUR.

---

## THE £1000 GAFF.

---

You have heard of the penny gaff but possibly not of the £1000 gaff. It is another name for that Pretty Theatre which so attracts me.

If the Pretty Theatre was expensive, those who supported it were wealthy. Nowadays they would keep race horses. One must have something to throw away one's money on, and also some place where one can meet those people one has just left a moment ago. At least I suppose so. I suppose so, because after thinking about this Pretty Theatre for a few years, I really am at a loss to know the true reason why the buildings were put up, for it was not a matter of just meeting together and having a little music and some dancing. It was a devilish serious undertaking compared with our modern notion of private theatricals.

Looking in the past three volumes of "The Mask" at the drawings and plans of little theatres that have been reproduced there, we see what finished things they were. There was nothing at all amateurish about the buildings; and since, very often, many of the first performers of the age were called to take part in the representations, there was nothing at all amateurish in the acting, singing, and dancing. So far as I know nothing was charged by the hostess, and in that sense it was amateurish, but in no other sense that I can see.

The most magnificent of the Pretty Theatres were in Paris. And the most sumptuous of these was built by the Duc d'Orléans.

Previous to the private theatres in Paris, there had been many a private theatre in Italy, but mere privateness does not make for prettiness. For pure privacy almost avoids display and most things that are pretty depend upon the tricking out.

Amongst the private theatres of Italy was the theatre at Vicenza, but this was built for an Academy and was a very serious affair. The next in importance was the theatre in Parma built by and for the Farnese family. One could only deal with such a building in a book with the title of "Georgeous Theatres." In Bologna, and in Venice, in Florence, and in Rome, private theatres had existed since the sixteenth century. Far earlier still, in the fifteenth century, Mantua and Ferrara had led off with these things, but all that is quite another story.

One must not confuse the doings of any of these princes with the pretty little trottings here and trottings there of the *filles* of Paris.

I do not think the Italians could be very pretty like that. What they did was too closely woven to be flimsy. There was too much design in their solid fabric for there to be a suggestion of trifling.

The private Italian theatre was a man's theatre, whereas the Paris private theatre was a theatre of the ladies and the *filles*.

And does it not reflect immense credit on them that they found it worth while building special playhouses for this game of theirs.

It is not until the eighteenth century that the game began, although the king naturally had his moveable private theatres in his palaces and these were found sufficient for the needs of society.

I do not know the date of the first French private theatre, but one of the earliest was that built by Monsieur de la Pouplinière for some lady or other. This was at Passy and was built circa 1732. He was a fabulously wealthy man and his château was the scene of prodigious doings. In his theatre at Passy he had an orchestra which was in use daily, and had, as director of this orchestra, Rameau, and afterwards, Stamitz, and Gossec.

M. de la Pouplinière was fond of playing on the flute and seems to have been a vivid little amateur, counting among his friends Voltaire, Rousseau, Piron, Lamotte, all of whom it appears wrote comedies for him. And then in 1737 he married Thérèse Boutinon who was twenty years his junior.

Another Private theatre belonged to la Marquise de Morville in Normandy at her château, circa 1737 to which was attached a company which, when it performed in Paris performed at the Château at Pantin, which seems also to have had a theatre about this time.

Still it is not until about 1750 that numbers of theatres begin to be erected in the country houses round Paris and the town houses in Paris; but then, and for fifty years after, they came along in hundreds.

At Puteaux in the house of the Duc de Gramont; at Versailles under Mme. de Pompadour in the house of the king; at Bagnolet for the Duc d'Orléans petit fils of the Regent; at Berney in the house of the Comte de Claremont; right in Paris in the house of Voltaire, on the second floor of the rue Traversiere.[6]

The Duc d'Orléans was the most fantastic of all the little amateurs, for he had at least six such theatres, perhaps more. In 1749 his theatre at Bagnolet; in 1754 his theatre in the faubourg St. Martin; this was built by the architect Pierre; in 1755 in rue faubourg de Roule, Pierre builds him one more theatre; in 1761 another at his villa at Menil-Montant; in 1767 another at Villers-Coterts, and in 1773 he surpasses himself and orders a magnificent theatre of architect Bronginard for his Follie d'Orleans in the rue Chaussée d'Antin. Its exact position was between the Chaussée d'Antin, rue de Provence and the rue Taitbout. Monsieur Fouquier said this was built in 1770, but what do three years matter! 1770 or '73, one is as apt as the other. It is the very midnight-hour of the pretty theatre development.

But the Duc was only the leader of the whole group of people crazy to have their own theatres, and the build went on at such a pace, that by the time the French Revolution was manufactured, that is to say in 1789, there must have been some two hundred to three hundred private theatres full to overflowing every evening in Paris and its environs.

After all it was more amusing, if you had nothing to do, to pass the time play-acting rather than playing cards and sipping coffee.

It seems to me also a rather more varied amusement than dancing the fox-trot night after night to an indifferent orchestra if any at all, or even to the most perfect gramophone.

Yes, there is distinctly more variety about it, and on that score is to be recommended to people today, who have so much time and so much money and do not know what to do with either except to go on to the stage and thus throw professionals out of employment.

But what a banging of doors there must have been in 1807 when Napoleon closed up all these theatres, and only two weeks given to take farewell of all the little relics which remained there.

For one must not suppose that, when the Revolution came, it made very much difference to these most charming performances and the more charming performers. They went on more or less in the same inane way as ever . . . . a nice hangman or two would be invited in, and what with the gigglings and the gurglings, I do not know that the show was not improved: One of the most frequented of theatres was that belonging to a charming butcher.

---

# PART V.

---

*Amour amour / Oh belle oiseau / Chante chante / Chante toujours.*

---

One cannot write the history of the Pretty Theatre in less than twenty-five volumes, and indeed, to do it full justice, it deserves thirty, for five volumes alone would have to be devoted to the portraits of those who have made the Pretty Theatre what it is—the dancers, singers, actresses who were so charming: the hangers-on who were so necessary, the intermediaries who were so adroit, and the rest who were so much in the way.

I may have time to compose these volumes if, as I hope to do, I inherit some £ 50,000 from a rich and, at present, unknown great aunt or uncle who left Europe sixty years ago and made a fortune in Brazil and has left me a slice of that fortune.

It will mean purchasing five or six thousand drawings, engravings, miniatures of the ladies and gentlemen who best represent this Pretty Theatre.

I possess only a hundred or so, and it is not enough. For there is not one Prettiness only, there are legions. Five volumes would not cover it, fifty would not, nor five hundred. Tis the great weed—a weed so popular that it is more often than not taken for the flower. Exquisite, Enchanting, Perfect, Divine; these are but a few of the ejaculations uttered in its presence. And yet it is only the Pretty . . . at times pretty vulgar.

Then how come to realise the power of this trifle unless we show it in all its finery?

Puritans—they who for the moment utterly despise the Pretty—have ever disparaged it—or rather her. Yet you have only to see her for a moment to change your mind, unless you too happen to be pretty and in the same Theatre or Dancing Academy.

Assemble the old Gods from high Olympus and pray them to perform for you some immortal play with music of the spheres and dances of the Hours or Seasons. Even as these are shaking your soul, lifting it from earth, will come a pretty thing posing as a goddess, and, in a few steps of the old dance after a few notes of the old song you, the Gods and all will be utterly charmed; you will find yourself beginning to speak French; you will utter the old familiar words, *Ravissante —charmante —charmante. Amour amour oh belle oiseau* . . . .

The old Gods know how to control their stage, if not their feelings, so that this momentary ebullition will not wreck the performance of the whole piece: after it is over it will be in vain for any of you to send round and enquire after the health of the pretty goddess.

She will have been garrotted by them silently and thrown into the ditch.

Even the Duc de Richelieu must stay where he is in his stall in the Theatre of the immortals on the other side of Styx.

But to descend again to the Theatre of Europe: the Duc de Richelieu, the Prince de Soubise, the Prince Carignan, Fitz James, d'Henin, de Vasse, de Jarente, de la Borde, de Harlay, Barrymore, de Saint Lubin, these and a whole host of such as these deserve to have their portraits in the five volumes because, if the Pretty Theatre's existence did not exactly depend upon them, (though it be made for them) they were always quite ready to lend a finger in the applause or a thousand francs for a carriage to take home one of the Pretty.

They lavished immense sums upon these pretty people and so their place in the book is an important one: their place in that Theatre is both before and behind the curtain.

Crudely stated, they haunted the theatre not so much for the sake of the Drama, the Music or the Dance as for the actresses, the singers and the dancers; and, crudely stated, even the French today are shocked at this.

There is not a shock in it, except perhaps when the statement is crudely made as I make it here. The attraction toward that which is pretty is a weakness and we should have no weaknesses—how true that is to those who have none. But a weakness for prettiness is one thing; a strong delight in it is another. The actresses, dancers, singers laid themselves out for *l'amour*, properly paid *amour*: were the gentlemen to whisper back, "Oh I don't know, ask Mama!"?

Yes, I would like to devote at least one volume of the five to the paintings, drawings and engravings which show us the salesmen and saleswomen, the purchasers and the goods.

What were the goods? Genius? no, I think not, for you cannot buy genius. Talent? . . . that too is not necessarily for sale, for how take home 15,000 francs' worth of Theatrical genius or talent in a coach. The Duke of Grafton could buy a drawing from Rolandson for £1 or £5, but he couldn't buy some of John Philip Kemble's genius; he must go and see it at work in a Theatre—he has only to pay a very small sum, a few shillings, and share what is before him with two thousand other admirers and remain seated quietly in the stalls or in the boxes.

But then Kemble is not to be found in the Pretty Theatre.

No, the Pretty Theatre is quite another thing, and you can give a lift in your coach or motor-car to that which is sold in it, the which we have come to call "favours."

These are sold by "favourites."

Although a true favour is something given, is a kindness beyond what is due and is not to be sold, in the Pretty Theatre favours were and are sold by the million. And the picture which best illustrates this is that by J. M. Moreau le Jeune called "La Loge à l'Opéra."[7]

It represents the sale of a ballet dancer.

Now whether it be wrong or right, illegal or legal, serious or comic to sell people (or yourself if you have no *mère fausse* to assist in the transaction) is not the question; but what has always been highly ridiculous is to call the sale a favour.

It is a sale and nothing else; so if any such sale take place, it should take place on the ancient basis of the slave traffic, on a frankly unrespectable basis; a hard deal or nothing. The Memoirs of dancers never deal frankly with this phase of their art.

If you are sold or sell yourself you *are* a slave, and dammé, slaves, being sold people, cannot possibly put on airs. Yet these airs have been put on, the virtuous airs, the airs of one bestowing favours, the giver's airs, the airs of one who simply could not possibly be sold, the "quite innocent" airs, the indignation airs at the mere suggestion, the pathetic airs, the airs of the lady, the womanly airs, the noble-woman airs, religious airs, above all the airs of the independent but quite respectable lady.

All these are airs, not actualities.

For the actually independent lady is as genuine as is a square deal: what she says and does is done squarely—in fact—and there is no other way to describe it—like a lady.

But the Pretty Theatre is not concerned with ladies or with things square but only with things fair, unfairly fair perhaps: a hard deal is, in the eyes of the bartering group which runs the principal side show of the Pretty Theatre, a fantastic notion from the country.

Ask Mademoiselle du Thé what she thinks of a square deal: whether she is open for sale on a square basis, and you will be laughed at for your pains. But she soon stops laughing to explain, and in an elaborate tissue of lies, that she is a pure woman, she says; misrepresented; she admits she has had seventy-five lovers, but these, she explains, didn't love her as she loved them, or did love her, and anyhow, she cries, "a predominant trait in my character is fidelity . . . . anyhow."

Fidelity is rare in anyone, — so rare is it that those who possess it and cherish it deserve too well of the whole world for that world to listen to trulls like the Pretty Mademoiselle du Thé talking about her predominant trait.

I adore Mademoiselle du Thé; I am writing a small "Life" of this able *Fille d'Opéra, vendeuse d'amour* which I shall add as an appendix to these chapters. No one could possibly appreciate her qualities more than I—: but I protest against the attempt to gull me. If she pose as High Priestess of the Art of the Dance, I am off: if she heckle me on the subject of morality, I am gone. I go to find a priest who is better fitted than is a prostitute to utter the word morality. Yet, bless your heart, morality is one of the lady's favourite themes. First she kicks her toe up to the ceiling, then she drinks her champagne steadily for two hours, and at last she launches into her pet topic, her morality and the immorality of the others.

Oh Mademoiselle du Thé, I'm simply shocked at you. I am afraid you are destined to be turned out of the Pretty Theatre for you are neither flesh, fish nor good red herring. You are a little fool, and we all thought you so awfully clever — so kind — so big-hearted: whereas one of the unnamed little pigs *de l'Opéra*, true to her colours, discreet and loyal in her *amours*, is, to quote the bard, a very different thing by far to the lump of iniquity big pigs are.

1. Edmund Kean when expressing obstinacy was wont to shut firmly his eyes and mouth, "squeezing his brows and eyelids tight" writes Mr. Gillicudy in his "Treatise on the Acting of the Elder Kean" (1859).

   "A damned determination not to see was what he expressed" (idem); and though I have never seen my editor contort his face in this way (thereby proving that Edmund Kean's as an artist was utterly untrue to nature) I have noted that he carries on most entertainingly when determined neither to hear, believe or tolerate any suggestion whatever. I cannot feel that I am as entertaining when I express obstinacy, though surely I am every bit as blind.

2. Even today I wince for the Theatre when Zola is so appalling rude about it. Yet I do not find him old-fashioned although it is the fashion to call him that. The thing which makes him seem so to people of today is that they have not read him. If Congreve be up-to-date it is because they do read him. Zola is now successfully disposed of after a struggle, and because he added grief and pain to his tale he is to be shelved. Had he spangled and powdered his heroine at her death and let her laugh a little more ironically, she and he today would be *à la mode*.

3. *Vide Mask*. Vol. X.

4. There is no date to the letter.

5. It lies on my table as I write this, and every consonant and every vowel in it breathe the practical business woman.
6. Here it was Lekain acted.
7. See *The Mask*, Vol. X Pl. 20.

# THIS LITTLE THEATRE by C. G. Smith. *The Mask*, Volume XI, no. 2, April 1925.

## BAKST.

he great Bakst is dead: and the famous Russian Ballet loses the last hope of regaining an important lost element.

When Diaghileff came to Paris and London "The Mask" was not able to find special reason for becoming ecstatic in praise of the Ballet or its Bakst: but it could and did appreciate that all the hysterical praise voiced by Paris was becoming to Paris.

It was so natural for Parisians to recognize and respond to this product of the Near East, for it could also do something in that line, so it could praise without becoming ridiculous. Whereas for a Public which tolerates, nay, appreciates, the London Theatre fare as does the London Public for twelve months a year, suddenly to pretend to have appreciated the famous Russian is not a little ridiculous. It is another case of the Maud Allen, Beggars Opera, Chauve Souris fever, when the patient becomes inarticulate for a period, and all friends are anxious.

Had the world never known greater dancers I could well understand a fine enthusiasm for Pavlova, Karsavina, Nijinski and the others. The twentieth century having seen the very genius of Dance, it seemed to "The Mask" an exaggeration to confuse genius and talent.

That M. Diaghileff had genius as an impresario, was the only genius in the group, must be counted as at least fifty per cent towards the success of this famous Ballet. He had the superb knowledge of the refined master-showman. He knew so well how to sell that which the world thrills to buy.

And examples of this exotic thing he brought with infinite care from a land which could produce some of the most vivacious men and women in Europe. These he decked beautifully out in Parisian finery, and he calls on Bakst to aid . . . . and Bakst did wonders. There was no one who could deck out dancers as he could; there were few, if any, who could contrive sceneries to match as he could. He was a pianter. I admit it: and I will also allow that painters of worth rarely leave their art to descend to the stage; but Bakst did so; and, descending to it, he took there such riches that the discerning public began to wonder whether the stage had not gone back a century and a half to that great epoch which the elder Bibiena inaugurated at his birth in 1657, and which Gonzaga closed in 1831 (dying at St. Petersburg, by the way).

For it is never to be forgotten that Bakst, as a scene painter, remained true to the old tradition. Supposedly a revelation, . . . something quite new, he was really doing what had been done before, and done superbly before; and now he came along and repeated it almost as superbly.

He was a scenic reformer of a stage which had grown feeble and commonplace in the stupid sense of the word: he allied himself with Benois, with Fokine and with the musicians; the performers, the dancers, were collected together, and all these remarkable Russians united by their Russian leader Diaghileff, who was determined to make a very real Russian effort.

This was in Moscow before anything had been heard of them. What happened? How was this determination and this enthusiasm met by their countrymen? Was it scouted? Were they derided . . . . or ignored perhaps? On the contrary. Russians were found who were prepared to finance them to success—Russian determination and talent found immediate response from the gentlemen of Russia, and this in spite of the damning evidence that they were all positively artists or experts.

No great dancer such as Isadora Duncan was in their ranks: no first rate genius of any sort; but all of them were spirited, determined, and very much aware of the high standard that they were sworn to reach: all were antagonists of the humdrum but highly respected cosmopolitan ballet of their own land. They were in fact rebels, but revolting to a good end. Had they been English, had some like spirit revealed itself in London, there would have been no financial support even if the spirit had revealed itself five or fifty years in advance of the Russians.

So it became Englishmen to praise these artists, . . . those Englishmen who preferred not to stand by their own men. It was essentially a fine democracy, this group known as the Russian Ballet; and so it was no surprise that as it wandered through Spain, France, England and elsewhere, it picked up new recruits. Unfortunately, when it added Picasso, Bakst seemed to fall off. In fact as it added internationals of all kinds, the Russians broke away. So it ceased to be the Russian Ballet, and indeed deserves to be known by the simpler and prouder title of The Ballet.

I do not recall the exact order of desertion and I do not know what sound reasons the deserters offered for running away; but I seem to remember that the first to bolt was the charming Madame Pavlova. Later Nijinski skedaddled: then Bakst, Karsavina and others. The great impresario was left in the lurch. That was quite living down to one of the traditions of the stage at its worst periods . . . . *tradizione traditore.*

There are quite a number of wonderful divisions and subdivisions in our Tradition. The main division is simple: Good tradition, Bad tradition: and I can but admit that to desert a leader is one of the worst items in the section Bad tradition.

I regret that I cannot see any way of accepting any reason which Madame Pavlova or Nijinski could possibly offer me for deserting the flag raised by Diaghileff. Yet the same old excuses doubtless were offered.

It is the Director's prerogative to engage who he will, arrange what he will, manage how he will. Once a performer or an artist *takes service* under any Director whatever it is his and her duty to remain faithful to him to the end. Even when he falls or faints, as many a leader has been known to, the followers must be staunch. All else is secondary; and failing this sense of duty all must fail. Followers must never question a leader they themselves have chosen to follow.

The Theatre would do well today to study a little its History. In Italy, in France, Russia, Germany and England the best efforts of great men of the Theatre have been rendered vain by the lack of discipline in their followers.

I do not want to seem hard, but I have to say a very bitter thing, and it is only bitter because it is true. The first to desert have usually been the leading ladies.

I can find every excuse that you can, and I can cap these with two or three more which perhaps will not occur to you; but when every excuse has been found I come back to my deepest conviction regarding our little world of the Theatre; which is that with the adhesion, the fidelity, of all to the director and leader, and with a real sense of discipline, our Stage can achieve what a nation, an army, or a navy achieves in the day of peril. It can pluck undying victory and everlasting glory for its cause and its people.

And until our European stage comes to know this once and for all, it can achieve merely petty victories, win only personal laurels, and these are plucked and won yearly and fade with the years.

I do not know how it was that Bakst came to accept service under other banners than Diaghileff's, but it was, and it remains, a grievous pity that his work was ever seen outside the magic circle of the Russian Ballet. I know nothing about this falling away and I am not curious to know. Neither do I know how the perfect Sicilian actress Signora Mimi Aguglia came to separate herself from Giovanni Grasso. Why did Musco ever dream of leaving that genius? No one admires the good Musco more than I do, but I do not admire his retreat. I admire no retreats.

And why do a hundred of the best desert their leaders every ten years? The most I may say is this. These leaders make no call, remembering that the world is old and tired and that self-interest is a mighty passion: so at the last they come to say "these people are not worth keeping. . . . let them go."

"Not worth keeping" is not strictly true; it is but partially true. Looked at as one looks at a coveted bicycle in a shop window—it may be true—"I haven't £ 10 . . . well, I don't think I want it; besides I can get another any where any day."

Perhaps the people are not actually worth keeping; to have to tempt them to stay by continually raising their salaries . . . . to have to blow spirit into them. . . . fresh force and will to abide faithfully, proves them a little poor.

"But then," asks one of them, "why stay faithful if not wanted?"

And here we touch the top of the question . . . . It is not I, or you, not Irving, not Diaghileff, who wants anyone:—it is the Theatre and Duty wants them and these managers represent Theatre and Duty. And that is the final argument which none of us must deny.

To Bakst this did not occur . . . . how could it. He must have felt the pull of the Theatre; it is an attractive siren. Yes, assuredly he felt attracted. Its call drew him gradually out of his studio . . . . away from his canvasses . . . away from his art. He was a painter, won over to the Theatre.

Compare him with Callot the French engraver. In Callot we have an example of a man utterly enamoured of the stage and Drama and to the finger tips *galantuomo*.

With what courtesy does this immense little genius approach the

benches at the back of the hall. One hears him saying "Permit me"—
they all make room for him. Enchanted, absorbed, he sits the entertainment through: when he leaves it is not to go and hob-nob with the
performers and amuse the actresses with sketches for a new costume.
When he leaves it is to record what he has seen, never to put on airs: he is
too great an outsider. These little records of his are more famous and more
valuable than all the costume designs by Berain, and do our European
Theatre more honour than all the Dramatic criticisms (in two volumes) by
Bernard Shaw.

And they set an example to others outside the theatre how to come to
look at the Theatre, and how to gallantly abstain from any closer intimacy
unless you are one of the troupe . . . . unless you belong to the tribe.

I suppose it is quite as clear to many another as it is to me, that one is not
an Englishman unless one be born of British parents: and in like manner
one cannot be a Theatre man unless one is born of it.

To become naturalized, to adopt a country, is possible; but even then,
unless with immense grace and with unrelaxing attention to ceremony,
surely the performance is gawkish and renders nil the result. To adopt a
land and to once forget oneself, to speak of "our land" . . . . no, I think
that finds us out. And to leave the art of painting to which one is born and
which, except for its parent architecture, is entirely self-contained and
complete by itself, and to push one's way into some other art is not
necessarily to play the amateur but it is to forget an essential fact.

And it is not quite good manners.

I will take Constantin Stanislawsky as an example of what I mean. Here
was a merchant—cloth was I believe what he manufactured. One day he
is attracted towards the Theatre, then drawn into it; becomes an amateur
actor . . . . quietly passes through a door into the professional playhouse;
finally becomes director; reaches to the highest position; but never for a
day does he forget that, somehow or other, he is still a guest. So he passes
here and there, carrying with him a grace, a certain modesty, *a way*, which
seems to say in every gesture, every phrase and every look, "How hon-
oured I am, how happy I am, to be allowed to be one of you."

His is an irresistible charm . . . . and sun or rainy weather it is ever the
same.[1]

To the painter Bakst no such grace had come. And so he never rose to
the position Stanislawsky won to. He is not what theatre people call "one
of us" as Stanislawsky will ever be.

And just as Stanislawsky felt as he did, and acted as he did, so does he, now that he is become one of the foremost leaders of our modern Theatre, demand of his followers the grace to serve and obey.

With what result? The tale is too sad to tell; but there are six chapters in it which are superb.

At the head of these chapters I would affix five names and there may be more.

LILINA.    KNIPPER.    MOSQUIN
KATCHALOFF.    SOULERGITZKY

and there are probably more chapters.

These are the names of two of his actresses, two of his actors, and one stage manager.

This fidelity of theirs is outstanding in the annals of the European Theatre.

It is this fidelity, this *esprit de corps*, this duty to the Stage, through discipline to the leader, that is needed in the whole European Theatre world if it is to advance.

The European Stage is advancing, but too slowly. Will the English ever come to recognize this? Why should such a great nation with so colossal a sense of loyalty, fail so in loyalty in the Theatre.

I accuse an influential minority among our workers of an inability to understand the word Duty and to endure. And I say that until every one in the theatre's ranks will come to understand and to endure, the work, while it may be good or bad, or indifferent as it is today, will suffer, and the calling will become a paltry one. It will remain the Little Theatre.

Leon Bakst was one of the greatest figures in this Little Theatre.

---

1. Irving, not born of theatrical parents, cleaves immediately and once and for all to the theatre: and ran no business in tandem.

## ARTISTS AND INTERPRETERS by X. Y. Z. *The Mask*, Volume XI, no. 2, April, 1925.

 n interesting note upon the late Leon Bakst in the "Ob server" *Jan. 4, 1925* caught my eye the other day and I give it here because it raises a rather curious question.

"A small point, that is nevertheless an important point with the designer of costumes, seems to have been overlooked in many of the obituaries of the Russian Artist, Leon Bakst. Bakst was not only an artist but also a workman. In scenic and costume designs he knew both the general effect he wanted and the exact means of obtaining it. A drawing for a dress by Bakst— sumptuous and beautiful picture as it often made—always remained a working drawing of the precise dress that Bakst intended, something that a workman could understand and cut from. In the day of amateurs, when a costume design is often a pretty picture first of all—a sketch for an idea of a dress, leaving all the real problems to be solved by the cutter out—this thoroughness and workmanlikeness was remarkable. . . . A glimpse at the colour-notes that Derain made for the charming "Boutique Fantastique" dresses, shows how much Derain owed to the cleverness (even the inventiveness) of the workmen who translated them into material. Bakst was too good a workman to leave any margin for the "inventiveness" of other people carrying out his designs."

This is all quite sound and I am among those who do not want too many "pretty picture" artists in a theatre. For these pretty nobodies are somewhat of a nuisance. Already too many of them have stowed themselves away in the new movement.

The International Exhibition of New Theatre Technique held in Vienna in 1924 offered us only too many such vanities. Anything less technical could not possibly be produced. Anyone who possesses a copy of the illustrated catalogue of that exhibition, can turn for himself to page 7, where he will find *two Figurinen* by F. Leger which would cause quite enough trouble all round. On page 42 is another such Figurine. This one is by George Grosz: and another by the same designer on page 43. Awfully clever, they may be: but far too troublesome. On page 55 we come to a couple of trifles by Oskar Schlemmer which might give a first-class cutter and his assistants five days unnecessary labour and cause some pain to the spectators afterwards. Then Herr Exter's [sic] little notation on page 68 is not exactly encouraging . . . . and four affairs on page 73 would, I fear, depress the staff, though it would not convulse it as would the error on page 80. Takuloff did that.

But these things would not only be troublesome to the technical men because all the difficulties had been shirked by the disdainful designer, but because they are worthless things.

Now suppose we take a design for a costume of great worth by a very famous designer, . . . . one by Inigo Jones (1573-1652): and suppose that this too is drawn without any indication the cutter needs: are we to throw that away too as useless. And are we to damn the whole system?

Let us first look a little more carefully into the methods of those older days. Doing so we find that as soon as Inigo has drawn a brilliant sketch of a costume he passes it on to the first interpreter. And this is *not*, as might be supposed, the cutter or the tailor.

*It is another designer.*

What does this man do? Does he interpret freely, changing here and there as he goes along as a protest against Inigo's genius? Not a bit of it. He positively makes an effort.

Now this is almost unbelievable. Yet that is precisely what he does.

He makes an effort to redraw it line for line, cuff, buttons, doublet, laces, knots, skirt linings, all as Inigo has done; only he makes each item clearer as a fact and divests it of all its fancy, its charm, *as a* drawing. He positively interprets faithfully and well.

I am by no means opposed to the opinion expressed by the writer in the "Observer" paragraph; but we must lay down no hard and fast law about anything of this kind.

While I think it *might* be good for *every* costume designer to learn to cut, stitch, pin, chalk, and generally act the tailor: . . . . you've lost your Inigo Jones at once, if you make it anything like a law.

A far wiser thing to do is to train *interpreters*. And I know no better examples to guide such interpreters than the copies which exist in the superb volume of the works of Inigo Jones lately issued by the Clarendon Press.

With but half an eye you can see there the whole process, and it is a process which could easily be learnt. All that is required is very long practice, continued exercise as copyist, and no flights of fancy; absolutely no "inventiveness." Therefore a superb training for beginners who have some talent.

Some of you may perhaps agree with me that the beginners start exhibiting in galleries and showing off in journals a little too soon. What would you have? Put them to work as *interpreters,*—as copyists—as the go-between twixt tailor and artist, and perhaps a big and troublesome problem has been solved.

This is perhaps what is being done nowadays in several theatres but it is not done *well enough.* Their copyists have not clever enough eyes. They miss eight or ten out of twenty points.

To sum up: while the Bakst method is first class, the Inigo Jones method is probably more valuable to the theatre, for it provides a training school in the wardrobe for the student, it helps the tailor and cutter immediately, and rids us of those silly exhibitions of gawkish calf-work which are beginning to grow into a nuisance.

---

Book Review. THE DANCE by Cecil Sharpe and A. P. Oppé. Unsigned. *The Mask*, Volume XI, no. 4, October, 1925.

---

his is a very delightful book which I, for one, would have printed on very much thinner paper. There is no other fault (if this be a fault) that I can find with the work of the publishers, which is done in a lavish manner, and with taste.

What is said in the book is exactly what was necessary to say, namely, that we have in England "sufficient material from which to develop a spectacular dance for the theatre which shall consist of movements at once natural and expressive, and possessing the advantage for England that they are cast in the dance idiom of our own country." All critics having any doubts could not do better than copy this statement and embellish it ten or twelve times in the course of each year. Foreign dances really do deserve a rest.

It really is time, I think, for an English ballet. I should hate to become sceptical, but I am sceptical for this moment. I am sceptical when I see a thing called the English International Opera Company holding itself up on foreign operas. It is quite absurd to call something which is not English, English. Call it what you will but do not call it English. There are heaps of other good names. And I dread lest an English ballet should be grown from Russian seed. It would be excessively stupid.

Cecil Sharpe, the author of this book, devoted long years of his life, with very little help from others, to searching for an English folk dance tradition, for he felt that, if he once found it and could give it shape, an English ballet would in time come into being.

I have often imagined an English ballet, and I have a little imagination and can sometimes spend half an hour watching the ballets which I myself create. Do not suppose me to be one of those superior beings who believe that all is created *solely* through the imagination. Before all, perhaps, there is the dancer, and I should be sorry for the public to be obliged to rely on me to cut the capers; but I can see these ballets—these English ballets. I see the curtain rising. I know the colour. It is not the colour of the Russian ballet, nor that of the French; it is the English colour right enough. I see the first movement: that is English, too. It is quite unlike anything the great Diaghilev brought to England from Russia. It is rather more easy; it is about six times as healthy. There was always something just a trifle sick about the Russians: a certain sickness soused in perfumery. Of its kind it is without question the very last word, but the kind has nothing whatever to do with the English ballet which, as you are doubtless aware, must have a melancholy all its own and a merryness not necessarily noisy.

And I am told that Mr. Cochran has started an English ballet. Well, with all due respect to Mr. Cochran, I very much have my doubts. Mr. Cochran, whom I have always thought owed much to influence of Mr. Duveen, is one of the most able men in the dramatic world to start a limited liability company, but an English ballet is not in his line. Mr. Cochran is an impresario: nothing certainly less—and not more. It was Mr. Cecil Sharpe who was the founder of the English ballet. Not that his rescuscitation of the Morris dance means very much. It would be a mistake to take the English Morris dance as revived by Mr. Sharpe too seriously, but there are things in it which can never be taken seriously enough. In a little booklet by Ralph Gardiner, called "The English Folk Dance Tradition," the author says that one of the great projects of the English Folk Dance Society is the creation of an English ballet comparable to those of Russia and Sweden. I do not like that word "project." Neither do I like the suggestion that a dance society is to be left to the creating of this long-waited-for ballet. I would rather Mr. Gardiner created it himself; or, if Mr. Gardiner is not a great dancer, that he should create it together with one great dancer, preferably a man. Now and again societies give us original performers but not habitually. The greatest French actor of the eighteenth century, Le Kain, came from a private society theatre, but somehow I look for a great dancer to appear any day from the ranks of a pantomime chorus in Huddersfield, or Nottingham, or Bradford. Such a man would not be in love with the Russian ballet. If anything he would rather fear it and be silent where Chelsea gushes. And to such a man this book by Sharpe would mean very little; and the truth is that all this book can do is to keep in front of our eyes the fact that there is such a thing as the dance, and that it was very wonderful in France, and was courageous in Italy, and charming in Vienna. Such a book can keep us all talking at the dinner table. It is like a little illustrated programme of an evening's entertainment which has lasted nineteen centuries, gone by in a flash like a bicycle goes by the window, in a flash. The nineteen centuries of Dance and Ballet have gone by in that flash, leaving England nothing behind.

I believe that there is really something true in the fact that one must be quick to catch a thing as it is going by; something true in it. Of course if you have a policeman at the end of the street and you give him his orders he will stop the bicycle, but what worries me is that he might not be able to arrest the intelligence of a couple of centuries . . . . still one never knows.

This book by Sharpe and Oppé contains a great deal of history. A number of dates, allied with a number of names, and illustrated by a number of superb reproductions; for there are seventy-five plates, and seven illustrations in the text, and the four coloured plates engraved and printed by Reiach are really charming; and these things all help to make it very well worth its price, and I bless the authors for giving us a good index.

Has the book sold well? I hear so often of books that do not sell well, and that always makes me worry about paper and the binding of books; and, as I said at the beginning I thought that this paper was rather too heavy, too rich, I must now point to an extra fault: I think the binding is too expensive. If paper and binding had been less, could not the book have come out at half the price — at 15/-. Such a price is more within the reach of another four or five hundred people. And, still thinking about paper and the binding of books, I wonder if it would not be possible to bring the book out for 5/-, giving a little less perhaps, and certainly eliminating more and more of the swank. It's swank that costs such a lot nowadays. Can't go to a theatre! Why not? Plush seats, Bristol board programmes, one shilling. Axminster carpets on staircase. Two hundred extra lamps for the auditorium. Costumes for the people who show you into your seat. Evening dress for the manager; motor car to and from the place. Hoity, toity. What is the meaning of all this swank? It is not worth anything, and yet millions of pounds are wasted on it. You tell me that nobody would visit the not-

Swanky theatre, that nobody would buy swankless books. I would not like you to consider me at all rude, but if you are a good friend of mine I tell you that you are deluded. If you had two or three days to spare (and if I had) I would go through all the details of the production of books and the management of theatres, and I would show you step by step where all this swank was unnecessary and how it totted up to the waste of many millions of pounds.

I only regret the swellness of this particular book because it is a book I should like to see many thousand people possessing. The same publishers issue another book on "Old French Line Engravings," this they limit to 1250 copies, and issue at three guineas and seven guineas, which seems to me a very proper thing to do, because old French line engravings are things which very few cultured people love to ponder over; and their book of "Old French Colour Prints," by Campbell Dodgson, also limited, is quite reasonable at three guineas; but "The Dance," which is a popular thing, belongs to the public, and the public should be able to buy all its popular things very cheaply.

---

## DISCOVERY AFTER FOURTEEN YEARS. AMALGAMATED DELIRIUM by J. B. [John Balance]. *The Mask*, Volume XIII, no. 1, January, 1927.

---

 n 1912 "The Mask" published an illustrated article entitled "The Best Theatre in London."

The author of the article was the well known Russian writer Edward Edwardovitch. He claimed that the best Theatre in London was Mr. Pollock's Toy Theatre, No. 73, Hoxton Street, Shoreditch, E. C.

He gave us a reproduction of an exquisite and ancient view of Mr. Pollock's house as seen from the outside, and several Pollock designs at their best.

Another article in the same number by D. Nevile Lees did full justice to R. L. Stevenson's 'discovery' of the Theatre of Skelt, one of Pollock's forerunners; and, in yet another article, Jack B. Yeats and his life-long love and service in the Skeltean-Pollockian cause was recorded by Allen Carric.

# A BELATED SURPRISE.

All this was done fourteen years ago; and now the journals of London are accepting the puff paragraphs of the Diaghileff press agents, telling how the said impresario Diaghileff, led by Mr. Sitwell, was taken to Mr. Pollock's shop and saw—literally saw—the said Theatre of which Edwardovitch wrote in 1912.

"It was," says the press agent, "a surprise for M. Diaghileff."

Toy Theatres exist in every land, and in Russia they have many pretty toys. These Russian toys have always served as inspiration to the artists of the Diaghileff troupe.

And now *our* Toy Theatres serve to "inspire" Prince Shervachidze who has designed his curtains, sceneries and dresses[1] for "The Triumph of Neptune" for M. Diaghileff.—So the English press agents tell us in the columns of the London journals.

And it is all not a little depressing.—I mean the fact that first Edwardovitch and now Diaghileff (both presumably Russians) were allowed by Mr. Playfair to get ahead of him, the first by fourteen years, the second by a head.

For really these toy playthings belong to the little Lyric up Hammersmith way.—To enlarge them to the size of Mr. Playfair's stage, would have been to make of them a natty little show; but to swell them up to the proportions of the Lyceum stage makes us almost sympathise with Mr. St. John Ervine in his Sunday morning reflection, as he gazes in his glass while shaving, that "Energetic men without taste are the gravest danger to any community."

In lending their services the Sitwells and Lord Berners will of course have saved the situation; but then they could long ago have gone to Mr. Pollock or "The Mask" and rendered the same service to Mr. Playfair or any Englishman with a fancy for toying. It would then have been an all-British Show—Penny plain and twopence coloured.

Somehow or other I like Russians very little nowadays.

# RUSSIANS: — YESTERDAY & TODAY.

Before they cut their Tzar to pieces and began troubling us all in every part of Europe and Asia I found many an artist who won my admiration: but it seems that you cannot be a Russian subject today and not serve the Soviets. Either as a spy or as a propagandist or as a plenipotentiary or as an ambassador (and all four jobs seem to be rolled into one nowadays), be you an artist or an impresario, a novelist or a clerk in a French or London firm, you've *got* to serve the Soviet. Which I consider very right and proper. Wherever we are, if we are Italians, we have to serve the *Duce*; if we be English, old John Bull. Right as rain, this.

That's why I don't like to see any Russians whatever in England.

Edward Edwardovitch may not really be a Russian; — M. Diaghileff too: both may be Czeco-Slovaks or Mussulmen, . . . . Heaven knows. I've lunched dozens of time with Edwardovitch, and I know also that I never did once ask him pat "are you an Irishman or what are you?" I let it slide. He looked like a Middlesex man if you know what I mean, — a good old London town man.

That M. Diaghileff would ever condescend to be aware of the existence of the Soviet is very doubtful; — for he is not the very aristocrat of impresarios? — Can you beat it?

As an impresario no one is a greater artist; and a kindly being is M. Diaghileff, that is certain.

So my theory falls to the ground — for no one so kindly or such an artist in "shows" could possibly serve anyone but a Prince.

For all this there lingers a far off faint sound of theatrical thunder in mine ears — something ominous — horrid.

It warns me somehow or other, — I cannot escape the almost imperceptible rumble I hear afar off. It does not seem to say "Take care, this man is a dangerous political agent" for I know that were impossible: it says "he is a friendly agent." That's worse.

He brings to England the very goods that England already possesses: he comes to our shores bringing his Ballets and our ideas; his Ballerinas and his Ballerinos. They settle in our land: they show us that we do not know how to dance or produce Ballets, nor how to be showmen. The whole troupe is loveable and charming — and laughs at us. I suppose.

Yes, I have heard M. Diaghileff laughing at us. He does it charmingly and we hardly deserve such an honour. So we all gather round him and assist. We take him to Pollock's shop and there he registers 'surprise' for us: we are entranced by that; — he twiddles his little finger and round we go.

Delirium — Amalgamated — actually English — Delirium.

* * * * * * *

Meantime, what about an English Ballet? what about it?

## A SUGGESTION.

But there again, what about English Journalism—what of English Theatre—English prose—English verse—English men?

I heard an outrageous suggestion made last week, by a true Englishman,
and he said he'd wipe three quarters of Fleet Street out of existence, three
fourths of the theatres, the verse-writers, prose-writers, and the rest—and
when asked why, he said that by doing so he would only be exterminating
the damn foreigner who is being allowed to spoil everything in London—
and that means England.

One has to repeat these things when one hears them—they *sound* so
awfully near the mark—But are they?

1. Why Mr. Jack B. Yeats was not asked to do this work is a blunder I find unforgiveable.

AN ITALIAN BALLET. SHAKESPEARE, OR A MIDSUMMER
NIGHT'S DREAM translated from the Italian of Giovanni Casati.
Unsigned. *The Mask*, Volume XIII, no. 2, April-May-June, 1927.

THE MASK presents to its readers an old but original Ballet in four parts,
entitled:

### SHAKESPEARE
### OR: A MIDSUMMER NIGHT'S DREAM

by Giovanni Casati, translated, presumably for the first time, into the
English language.

This Ballet, or *Ballo* as such things are called in Italian, was performed in the spring of 1855 at the inauguration of the Teatro Paganini in Genova, on April 9th.

Thirty performances of it were given, which is, for the place and time, a fairly long run.

The cast is given below. To this we can add the names of the Stage manager, Giuseppe Righetti, Conductor, Nicolo Uccelli: Prompter, Pietro Giannetti, Scene painters, Carlo Fontana, Costantino Dentone and Antonio Leonardi: the *Figurista*, Cav. Giuseppe Isola: the Machinists, Novaro, Ansaldi and Daguino: the *altrezzista* Rollero: the head tailors, Cavvera, Bremi and Poggi: the *Berettonaro*, Bremi, and lastly the wigmaker, Carlo Piazza.

This Antonio Leonardi went later to America where he took up his abode. Whether he painted scenes there I cannot say. Mr. Hornblow does not mention him in his two volume "History of the Theatre in America."

Dentone was living in 1875 in Via Balbi, Genova.

This Teatro Paganini was built in 1853-55 from designs by the architect engineer Tommaso Carpineti, the first stone being laid on June 28th, 1853.

The *Platea* measures 16 metres 70 centimetres by 18 metres 20 centimetres. It has five circles of boxes and a *Loggione* or Gallery, and every circle contains twenty-nine boxes.

Together with the theatre were built two cafés and a billiard room; a large vestibule and a Ridotto in line with the fourth circle.

It was originally illuminated by gas and had a magnificent Lustre with seventy-six jets suspended over the *platea.*

It was named after Nicolò Paganini the violinist, born in Genova in 1788, dying at Nice in 1840.

It is one of the finest theatres of Genova which city can boast better theatres than it can theatre-goers.

---

*I derived the subject of this Ballet, not from Shakespeare's drama "A Midsummer's Night's Dream" but from an Opéra Comique[1] by Messers Rosler and De Leuven, which bears the same name.*

*I ask indulgence that it was an inevitable necessity for me to give somewhat in detail the present programme. —G. Casati.*

---

| CHARACTERS. | ACTORS in 1855. |
|---|---|
| WILLIAM SHAKESPEARE | *Lodovico Montani* |
| ELIZABETH OF ENGLAND | *Carolina Bagnoli-Merli* |

MISS OLIVIA, court lady                          *Antonietta Kurz*
FALSTAFF, keeper of the royal
    park of Richmond                         *Antonio Coppini*
LORD LATIMER                                     *Pompeo Merli*
JEREMIAH, host                                   *Vassallo Pietro*
TOM, his son                                     *Virgilio Calori*
NELLY, his niece                                 *Carolina Mengoli-Massini*

*Sailors — Tavern men-servants and servants — Masqueraders — Actors —
Actresses — Cavaliers— Boatmen — Ladies — Courtiers — Gamekeepers, etc.
The scene is laid in England. Sixteenth century.
The music of this Ballet is expressly composed by the Maestro Paolo Giorza.*

---

## PART ONE.

---

*The Mermaid Inn—common room; at the back door opening on to the
Thames—In the centre the entrance door; to the right another door, which
leads into a cabinet; tables, benches, etc. To the sides the portraits of
Elizabeth and of Shakespeare—At the back, a raised gallery where a most
sumptuous table is spread.*

Many sailors are grouped at various tables eating, gaming and
drinking—Enter Shakespeare, also in a sailor's costume, and exchanges
handshakes and greetings with the jovial party, improvising some interesting little tales.

The pretty waiting maids of the tavern move about the room, intent on
replenishing, so soon as empty, the glasses of their guests, who, a little
heated by the frequent libations, would like to recompense them with
kisses and jests, which they provoke and repulse at one and the same time
with feminine coquetry—Shakespeare certainly does not show himself the
least enterprising of the company, nor the graceful Nelly the least roguish
and lively of her companions.

Jealousy of Tom, her *fiancé*, which increases the good humour of the
great poet.

Shakespeare proposes a toast in honour of Queen Elizabeth. All accept
with enthusiasm—Tom alone refuses with a gesture of contempt, at which
Shakespeare, offended, challenges him, after a sharp interchange of
words, to a boxing match.

This is accepted by the other, who is only too eager to find vent for his ill
temper—but who is beaten after a short encounter.

*151*

In the mean time there enter the tavern throngs of maskers decked out in various and bizarre fashions, returning from a wonderful fête given in honour of Elizabeth, and make a great deal of noise and riotous fun.

Jeremiah, the host, invites the masqueraders to give their orders and to use despatch because his tavern is engaged for a select gathering of artists and gentlemen who are giving a great supper there to the luminary of England, to William Shakespeare.

At these words the poet recalls to mind an invitation which he had forgotten, ascertains that the meeting place is fixed in that tavern, and hastens off to don his own costume.

The masqueraders, hurried off by Jeremiah, go out after him—Enter Falstaff, who, as head of the banquet, wishes to see, to taste and to approve the preparations and the selected wines, repeating then the order already given.

After this accurate and conscientious examination he ascends into the banquetting gallery accompanied by all the heads-of-staff of friend Jeremiah.

Lightnings, peals of thunder, torrents of rain—Enter, by the common door, Elizabeth and Olivia, the latter is prey to intense agitation while Elizabeth on the contrary laughs at her fears.

The Queen, wishing to be present in *incognito* at the fête which her good people of London were giving in her honour, had repaired to it masked, with her faithful Olivia and two gentlemen of the court; from thence she passed on to the theatre where there was being performed "Macbeth" by Shakespeare, of whose genius she is a warm admirer; but on leaving there, separated from their cavaliers, followed by some drunken sailors, overtaken by the storm, they were forced to shelter in that tavern.

Elizabeth, to reassure her trembling companion, shows her a parchment which she always carries with her, in which the high Sheriff orders every citizen of London to lend assistance and valid aid to the presentor of it; but, the storm being over, Olivia implores her not to linger any longer, confessing that, more than anything else she fears the jealousy of her noble cavalier, Lord Latimer, who is waiting that evening at the court circle where she has to return him the bunch of flowers which he presents to her every morning, receiving it back in the evening; .... a bunch which she wears at her girdle.

The two women turn to go out—but in that moment Falstaff enters. On seeing him they hastily replace their masks—Olivia's terror increases lest

Falstaff recognize her; Elizabeth laughs and communicates her plans to her.

—Falstaff is the general keeper of the Royal Park of Richmond the key of which he always carries with him—he must thus reconduct the Queen to her own Palace without recognizing her.

Falstaff, seeing two women, sets himself to play the fascinator and to act the lover—and invites them into Richmond Park, the key of which he offers to them—the two women accept and ask his arm; but as they are about to go out lively music is heard . . . . It is the guests who are arriving.

Falstaff hides the two women in the cabinet, promising to come and fetch them from there so soon as it shall be certain that his companions, all occupied with wine and gaiety, are not noticing him.

Into the *Sala* come the guests, Actors, Actresses, Dancers, Gentlemen; among them Shakespeare and Latimer:—Jeremiah and Tom announce that the repast is served:—the latter is embarrassed on recognizing in the great poet the sailor with the strong fist.

The guests all ascend to the upper floor save Lord Latimer, who remains wrapped in this thoughts, and Shakespeare who questions him on the cause of his melancholy—Latimer confides to him that he loves and is jealous. —Shakespeare laughs at both the love and jealousy, calls all women fickle, and invites him to drown his sorrow in wine—Latimer refuses—Shakespeare, called by his friends, mounts to the upper floor where the gaiety is already at its height.

A little before this Falstaff will have entered and will have hidden himself in one of the adjoining rooms—When Shakespeare has gone out he believes that there is no longer anyone in the ground-floor room, and, without seeing Latimer, hastens to liberate the two women.

Olivia, on perceiving her lover, utters a cry and throws down a little bunch of flowers—Falstaff, believing it is a gift intended for him, picks it up with transport and lays it away against his heart—Olivia staggers and falls back on a chair—All surround her—Latimer is seized by a suspicion which he soon drives away.

At that moment Shakespeare enters, half drunk, following Nelly. He sees the two masks and wishes at all costs to present them to his friends—Falstaff replies that those two ladies were about to withdraw in his company—Shakespeare retorts that no one should go out from there that night.

Elizabeth with the imperious gesture of the Queen orders him to clear the way for her—Shakespeare in reply locks the door, removes the key, and, drawing his sword, declares himself ready to oppose the exit with force; he then enjoins upon Falstaff to return to the banquet: on Nelly to conduct Olivia to her rooms as she stands in need of her assistance: on Elizabeth to remain there with him.

All obey. Latimer goes out with Falstaff—The Queen casts a menacing glance on the audacious fellow who dares to impose his will upon her, but, seeing the alteration of his lineaments, feels in her heart a profound compassion for that genius which is so miserably being lost unless a friendly and protective hand succeed in saving it—and remains with him almost to carry out a project of her own.

Shakespeare, left alone with her, implores her to remove the mask—but in vain.

She reproves him for so degrading the genius bestowed upon him by God—talks to him of the future, of glory, of the theatre, of art.—But Shakespeare replies that, betrayed by love, by glory, by art, he neither believes nor hopes any longer save in one sole comfort, . . . in the bottle which he clasps tightly and from which he gulps down large draughts. Elizabeth orders him to leave her—Shakespeare promises on condition that she remove her mask—The Queen refuses—and the great poet, whose reason is clouded by the fumes of wine, staggers, sways, and falls drunk upon a chair.

Elizabeth, having removed her mask, contemplates him with a sense of noble and generous pity—and decides to save him from the abyss into which he is about to fall. —But on hearing people coming she replaces the mask and withdraws into the room on the left after having taken the key from him.

The guests rush in, all somewhat excited by wine, following Jeremiah who does not want to serve them any more to drink—Falstaff is the rowdiest of them all. —

In the meantime the watch is heard approaching—General confusion. Elizabeth takes advantage of it to place unseen a parchment on the hilt of Falstaff's sword—then she retires rapidly and unobserved with Olivia.

Jeremiah implores his guests not to expose him to the rigours of the law by remaining longer, and notifies them of the approach of the watch. — "*What do you fear?* exclaims Falstaff . . . . *here am I and my sword*"; but, in striking on the cross-piece, he finds the parchment, reads it, and is struck dumb. —It orders him in the Queen's name, under pain of death, to transport Shakespeare instantly into the royal park of Richmond. — The guests in the meantime have all withdrawn.

He, having called four of his men, hastens to execute the orders received — while the four men lift Shakespeare up the scene changes.

---

## PART TWO.

---

*The Royal Park of Richmond — In the background the Thames — to the left a Gothic Pavilion with a door to which one ascends by a few steps. Moonlight night.*

The four men transport Shakespeare, and lay him down in the open air; they then retire. —

The royal gamekeepers assemble there from their nightly round — Falstaff arrives, still disturbed by the emotions of the night. Having gathered the gamekeepers around him he gives them strict orders — no one is to approach the royal park that night: he is answerable for it with his own head.

So saying, he turns his head and sees Latimer before him — Terror of Falstaff who implores him to go away, informing him of the orders he has received and the terrible responsibility which weighs upon him.

But Latimer, in prey to his jealous suspicions, wishes to ascertain whether they are true; thus he promises him to retire on condition that he tells him who were the two masked women of the tavern.

Falstaff, to whom it seems too good to be true to free himself from so great a danger so cheaply, confesses with a mysterious air that they were his lady loves — and to convince him more firmly shows him the bunch of flowers. Latimer recognizes it; and, beside himself with rage, snatches it out of his hand and draws his sword; *"Very well, says he, since thou art my rival thou must fight with me."*

Falstaff, in whom courage is not the principal virtue, not knowing how to get himself out of the difficulty, confides to Latimer that the women were not at the tavern for him, but rather . . . . *For whom?* cries the young lord furiously . . . . Falstaff, hard driven, rolls his eyes, around, pale with terror, sees Shakespeare who is sleeping, and pointing him out to Latimer, —*For him* . . . . he exclaims.

Latimer is about to throw himself upon the sleeper when the Queen appears upon the threshold of the pavilion, followed by Olivia, both dressed in white and covered with white veils.

Falstaff sees her, restrains Latimer, and drags him away almost by force—The gamekeepers disperse.—Elizabeth communicates to her friend the plans laid so as to succeed in her generous intention.

A sweet and mysterious melody awakens little by little the drowsy poet——He looks around as though bemused, seeking to reconnect his own recollections, and sees the park peopled with white and airy apparitions which sport and frisk before him.

Elizabeth from the highest step of the pavilion controls with the sound of the harp the movement of those apparitions.

Then, turning to Shakespeare, it seems that she says "*I am thy genius which speaks to thee yet once again before abandoning thee —Let the man with his frailties and his vices disappear, and let the poet be born afresh.*"

Then the apparitions, ever obedient to the signs of the Queen, present before his eyes some pictures from his most celebrated tragic poems— Romeo and Juliet—Othello—and Macbeth—which ends by exalting his mind and his heart.

Then he, kneeling before Elizabeth, says to her—*Oh thou who hast restored to me strength, genius, hope, courage . . . . ah! complete thy work! unveil to me thy features and reawaken me also to love . . . .* —and beside himself with emotion he is about to raise her veil, when the Queen, repulsing him, exclaims "Back! wretched man, someone approaches."

Latimer in fact is approaching—but Olivia thrusts herself between Shakespeare and Elizabeth, who retires hastily—Shakespeare does not perceive the change, and repeats to the woman who was standing before him ardent protestations of love. Latimer, furious, rushes upon her, tears off her veil, and recognizing Olivia, overwhelms Shakespeare with reproaches, challenges him to a duel, and forces him to defend himself.

Falstaff rushes up with the gamekeepers—Olivia goes in search of the Queen, who alone can avert a disaster.

The two adversaries contend in spite of the opposition of Falstaff, who reminds them that it is a crime punishable with death to fight a duel in a royal park—Shakespeare presses hard on Latimer who falls back between the wings.—Falstaff and the gamekeepers thereupon rush up.

From the other side comes the Queen. —Shakespeare, who believes he has killed his friend, reappears greatly agitated, encounters the Queen, recognises her, and turns and rushes rapidly away like a madman.

General tableau.

# THIRD PART.

*Reception hall in the Palace of Whitehall. Entrances to right and left.*

The Queen and Olivia, ignorant of the result of the duel, because the Queen saw only the flight of Shakespeare and is completely oblivious of what may have happened to Latimer, await with great impatience the arrival of Falstaff, whom the Queen has had summoned.

Enter the intrepid guard, still bearing the traces of the terrible proofs to which his courage has been put. The Queen orders him to give her an account of what took place the preceding night in the royal park of Richmond. Falstaff, who fears for his life if the Queen (who he believes to be ignorant of everything) should come to know that the park was invaded despite her orders and that a duel was fought in it, declares that, thanks to his active surveillance, nothing unusual took place. But the Queen makes him swear upon his life what he asserts, and threatens to punish him severely if he should have lied.

At such words, Falstaff, trembling from head to foot, throws himself at her feet confessing everything; but he reassures her regarding the life of Latimer, relating how the young Lord, who was believed to be severely wounded, had but tripped and fallen on the grass. —Joy of Olivia and of the Queen at this news.

Elizabeth accords her favour to Falstaff on condition that he will always and to everyone maintain that nothing took place that night in the royal park of Richmond and that he did not see there either Shakespeare or Latimer, or the Queen, or Olivia.

Falstaff, bewildered between fear and surprise, repeats mechanically the words of Elizabeth; his amazement increases on finding in his hat the key which he had given to the two masqueraders and which the Queen placed there without his being aware of it.

In the meantime Elizabeth seats herself at the table, and writes a note in which she explains everything to Lord Latimer, reassures him as to the love and fidelity of Olivia, and recalls him to court, enjoining upon him absolute silence respecting all that took place.

The note has hardly been despatched when an usher announces William Shakespeare. He is introduced.

The Queen thanks him for the promptitude with which he responded to her invitation to present himself at the Palace. *I wished,* she continues, *to take advantage of a solemn fete, which gathers around me all that there is of noble and eminent in the three Kingdoms, to receive at court, and see for the first time, the great poet who does honour to England.*

Shakespeare is amazed by such words and humbly reminds Elizabeth of the visions of Richmond park and of her generous counsels. The Queen replies that certainly his imagination caused him to take a dream for reality. Shakespeare insists, and cites two witnesses, Miss Olivia and Falstaff.

Both of them reply with a decisive negative to all his agitated demands. Shakespeare then throws himself at the feet of the Queen and says to her—*Even were it all a dream there is one fact which is, alas, real. —I have slain Latimer.*

Latimer at that moment appears on the threshold; Elizabeth points him out to Shakespeare, who, in despair, fears for his own reason, and . . . . *since*, he exclaims, *that which consoled my life is but a dream . . . . I renounce life.*

The Queen then draws him aside and, . . . . *No,* says she, *you have not dreamed, live for England . . . . and for me.*

She then calls Latimer and Olivia to her, unites their hands, and presents to the bride and bridegroom a rich casket; presenting another, no less rich, to Shakespeare. He opens it and discovers a wreath of laurel.

"*Oh! I am not worthy,* exclaims the great poet in confusion, going down on one knee; "*Yes, you are,* responds the Queen, *it fell from your head, I replace it and fasten it there. From this moment you will always find in your Queen a protectress . . . .* ". "*And nothing more . . . .* " asks Shakespeare with emotion. "*And a friend in Elizabeth*" replies the Queen in a low voice; and in thus saying she encircles his brow with the rich crown, and orders that the day be celebrated in which the Queen of England, in the name of the country, thanks Shakespeare for his works.

From within is heard the music of the festival. Elizabeth, taking Shakespeare by the hand, introduces him into the Great Ball Room.

---

## PART FOUR.

---

where the supreme poet is feted and applauded by all.

1. First performed in Paris April 20, 1850.

Book Reviews. THE STAR OF PICCADILLY by Lewis Melville,
ENEMIES OF SOCIETY by Charles Kingston, SOUVENIRS DU
VIEUX COLOMBIER by Berthold Mahn, SOME STUDIES IN
BALLET by Arnold Haskell. Unsigned. *The Mask*, Volume XIV,
no. 2, April-May-June, 1928.

lthough we would have supposed that old Q's life
would have furnished Mr. Melville with countless doc-
uments, one more interesting than the other, it does not
seem that there was much for this most entertaining
writer to go upon. Old Q's existence was almost a
round of dull events. His friendship, his wagers, his
flirtations, his liaisons, his reputation we hear of in this book, but the whole
life amounts to little compared with, let us say, the life [of] Mrs. Jordan or
Lady Hamilton's career. It is dull; and, what is more, there's no thread
connecting his wagers, his friendships, his liaisons and his flirtations, and so
his reputation suffers. It was a bad reputation, now become no better than it
should have been.

Truly difficult for a Michael Angelo or a Casanova to live up to the
common repute.

One hears too much of a Michael Angelo, and so, in a Piccadilly way,
does one hear too much of old Q. Angelo survives it; Queensbury falls flat.

It is not Mr. Melville's fault for we know how well he can string together
facts which are interesting about such figures as Nell Gwyn or Beau Brum-
mel. His historical works on these and other like people become romances.
With old Q he had nothing to string together or he could have done it.

Mr. Charles Kingston in his "Enemies of Society" has an amazing mass
of very good material, and very well he handles it. His are true tales. That
touching the *Famous Jewel Theft* by Mr. and Mrs. Torpey is very pleasing:
and *The Murder of Madame Laurent* is most thrilling.

There are eighteen tales in all, twelve to fourteen of which are all you
could possibly wish for.

The author is apt to use comic phrases now and again which somehow
fail in their effect of heightening the melodramatic tension.

More successful when detailing the incidents of a robbery, he is only
surpassed by Mason of "The Villa Rose" when it's a murder because he is
tied to his facts.

Some good illustrations, mostly portraits by Spy, of Rufus Isaacs, Sir H. B. Poland and Sir Frank Lockwood add something to the book.

And Aubrey Hammond's drawing of "Old Q" which I had almost forgotten to mention almost makes me curious again about that old Piccadilly Lord. Aubrey Hammond is apt in his designing; that's because he's an artist; but you are never made too conscious of this in his popular work,—and it is growing more and more popular, and a very good thing too.

The fifty-five drawings which M. Mahn has collected together so as to show he remembers the Théâtre Vieux Colombier of Paris merely show me that he never even saw it. He was looking at himself, admiring the point of his pencil or his pen; but what Copeau was really trying hard to do is not in any way recorded.

Compare M. Mahn with a good draughtsman recorder of theatricals— with Daumier or with Callot or with Cruickshank or twenty others whose names occur to you.

These men were keen to record an incident, a place, a scene, a bit here and a bit there—a reality every time.

M. Mahn *records* nothing; he makes no effort to; he just scribbles.

The book does Copeau an injustice.

Copeau may not be a great actor or a great producer, but he was ever a very serious man trying to do his level best at this Théâtre Vieux Colombier.

I would have liked to possess fifty-five designs showing us the stage during rehearsals, Copeau at work there; Jouvet discipling around him, and all the other assistants busy at their work. —And everyone was very busy, very keen; the work was serious.

M. Mahn turns it all to froth.

And so I prefer a hundred times more Mr. Arnold L. Haskell's records of some of the Russian ballet dancers, which is issued sumptuously.

His records are photographs around which he writes, and both his opinions and photographs are interesting.

Alicia Markova as photographed by Raphael is enchanting—and, what is more, it's a good record.

In much that he says Mr. Haskell is very right, and if there had only been an English Ballet to write about this author's critical faculties and enthusiasm for dancing would have had a proper chance. As it is we can't be expected any longer to be enthusiastic about a group of foreigners who have given us quite the wrong notions of dancing.

We mustn't dance that way. Nothing resembling Mentchiova or Pavlova must be our model. English dances say one thing, Russian another.

Would you have our coming Shakespeare writing plays to the model Tchekov offers? Are we so utterly tongue-tied, brain-frozen, leg-bound and blind that we must ape the foreigner.

I know we are not. What on earth makes us do it?

---

## A LETTER ON RECENT TRAVELS THROUGH EUROPE. *The Mask,* Volume XV, no. 2, April-May-June, 1929.[1]

---

Dear Semar,

In these last moments—people call them months sometimes—all sort of absurd things, and delightful things and people, lovely things and people, have I seen and heard, and it's when the full tide comes on that I have at times written to you. In 1908 . . . wasn't it? . . I wrote of München and Moscow and England.

These last months I have been in Paris, in Berlin, Weimar and London. Add to these Heidelberg, Mannheim, Boulogne-sur-Mer, Karlsruhe, Lyon, and Cormery and a place called Schwezingen.

I went to all these places quite alone, but in every place I met friends and strangers, and one quite strange sort of being of whom I may tell you something or no if the light permits.

It was when listening to the immortal song "C'est vous" that I met the strange being—in one of those ultra modern places in Paris . . . but it would take ages to tell you the story and so we will come to that next quarter, not now.—

In Mannheim I bought one interesting book on the Theatre published in the early part of the 19th century, wherein a "producer" of that day had described, step by step, how to produce an opera; he manages to fill some two hundred pages describing how it is to be done.

The book is the only remembrance I have of this place . . . excepting a very bright half-hour in the museum when Miss Stoll, the assistant of the director of the archives, told me many an interesting thing about the old Theatres of the place.

I then went on to Paris; there I met with another curious figure . . . a certain Englishman who styles himself the Comte d'Angleterre.

I could write a history of this man, but I doubt whether I shall have the time. An austere being devoting his time, strength and money to others, he passes almost unnoticed amongst those celebrities in Paris who are said to be somebodies.

In Paris too I came across that remarkable theatrical genius M. Diageliev. I have never seen anyone look older than he can look at 12 o'clock midday and then at 8 o'clock the same evening look and be the youngest man in the city. He invited me to his box at the Opera House to see four of his ballets . . . . four on the same evening . . ! I almost think that four is two too many.

A most enjoyable hour and a half I spent following the two first ballets, "L'Oiseau de Feu" and "Apollo," both composed by Stravinski. I for my part preferred the "Apollo" to the other.

I can imagine no more delicate piece of work than the arrangement of the different sections of this second ballet, this "Apollo."

Everything conspires in it to cheat us—but all is done openly and beautifully.

The arrangement of this Ballet was by *Georges Balanchine*, a man of a fine creative talent. The dancers were Serge Lifar and the three ladies, Danilova, Tchernichera and Doubrovska, and all four enchanted me.

There was only one fault in this ballet and this one fault is the unwillingness or inability of the arranger to make his ballet *in one piece*. It was broken up into ten or twenty or thirty sections. Nature in this respect does better than he. Clouds—seas—rain storms—sciroccos—always proceed without a break; no matter what the contrasts or what the harmonies, in nature all goes on from its start to the conclusion of its performance; there is no break, there are no jerks—no goings forward only to go back—no goings round—all advances and always.

And when I came to London and visited the Exhibition of Dutch Art and stood before the mighty landscape (No. 227) by Philip Koninck I realized that great painting also proceeds from start to end in a single unbroken series of advancing waves. It may take hours for the spectator to follow these; it does in Koninck's landscape; but the rhythm never suddenly breaks—not once.

I thought this the most wonderful painting of all the 921 items of the show. Its manner is the grandest manner of Shakespeare or Bach—and this explains why hardly anyone stopped to look at it, and there must have been some 1300 people at Burlington House on the day I went in.

The Catalogue, which honours some of the artists by a word or two of mention, does not stop to speak of Koninck. He was born in 1616 and died in 1689.

The success of M. Diageliev's Paris performances was greater than ever . . . and indeed this is not hard to understand, for it is today the best ballet in the world, and never was the troupe stronger nor the inventions of M. Diageliev more happy.

My only reason for not waiting to see the whole four ballets is that I had had enough. I didn't want to forget the loveliness of "Apollo."

I sometimes wonder why it is that the spectators are not given two ballets and then asked to say which of the two they would like repeated. I would have called for "Apollo."

In Berlin there was a production I would willingly have seen twice over . . . the German version of *"The Beggars' Opera,"* but I fell ill and could not. In Berlin I nearly died. None of my friends knew of this at the time and so it does not matter.

In London, I saw "Journey's End" at the Savoy Theatre; . . . a money making piece well done by actors.

In London I heard of five people each of whom is going to "save the British stage." One is a rather lame copy of Irving's less intelligent son; another is a hairdresser; a third drops his Hs—and so on.

My one disappointment was on discovering that at the Ambassadors Theatre the brilliant young actress Miss Marda Vanne was out of the cast.

I had long promised myself I would see her work.

While the flimsyest excuse is for me excuse galore for mentioning Miss Marda Vanne, I shall have a very grave reason for doing so soon and shall come to that in the next but one issue of "The Mask." For I shall then prophesy!

As I have always been labelled a prophet I intend to prophesy with care. I shall prophesy that if Miss Marda Vanne returns to act in England she will be seen as . . . . and I will even prophesy that she will do it better than did Sarah Siddons or Sarah Bernhardt.

I shall name the part in the next but one number.

Now who any longer says I am a prophet? . . . for what prophet risks all on a single cautious throw like this. Call me a gambler in future.

I have also discovered a "Hamlet" . . . a man fitted to play it surprisingly well . . . an Englishman, and one who never dreamed it possible, does not now dream it, for I've not yet told him he was born to play it—and better than John Kemble.

In Paris, by the way, I met one of the Footes—a descendant of the great comedian of the 18th century Samuel Foote. We lunched together at the Café de la Paix and he showed me a snuff box which came down to him from his great grandfather.

In Paris I was reminded of that line . . . is it by Dryden or by Pope? . . . *"Some men to business, some to pleasure take"*; and indeed no where else can the two streams of serious and playful men be so clearly defined—nor more markedly divided.

If anything your Parisian is more solemn than he was, and more charming.

1. [Partially reprinted in *Dance Index*, Volume II, no. 8, August, 1943.]

## ON CREATING AND DESTROYING. A NOTE ON LAMBRANZI AND HIS BOOK OF DANCES by J. S. [John Semar.] *The Mask,* Volume XV, no. 2, April-May-June, 1929.

 e give as our Frontispiece this quarter one of the designs from Lambranzi's "Nuova e Curiosa Scuola di Balli Teatrali," which appeared in 1716. In this dance . . . A Raguadon . . . Harlequin is playing the joke that Launcelot Gobbo plays on his father Old Gobbo in Shakespeare's "Merchant of Venice." Old Gobbo is also blind, and bringing eggs or something to market in a basket.

Lambranzi has always puzzled *"The Mask"* since it first heard his name; and when in 1923 it published a design from Lambranzi's book which was, we believe, the very first to appear in any English publication, it made no pretence that it could inform its readers about the author, the book, the designer or anything at all.

Now Mr. Beaumont, . . . . Mr. Cyril Beaumont the writer and historian of the Theatre and Mr. Beaumont the publisher of 75 Charing Cross Road, . . . . have together, in their dual yet united individuality, brought out a

reprint of the work with the illustrations all in order and handsomely reproduced, and only six years after "The Mask" called attention to the existence of Lambranzi and his book.

How slowly "*The Mask*" moves, you think, its wonders to perform. We
rather think that six years is a bit rapid.

There is a certain theatre person in London who breaks his word and
whom for that we intend shortly to damn for a weak-kneed nobody: but
he can't possibly be exterminated by that so suddenly that you witness any

*Harlequin and The Blind Man, from Lambranzi's* Balli Teatrali, *1716. From* The Mask, *1929.
Vol. XV.*

theatrical, any immediate catastrophe: he will hang on for quite three or four years.[1]

Yes, we kill quicker than we can create.

Beaumonts and Lambranzis are not easy to create, whereas Joneses, Smythes and Rubinsohns puff out pretty easily.

To do this without care or thought, to wildly create or as wantonly destroy, would be on our part to sink Journalism to the level of the "Daily Bubble."

We have ever been proud since we began in "The Mask" work in 1907 to do as well as possible with our little journal in the honourable field of Journalism . . . and we believe that here and there, in and around "The Mask," are to be found some original nice touches unique in journalism.

"The Review of Reviews," in saying "The Mask thinks what it says and thinks a long time before saying it," pays a compliment we are happy to fancy we have earned—and we are thinking long before we decide to kill or mutilate any Joneses Smythes or Rubinsohns.

---

1. Now don't all rush to try on the cap, although quite a few of you have been so very unreliable, to say the least of it.

---

Book Review. CHIC AND THE POETIC. 1930.[1]

---

 t is a teasing thing to discover that, though I know the theatre well—since I belong to it—I am considerably puzzled by this book on the great Marie Taglioni. The report seems to me to be all that it ought not to be.

Assuredly, a stage performance by one who can perform well has a strange effect upon those of us who are looking on and listening: we are made to say and do the most surprising things. For example, we write articles or books about a great performer which we should never write about some great artist. We write about the artist's *work*, but we write about the performer's person . . . always the person. And so really, in the final estimate, the whole thing is worthless. For if we are to write about persons, would it not be saner to study the very highest persons, and write of them—of Julius Caesar, perhaps, or of Francis of Assisi. We don't take cheap books and enthuse about them, as we enthuse about the performances of not very worth while persons. Taglioni and Fanny Elssler do not seem to have been in the very slightest degree comparable to Joan of Arc or Queen Victoria; and yet for a number of years the spectators, including writers like Gautier and Thackeray, when in the presence of the two dancers, seemed to lose their sense of proportion. When critics wrote of Taglioni (though, strangely enough, only one great writer ever wrote very well of her, and that was Thackeray—all the others being madly on the other side, the side of Fanny Elssler) they wrote of her as though she were greater than Moses, David, or Elijah. As an inspiration, Taglioni was not unimportant: for in whatever city she might appear, there seems to have been a free fight until she left. Briefly, when city folk spy a great performer coming to their town, the whole place decides to turn fool.

"Will the young folks ever see anything so charming, anything so classic, anything like Taglioni" wrote Thackeray. Well, the young folk have seen it, from 1905 to 1912, and now, in their middle age, they speak of it—assuring people, in tones which allow of no contradiction, that nothing like it will ever be seen again. Why is it that the stage should make fools of us all? I, too, have raved about performers, and I shall continue to rave about them: but whenever I do so, I am well aware that I have lost my head. Barbey d'Aurevilly, the chronicler of the "Nouvelliste," publicly praised the "audacities of Fanny Elssler," and swept away "the idolatrous memories of that pair of compasses, composed of little flesh and much bone, called Mlle. Taglioni." Yet he says in his diary, written at the same time: "I love Fanny to the point of telling lies for her. . . . so I have slaughtered Taglioni on her altar."

I am as good a spectator as you—as impressionable as you—the whole audience should be that—not so the critics: and it utterly kills the Theatre when the critics fall into the bad habit of losing their heads to persons.

This book on Taglioni, so delightfully written, so full of information, is the best memorial that exists of the celebrated dancer. André Levinson, through his art, recreates for us a period we love to see again. Of course. But when you close the book, you feel that something was in those days very ridiculous in the state of Europe.

I am not at all sure that the dramatic critic is necessary. I begin to believe that the public alone should be admitted to theatrical performances, there to shout with joy or scream with terror during the spectacle. I feel that we should not delegate people to attempt to put into cold print, the same night, what it is they *think* they have seen. Even for the critical, the thing to do after such a show is to go out of the playhouse and drink deep; there is nothing else will serve, till the Dionysia and its liberty to run wild for days at a time in our Athens, be restored. Theatre essentially belongs to Carnival time, and in the old days when mankind invented Theatre, it knew what it was doing when, at the same time, it fixed a period for it to begin and end in.

Feeling a bit Bacchic about it all, the glorious Théophile Gautier plumped for Fanny Elssler—who was chic, who was "a pagan dancer," in distinction to Taglioni, whom he calls "a Christian dancer." Not so did the lovers of Taglioni feel about Taglioni. They thought, they felt, emotionally of her, as of a spirit . . . "so poetic" . . . "so divine." They should have realised that Taglioni was only a weaker, sweeter, pagan dancer than was Fanny; that and no more. To do more—to dance the very truth itself, not merely its saucy, *chic* side or its sentimental, poetic side, never has occurred to anyone since Greece died.

This book reminds me that we should not rest so content to leave the theatre where it is—we should call for something from the performers which shall help to place the theatre, with its dance, song, and act, level with the work of the great writers and the great architects. We never love Sir Christopher Wren to the point of telling lies for him, so as to slaughter Lutyens; we never fool ourselves about Milton or Defoe. The fine arts are still great and fine; their concern is with truth only. This book on Taglioni once more tells us, and should tell the critics, that we must wake up and bring the theatre nearer to the great arts.

1. ["Marie Taglioni," by André Levinson. With 13 Illustrations. (C. W. Beaumont.) A trimmed copy of this newspaper review was a gift from Ben Weinreb of London to the editor. There was no expedient way to identify the source or date without delaying its publication here.]

Book Review. HER EXCELLENCY PAVLOVA. *The Week-end Review*, August 1, 1931.

wonder what it is that everyone in London is saying about this book?[1] I can well suppose that the author is hardly ever mentioned, and that all the talk is of Pavlova—the known Pavlova—the woman fated to give up her life to become a celebrated name. Yet the writer of the book, who was her musical director, deserves a great deal of praise for his work so well done.

Pavlova made her home in London, but we must remember that everyone has heard of her, in Russia, Austria, Italy, France, Germany and Holland, and in America and far Eastern cities, and many claimed that they knew her. She was ever kind and gracious. Her reputation was always growing greater and greater, and she positively ran away from it, and kept running away from the more exasperating obligations of that ridiculous popularity which the public thrusts upon a famous performer, especially in London and Paris. Her best work as a dancer was not appreciated—if she had a worst, it was *that* the public "bravoed."

Had she written the Book of Job, or one of Mozart's compositions, or been a model mother, the publics of the big cities would have taken bare notice of her, yet these three things are more difficult to accomplish than to dance excellently. But because she was a performer, one who appeared in the flesh before the collected intelligences of the enlightened crowds in the great cities, between the years 1905 and 1930, she became very well known and noticed so very much that ten or twelve new terrors were added to the ejaculations "Oh!" and "Ah!" She was much too good to fool away her time so as to please a public which is never content until a performer has done what *it* wants.

She was an excellent fine creature—not in the least pretty. Four photographs in this book show her looking rather like an Indian peasant . . . "the worthy niece of Mr. Gandhi," I should have sized her up, had I seen her carrying the bundles of hay and stacking them, or feeding the animals, as these photographs show her. Her skin is tight-drawn across a nicely-shaped bony skull—nothing fleshy—plain to ugliness. Had I met her in some village inn up north, and had she turned to me and said, "I be just a-goin' to get thee a coop o' tea," I should have been in no way sur-

prised—and a cup of tea would have seemed to me to fill the bill exactly
. . . but I defy anyone to find in these four rustic photographs the person
we thought to be the celebrated Pavlova. Alas, instead of this fine reality
offering a few of us some real cups of tea and introducing us to her sons
and daughters and swans and living a happy life, she was, by a cruel fate,
forced to dance, so as to give millions of us a series of semi-imitations of all
sorts of things. These were: "A Frenzied Greek Bacchante" — "A Butterfly
dancing with the flowers in sunshine" — "A Dragonfly" — "A Californian
Poppy" — "An Oriental Courtesan" — "The Spirit of Time" — "A Tennis
Player" and "A Swan."

She was a remarkable person—a very intense worker—and when she
*had* to, she made herself an excellent dancer, and kept herself excellent by
discipline, and did all sorts of difficult dancings well; but I do not think she
would have failed had she been put to some other craft, to making dresses,
or weaving, or to the goldsmith's craft. I think she would have succeeded
always. For she was not a born dancer. There were several, if not like her,
not at all unlike her, both before her time and after.

She was well taught in the Imperial Ballet School; but she and her
fellow-pupils would never have been subjected to the ordeal of that tuition
had it been supposed for one instant that the pretty creatures being fab-
ricated by that terrible process were one day going to leave St. Petersburg.
The really extravagant sums of money which Indian Princes and Russian
Tzars devoted to their ballets were not spent from any particular desire to
learn what the ladies had to say with themselves after they had been
trained, nor from the slightest understanding of the possibilities of the
Dance as an art; but simply from the desire to own as good ballet dancers
as they had good racehorses and good soldiers. "Each animal to its own
purpose" was their motto; and they supplied stalls, barracks and villas to
lodge all these, so that no possible harm could come to a single ankle,
fetlock or rib.

Then (in 1905, not 1907) the great dancer of the world visited Russia
and was seen by Pavlova; and once seen, so greatly did all lesser dancers
admire, that they took on something of the style—caught at what they
could—were entranced—swore it was the one and only way to dance—
swore she *was* the Dance. The great dancer had pulled a veil aside—one
glimpse was enough.

Pavlova, with her deft Russian powers of imitation, caught up the pattern of the idea and displayed it all round St. Petersburg. It was said to be

American! Not a scrap of it: it was individual. The applause rose to crescendo on crescendo—dancing folk thought this new dancing was a new trick which could be acquired: it was much more, and most attempts at copying it had disastrous results; that was in or about 1907. Pavlova left Russia about then and went to Paris—danced in the touring Ballet company which Diaghiliev organised; and after a short time, she left Diaghiliev, too.

I always think I saw her dancing at her best at the big theatre in St. Petersburg in 1905—or 1906, was it?—just before she joined Diaghiliev. The conventional background, that of the St. Petersburg Theatre, was the best setting for her delicate performance: her slight charm needed a solid, rather stiff, background against which to display to perfection the little thing she had to do, and did so well. When I saw her some years later, in London, I thought she was rather less excellent than she seemed in St. Petersburg. She had fine, thin wrists, and never became stout—I remember noting how very thin were her wrists and how thin were her arms—that was when I saw her in Russia. In a description of her rather before that time, by Prince Georg Kotschubey—a very delightful description—he refers to "her thin young face." He should be writing a book about her, for surely he could well describe those early days we need to know more of.

Meantime, the facts recorded so admirably by Mr. Hyden in this book make most interesting reading, as well as being of real importance to the history of the Dance. The photographs, which too often betray theatrical people, are here full of charm. I have referred already to four of the most interesting of them; but they are only four out of seventeen. Two wonderfully sweet portraits show her "at rehearsal" and "in her dressing room"—the hard-working little lady in her most intelligent mood. Other pictures reveal quite other women, and yet all are Pavlova. The intelligent Russian ladies who become performers perhaps do not possess such symmetrical features as the more beautiful English or Americans; but they have studied more, and part of their training for the stage is to know how to make themselves look what they like. So that in one photograph, facing page 70, you see the excellent, but plain-looking Indian peasant transformed into the sweetest of little English girls, in high-heeled shoes, and looking like a chocolate-box piece of perfection.

The book as a piece of printing is good, and really good paper has been used, so that a pretty book, well worth its 8s. 6d., is the result. The binding is the most original and the best I have seen on a lively London book for a very long while; and it is by the books that the dancer will be judged in years to come, so it is well to print and bind them well—and to write them as well as possible.

1. ['Pavlova.' by Walford Hyden. (Constable.)]

## MADEMOISELLE GUIMARD AND HER PRIVATE THEATRES.
*The Dancing Times*, December, 1933.

ademoiselle Marie-Madeleine Guimard was born in 1743,[1] and died in 1816; so she lived through the reigns of Louis XV and Louis XVI, the Reign of Terror, the Consulate, the Empire, and the first months of the Restoration.

No French *danseuse* of the second part of the eighteenth century was so famous as she—and she was famous for many things besides her dancing, in the same way that Sarah Bernhardt was famous for many things besides her acting. La Guimard was famous for her many protectors; for her suppers; for her charity; for her leanness; and above all, for her houses in Paris and in Pantin, and for the theatres they contained.

About the country house at Pantin everyone seems rather uncertain— except that it belonged to the Prince de Soubise, her fourth protector. I have never seen the plans, or reproductions of the plans, of this house at Pantin, or its position in the town, or a plan of any theatre which may have been therein. But Collé and Bachaumont, who lived at the time, both say that performances were given at Mlle. Guimard's theatre at Pantin in the winter of 1769-70. They refer in detail to these performances—they say that the music was excellent—that the piece of which they speak had not yet been given in any other theatre; but they do not describe the theatre.

The duc d'Orléans, who had a fancy to buy this house and theatre, sent down his architect, Piétre, to measure it up. This was in 1773. Piétre wrote

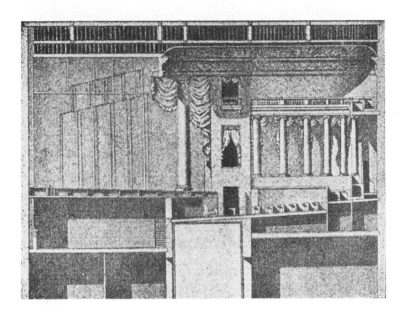

Above: *The Private Theatre of Mademoiselle Guimard. Built in 1772 by Architect Le Doux in her house. Inaugurated on December 8th with Collé's* La Partie de Chasse d'Henri IV *followed by* Pygmalion. Below: *Ground Plan of the Private Theatre of Mademoiselle Guimard. From* The Mask, *1925. Vol. XI.*

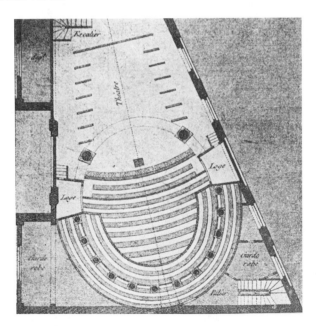

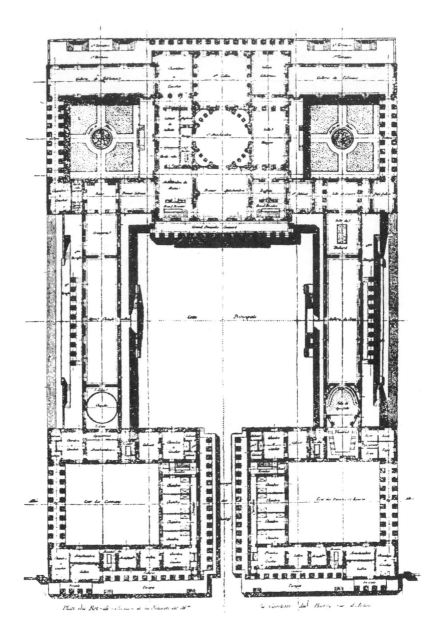

*A Pretty Theatre. Project for a house for Mme. La Comtesse Du Barry (1768-69): Architect Le Doux. The Theatre in this project of 1768-69 should be compared with that built by Le Doux for La Guimard 1772 on a piece of this ground along the Chaussée d'Antin. Compare also with the Private Teatro of Cardinal Ottoboni built by Juvarra some seventy years earlier in Roma, about 1705. From* The Mask, *1925. Vol. XI.*

out two folio leaves, called *Mémoire sur la salle de spectacle de Mlle la Guimard,* in which he states—according to Edmond de Goncourt, M. Capon, MM. d'Almeras and d'Estrée, and Signor Bruno Brunelli—that the theatre was "infinitely small," could hold 234 spectators not counting those in the six boxes, that its length *from the back of the auditorium to the front of the orchestra* was 157 feet and a few *pouces,* and that its width was 21 feet, 8 *pouces.* Now if you suppose these measurements to be correct, and draw them out, this is more less the shape of the auditorium of that famous theatre:—

*157 feet long*

*21 feet high*

But these measurements cannot be correct, for 157 feet is not "infinitely small"; and as I cannot show you any designs for this theatre, we must be content with those of the Paris theatre, which are available.

The Paris theatre was in the rue de la Chaussée d'Antin[2] and was built by the architect, Le Doux, in 1772, and inaugurated on December 8th with a performance of Collé's *Partie de Chasse d'Henri IV,* followed by *Pygmalion.* This theatre was not inside the house itself, but in an annex at the left-hand side as you enter the courtyard in which the house stood.

House, courtyard, annex, theatre and all had been specially built for Mlle. Guimard at the expense of one of her admirers—de Jarente, Bishop of Orléans, who was apparently her fifth protector. She was extravagant, and seems to have ruined one of her admirers, M. Benjamin de La Borde; but this does not appear to have dismayed the Bishop of Orléans, who lavished money on her. And the two designs given here show us the interior of the theatre which he gave her—its auditorium and stage, complete and professional in appearance.

Here some extraordinary performances took place, and in these boxes sat the guests of la Guimard (for the performances were not to bring in money, but to give pleasure). The only things that do not show are the famous *grilles* in front of the boxes. These grilles were put there to save the faces of those ladies who liked to see and listen to "naughty" plays, but were far too "good" to be seen looking and listening; so they sat behind grilles, enjoyed themselves vastly—and, on going out into Paris, damned the show and their hostess, saying how improper it all was, as, doubtless, it sometimes may have been.

When Beaumarchais' "Marriage of Figaro" was privately performed in the hall of the Hotel des Menus-Plaisirs in Paris (public and even private performance having been prohibited by Louis XVI), the duc de Villequier asked Beaumarchais for a private box—one of the stage boxes—with a lattice-work grille in front of it, so that the ladies of his party might see the play without being seen. Beaumarchais replied to the duke that he had no respect for women "who allow themselves to see a play which they consider improper, provided they only see it in secret," and that he could not lend himself to such caprices. He added: "I have given my piece to the public to amuse and instruct it, not to afford semi-squeamish persons the pleasure of going to it and thinking well of it in a private box, and speaking ill of it in society." He added even more, saying: "The pleasures of vice with the honours of virtue! Such is the prudery of the age. My piece is not a work of an equivocal nature; you must admit this or avoid it. I salute you and keep my box."

This portion of a letter gives some idea of the spectators during the last part of the eighteenth century in France; but it cannot give any idea of Mlle. Guimard herself—who, if she was capricious, was not a "semi-squeamish person"—but for all that, being one of the most tactful of dancers, supplied her theatre with these same lattice-work grilles.

I question if she was even capricious, for she has to her credit the fact that she was never late at the theatre, never missed a performance, and was altogether the perfection of discipline in that very undisciplined group, the members of the ballet of the Opera House—to which she passed from the Comédie Française in 1762.

That she was a woman of character seems evident, for when the Revolution came she was not, like so many of the friends of the aristocrats, involved in any of its troubles. In the year of the fall of the Bastille, 1789, on August 14th, she married the dancer, Jean-Etienne Despréaux. Despréaux was, from all accounts, a charming person. He was five years younger than his wife, and had been ballet master at the Opera. He became stage manager there in 1792, director of public fêtes in 1799, and inspector-general of the Court entertainments in 1815. Besides all this, he invented the musical chronometer. He wrote songs, and Baron de Frénilly, who knew him well, says that he was the soul of all pleasures, a genius for minutiae, and that his only fault was that of having buried some charming songs in two octavo volumes.

Before Despréaux and Mlle. Guimard could marry they were both obliged to renounce their profession, which seems a dreadful thing to people living in this year of freedom, 1933. But it was the pleasant eighteenth century, with all its freedom, which imposed this and all sorts of penalties on actors and other performers (at least in France). Whenever a performer had to do with a priest (unless he was the Bishop of Orléans, for example), the priest made this condition, that the performer must renounce his sinful calling before having anything to do with marriage or burial or anything which had to be carried out on holy ground.

Before she married, Mlle. Guimard sold her private theatre and her Paris house, and in order to get a good price, she raffled it at so much a ticket. Thirty thousand *livres'* worth of tickets were sold it is said, and the winning ticket—No. 2175 fell to the Comtesse du Lau, who had only bought one ticket. The Comtesse instantly sold the house, theatre and all.

Once married, Despréaux and Mlle. Guimard did a very sensible thing by slipping quietly out of Paris, where burnings and hangings and other slaughters were going on, and walking up the hill to Montmartre, which was then in the country, there took a house there in which they stayed for four years. It was in this house that Despréaux wrote many of his songs, describing in one of them how he and his wife were taking to country tasks, "holding the spade and the watering-can." He tells us that the place where they lived was so steep that the Republican patrols did not trouble to climb up there and that the occasional sound of a cannon-shot was the only thing to remind them of the agitation in the town below. While they stayed in Montmartre they gave dinners once or twice a month, inviting only those friends who would agree not to talk politics, and each one had to bring a song. These meetings they called *les diners du Vaudeville*. It is in one of Despréaux's songs that we get the date when they left Montmartre—December 22nd, 1797—he excusing himself for not attending the monthly meeting "during his removal."

\*                         \*                         \*

When they grew older and la Guimard could no longer dance, Despréaux used to entertain his guests with what came to be known as "Despréaux's *petites jambes*." He somehow procured the beautiful model of the old Opera House of 1781, which had been built in the space of three months at the Porte St. Martin. This miniature theatre had somehow survived the Revolution, and he got hold of it. Besides showing the stage, with the curtain and scenery and everything handsome about it, it showed portions of the front of the house, in which the boxes were filled with little figures of ladies in full dress. De Frénilly says that: —

"Despréaux possessed the art of imitating to perfection the dancing of all the famous dancers of his time. But he did this not with his feet but with his fingers. When the first and third fingers of each hand were dressed in beautiful little white silk stockings and tiny shoes, the rest of the hands being covered up, he could make them execute *pas de deux* to perfection. This illusion was produced in the following manner. The Lilliputian Opera House was placed in the middle of the drawing-room; the orchestra, in a corner of the room, struck up a ballet tune; and Gardel, the former director of ballets, cried out: 'Raise the curtain.' The curtain rose, but stopped at the height of Despréaux's fingers, that is to say, at the height of the dancer's knees. Whereupon there was a quarrel between the manager and the stage decorator. It was found, however, that the curtain would not go up any higher, so, for once, the audience was requested to be content with things as they were, and the ballet opened. Such, then, were Despréaux's 'petites jambes,' which the spectators recognised as imitating the 'Dieu' of the ballet (Vestris), Mlle. Guimard, Mlle. Herle, Gardel, Nivelon, Mlle. Allard, Mmes. Perignon, Clotilde, Miller and Duport. It was difficult to obtain this performance, which greatly fatigued poor Despréaux, and it required all the friendship which I inspired in him to get him to consent to give it in my salon to a small company of intimate friends."

1. At least four historians disagree as to the exact date. One puts it at October 2nd, another at December 27th, a third says it was in 1753, and a fourth that it was in 1745. And these historians are Mons. F. de Mesnil, who wrote "La Danse," Mons. Adolphe Jullien, celebrated for his histories of the eighteenth-century théâtre, MM. d'Almeras and d'Estrée, who wrote "Les Théâtres Libertins," and Professor Garollo.
2. This house and theatre were on the left side of the rue de la Chaussée d'Antin as you go up from the Boulevard des Italiens. To-day, the beginning of the rue Meyerbeer, the first turning on the left, is the exact spot where this theatre stood.

MARGIN NOTES. *Dance Index,* Volume II, no. 8, August, 1943.

(These notes were made by Craig in his bound copy of the French illustrated theatrical review *Commoedia Illustré,* for the early seasons of the Russian Ballet in Paris from 1909 to 1914. Craig made these notes in pencil in the margins of the pages during 1913. There are later comments indicated. These Volumes are now in the Dance Archives of the Museum of Modern Art.)

1. (*In the front of the Volume.*)
1911 to 1913—Showing perhaps (better than) as well as, any other document exactly what was happening in the new movement as expressed by the following men and women:
  *Fokine, Nijinski,* Karsavina, Mad. Fokina
  Bakst, Roerich, Visconti[1] (?), Bolm
  D'Annunzio (?), *Antoine,* Ida Rubinstein.
  *Rheinhardt*, Maria Carmi (Princess Matchabelli)
  De Max
  Jean Morax
  Bernhardt (?), Tellegen.
(I question some of these as representing anything in the new movement. The names *italicized* are the principal figures.)
(Note how Meyerhold was overshadowed in these years—in Paris!)
                                        (E. G. C.—1935)

Now we have at a glance more clear idea *how much* of (and what class of thing) the new movement got into the great city of Paris.
    We know that Isadora Duncan got in and left her mark but her presence was unable to prevent the pandemonium which a big city seems to crave for.
    But there are some important people who did not go to Paris:
    Stanislavsky's company of actors
    The Irish Players from Dublin
    Dalcroze's company of dancers
    Still, even all these as visitors would have amounted only to a passing fashion and made Parisians "rave" for a month or two.

But Appia, not a word of him, and he is the greatest scenic figure of the new movement. Of E. G. C. we do not hear either—not to be with D'Annunzio and Bakst in Paris is lucky. To be left with Appia and the others is a good sign.

The "new movement" amounts to nothing when you've considered carefully what (there) is in this volume.

Why nothing (?). I will tell you in two words.

It's a *new theatricalism* which the whole things amount to.

—a new falsity

—it is beliefless—

In this volume you can see what their method was.

They thought they could imitate so well as to deceive us into believing it was creation.

They went to see the Indian statue's pictures dancers and did an Indian affair.

They went to see the Egyptian statue's pictures dancers and did an Egyptian affair.

They went to see the Grecian statue's pictures dancers and did a Greek affair.

They went to see the Turkish statue's pictures dancers and did a Turkish affair.

They went to see the Italian statue's pictures dancers and did an (Italian) affair.

The list is as long as the list of nationalities.

They had no belief in themselves and in principles.

They put on and put off anyone's elses' *belief*.

We will do it "like this" they said on Monday

We will do it "like that" they said on Tuesday

They could do it anyway.

They were not doubtful if they could manage it.

They were sure of themselves, very.

Very sure they could disguise anything.

How far were they successful (?)

They disguised everything and created nothing

*We believe that is to have failed.*

(E. G. C.—May 1915.)

2. *Notes on illustrations in the text.*

On Bakst's costume design of Ida Rubinstein, martyred as Saint Sebastien. *Sickness.*

On Bakst's color sketches for Le Martyre de Saint Sebastien: *Compare photograph:*

*All is lost.*

Costume is not dress (but only) a cover: Costumes is that which uncovers the Soul.

The flesh and bones are the costume of the Soul. Reveal them then— without exposing that which is mute and must remain so.

(E. G. C. — 1911)


On four photos (Bert) of Nijinsky and Karsavina in *Le Spectre de la Rose:*

These four photos are charming indeed and represent all that is best in the Russian Ballet.

And yet Karsavina seems to be the very essence of insincerity and of vanity of a dull kind.

—but Nijinsky!!!


On a photo of Vera Fokina:

Possibly the best brains of the group. Her fat hands and whole person well under control and does not make mistakes.


On a photo of a Dancer designed by Leon Bakst for the Paquin (dressmaking) Pavilion at the Exposition of Turin 1911:

The awful effects of following the footsteps of Isadora Duncan.

The mixing of art-dressmakers-royalty-naked ladies-dancing and prostitution:

If pleasant things each in their own place how unpleasant when mixed in this friendly fashion.

All for commerce.

This kind of thing it is which makes us hate and wage war on commercialism. And this is only the fringe.

(See illustration of these designs with Craig's notes—p. 105)


On a cover in color of *Commoedia Illustré* for June 1, 1912, showing Karsavina and Bolm in costume for "*Thamar*":

Senseless if you will consider it for a moment.


On Nijinsky's costumes for *Le Dieu Bleu* (Bakst):

Compare this first with the Indian plate 30 in Coomeraswamy. (The

Mirror of gesture) after with the protographs facing (Nijinsky photographed in the finished costume).[2]

On a color plate for the decor of *Le Dieu Bleu* (Bakst):
The worms on the twig are rather unconvincing.
(The sketch) Not a bit like the result achieved. I saw it in 1912.

(E. G. C.)

On photos of dancers in costumes for *Le Dieu Bleu:*
Some good dresses.

On the dancer Baranovitch II:
Stupid woman, good dress.

On sketches by Roerich for *Le Sacre du Printemps:*
Roerich is the best of the Russians as decorators of painted scenes and costumes.

On the description with illustrations of *La Pisanelle* or *La Mort Par-fumée*, words by D'Annunzio (Italian), music by da Parma (Italian), decor and costumes by Bakst (Russian), dances by Fokine (Russian), musical direction by Inghelbrecht (German).
And interesting this series of pictures, for it shows how much or how little the great Meyerhold could do without his own theatre, his own company and his liberty.

(E. G. C. — 1915)

On a review by Louis Delluc of *La Pisanelle* (20 June, 1913)
"Is there nothing about Meyerhold?"
(The review had mentioned all the collaborators except the director-in-chief.)

*3. Notes by E. G. C. in The Art of Nijinsky by Geoffrey Whitworth
(1913), with Gordon Craig's bookplate. Florence 1913.*
On a quotation from the article on Ballet published in the Encyclopedia Brittanica (1910 page 1).
Only in an atmosphere of *ceremony, courtesy and chivalry* can the dance maintain itself in perfection. Right (Italics of E. G. C.)
Page 9: The young Nijinsky soon *began to manifest the character of genius.* (Italics of E. G. C.)

and later on he blazed them by deserting the ranks of the Russian Ballet in Diaghilev's personal direction.

Page 17 and 18:

Nor must we forget the liberating force which sprang from the art of Isadora Duncan, whose heroic practice has done far more than any precepts of philosophy to widen our ideas as *to the intellectual and spiritual possibilities of the dance.* (Italics E. G. C.)

Not that—Isadora Duncan has not dealt with the dance intellectually, nor spiritually—but personally. The age saw to that!

1. Scenic designer: Designed decor for Fauré's opera *Penelope*, Monte Carlo. 1913.
2. Craig's intention was to show how little the dead photo resembled the highly stylized sketch.

# PART III.

GORDON CRAIG ON ETHNIC DANCE

Book Review. THE JAPANESE DANCE by Marcelle Azra
Hinckes. Unsigned. *The Mask*, Volume III, nos. 4-6, October,
1910.

his Brochure, for all its brevity, shows no little learning
and treats of a subject very interesting to those who
would know something of the Theatrical Art of the
Japanese, since, although the modern drama has now
"become entirely separated from dancing" it was from
this source that it sprang originally, and the fine influ-
ence is yet traceable in the fact that "on the Japanese stage the mimetic art
is as important as the spoken word."

From a remote period the Dance in Japan has been of paramount
importance historically as well as esthetically, and ever closely associated
with the religion of the country. In fact in a land where "the very gods
danced, before ever mortal feet had learned to tread a measure" it was
inevitably woven closely into the fabric of the nation's religious, artistic and
daily life, and to it the country owes its finest dramatic literature, the
"preservation of the classical Japanese language in the poems written
several hundred years ago to accompany the *No* dances," its masks, its
stage, the construction of its theatre and the birth of those wonderful *No*
plays which are supreme examples of brevity and fine tradition in dramatic
art.

It should not be forgotten, however, that the so-called "Dance" of
Japan is a thing widely differing from that exercise which Europeans understand by the word, . . . an exercise which the Japanese would call
gymnastics and class with Ju-jutsu or the ancient acrobatic "Vengakuo."

The Japanese dance, like the ancient Greek as we imagine it, is entirely
of a pantomimic nature and "strives to represent in gesture an historical
incident, some mythical legend or a scene from folk-lore."

By symbolical gesture and a rhythmic, highly-conventionalised, regu-
lated movement it suggests, gives visible expression to, ideas and emotions, but in so delicate and distant a manner as to require, not only for its
appreciation, but almost, one may say, as a condition of its existence, a
particular temper and mental attitude on the part of the spectators, a unity
between actors and audience; and the need of this preparedness on the
part of the onlookers can be the better understood if it be remembered

during the "apparently meaningless gestures and sleeve-waving and fan-waving and stamping of feet" that "every movement, every turn or twist of the hand, the arm or the body has some significance as clear to the Japanese as spoken words and that the subtlety of the Eastern mind detects various shades and degrees of emotions in dance movements which we neither look for nor understand."

The bare-legged dancer, . . . the lady whose success lies largely in the scantiness of her costume, is unknown among the dance-artists of Japan, where even the feet are little seen, taking, especially in the religious dances , but slight part in the action ; and formalised gesture , rigidly pre-scribed postures, dignity, perfect control of movement attained to by rigor-ous physical training, smoothness and that appearance of ease which is the outcome of long discipline, are salient characteristics.

The fact that the body itself is never seen and that Japanese dancing is yet so fine a thing as it is and was dispels once and for all the illusion that it is necessary to the dance for the movement of the natural body to be seen.

The European dance may affect us, give us the same pleasure, as the graceful spontaneous movements of lambs in a meadow, of children run-ning on the seashore, of young leaves waving in the wind; but the Japanese, with its strict ritual, its noble conservatism which still preserves traditional postures without change or modification, its obedience to a fine tradition, its perfect control of its material, . . . . that is, the human body, approaches more nearly to the stately and splendid ceremonies of the past, of which, among us, some trace yet lingers in the symbolic gestures of the priests celebrating mass, and it thus partakes more nearly of the nature of an art.

Miss Hincks discusses her subject under three headings, Religious, Clas-sical and Popular.

Under the first of these are included the religious temple dances origi-nally introduced from China, and of which the most interesting and impor-tant was that of the Shinto Shrines, the "Kagura" whose strains were supposed to be those which, according to legend, lured the Sun-goddess from the cave and originated all the dances of succeeding centuries.

For the performance of this "Kagura" stages were erected at all the principal Shinto temples, each temple having its staff of dancers; and on these stages and from these dances, to which marionette shows were later added, was developed the modern Japanese Theatre, . . . a theatre born of the actor, not the poet, of movement, not the spoken word.

Passing on to the Classic dances we find their origin is neither as mythological nor as remote as that of the religious. They seem to have developed under the influence of the Buddhist priests, who, finding the love of music and dancing too deeply rooted in the Japanese nature to be eradicated, turned them to good purpose by wedding them to religious poems teaching "the instability of life, the vanity of all things human" until there finally emerged those No dramas which show a marked affinity with the Greek, and which, to the cultured Japanese, are so sacred, so jealously guarded from the invasion of the modern and realistic spirit which is fast dominating every department of the national life.

These dramas, in which "nothing of a commonplace or frivolous nature is ever represented" are acted on a stage and "are partly sung, partly recited, and performed by dancers, or what in Europe might be called actors, were it not that their gestures are to a certain extent rhythmical and conventional, and by a chorus which sits on one side and sings and recites but takes no part in the proceedings," while the hero "dances or strikes appropriate attitudes, both his paces and postures being slow and solemn."

Only men are permitted to act in the No dramas and the scenery is scanty and simple, . . . . merely a suggestion; but the costumes are rich and stately and masks are always worn.

The No drama is, in fact, with its beautiful monotony, its freedom from violent passion or play of emotion, its simplicity, symbolism and spiritual suggestion, a highly conventionalised form of art, a relic of that which was finest in ancient Japan, the language, costumes and postures being still those of eight hundred years ago.

Of the three classes of Dances the most ancient and primitive is, however, the Popular dance, since, before arts, civilisation or even formalised religion spring up in a country, it is the instinct of primitive peoples to express their emotions by dances, and the "bon" dances, varying in detail but uniform in their main features, are danced in conformity to the Shinto cult in August, to welcome the departed spirits which are supposed at that season to revisit the earth.

In these dances "the peasants form a great circle, a living wheel, which revolves now slowly, now swiftly, whilst they posture and express their feelings by means of sleeve-wavings and conventional gestures . . . . Little fairy-like figures glide about in the white ghostly moonlight, their long soft sleeves waving like wings; their rythmical and precise paces are silent and muffled, their gestures are mysterious and expressive of worship, and their song mingles with occasional soft hand-clapping."

We should like to give more details of these dances which Miss Hincks describes for us in so charming a manner, but must refer our readers to the book itself, and would advise all students of the stage, having read her account, to follow up the subject for themselves, since in this matter of the Drama Dance is perhaps of paramount importance.

## MR. CECIL SHARP AND ENGLISH FOLK DANCE by Edward Edwardovitch. *The Mask*, Volume V, no. 3, January, 1913.

nce walking with my little boy in Genoa on a warm summer night I was attracted towards a dark archway by the sounds of rhythmical noises. Under the arch we witnessed a jolly sight.

A ring of dark niggers, their black arms and heads glistening in the sparkles of light which came from a bad lamp; all of them clapping rhythmically with their huge hands. . . . Such an easy charming sound, and one of them in the centre of the ring dancing like only a black man can dance, . . . dancing like the very dickens.

We both of us drew nearer and watched.

The dancer leaps and glides, . . . and glides again and falls; boils up again and bounds round the ring; then simmers; finally falls only to rise instantaneously; then tumbles into his place in the ring and starts his rhythmic hand music. Almost before he has left the centre a second has filled his place, . . . a poorer dancer, but good for all that.

The excitement is not so great, so the first dancer returns to the charge, capering round his fellow in the centre , aiding and abetting him . . . . What a noise, what an experience, what inspiration!

The feet of these dancers pound and shuffle for me to far subtler rhythms than ever any other dancers have yet done, . . . . and I have seen and listened to many.

Their stage was the most profound I have ever seen, their choice of place and time subtler than that of even the greatest of Russian or Greek dancers.

Oh, how they laughed, and how we laughed, and how wild the dance grew. Immoderate and yet masterly. . . . What faces too, . . . quite unforgettable. And ever since having witnessed this ecstatic demonstration we ask ourselves and each other, on seeing each new dance or dancer, "is it as good as the black men that night?", and then we grin at each other and shake our heads.

And Mr. Sharp's dances and dancers? We both saw them, and we both liked some of them. We liked two men who gave us something strong and strange; . . . something really exciting: and another men's dance made us feel something like swing. But we were left to think too much. And we thought if only our black fellows would come in and swing along in that irresistable gliding shuffle how all the senses in England would open and how the Imagination would call aloud for liberty.

Mr. Sharp's dancers are not free. Perhaps it is part of their charm. I am sure those who from conceit have revolted from Sharp are not a scrap freer, and I don't even suggest that any of those picked men who are now under Sharp should break loose from him. But from themselves, yes! From fogs and swamps, oh yes. One can't dance in a fog or on a swamp, nor with the blinds down, nor in a brown study.

Up with the blinds . . . . up with the sash of the window, . . . out on to the green, . . . away over the hills . . . . mad if you like, but not sane. A sane dancer is like a sane donkey ride; a ridiculous affair. To assemble in evening dress and white kid gloves and go on like the Rabbit in "Alice in Wonderland" is sane. That's what men do at most dances. It's a pretty way to pass the time, and quite sane.

What then are Mr. Sharp's dancers doing in even approaching the conditions of those party-dancers?

They dress up, bells and white suits and bows. They have a look in the glass, . . . "Am I quite tidy?" Then with a determined air they go to their self-inflicted doom, conscious to the last.

Now I don't want to be unfair, but I do want to speak to some purpose. And no amount of flattery has any purpose in it but gain.

I'd rather lose than gain in this Instance, so long as I don't lose the respect and good feeling of those men who danced the morris so well the other day.

I don't compare these dancers to those of the Russian Ballet. There is no comparison. These Englishmen beat the Russians hollow, . . . . the Russians being hollow to begin with.

But I compare them, . . . am forced to . . . . with my black men that night in Genoa, and then the cat is out of the bag. The Englishmen lose.

I don't want them to lose. Bend them, . . . . loosen the latches, take all the doors off their hinges . . . . down with the barriers; they are false and futile. Loosen yourselves, loosen . . . . ! You have the strength, . . . . hide it lest we are led to believe you are merely stiff.

Bend! . . . . It is not so unbecoming. Risk falling at each bound; fling yourselves upon the shadows and strike them into fire. Wing yourselves with the truths you have absorbed through your master. You will not fall.

This you can do if you will not deny life, if you will play with life as you dance. Take it for your partner.

That is what the Black men did. They dared a figure into the ring with them. They allowed it to trip them up; recovered themselves, and tripped it up, . . . . raced it, confused it, coquetted with it, parodied it, caught it in their arms and threw it up to eternity, as one tosses a coin.

If you would dance you must take Life as your partner.

Honour Cecil Sharp your master, . . . . but for all that take Life as a partner.

---

## ASIA AMERICA EUROPE. *The Mask*, Volume VIII, no. 8, October, 1918.

---

 n the preface to a companion volume to this "Dance of Siva" Dr. Coomaraswamy spoke of me as one "who understands so well the noble artificiality of Indian dramatic technique," and mentioned, quoting part of a letter that I had written to him, that I had "frequently asked for more detailed information" on the subject.

This must not be misunderstood by those few good workers along my path. And so that their attention shall be in no way attracted away from the work we have in hand I have thought it time to turn to India and say a thing I have for long wanted to say. You must not be too critical with me, for I admit that for me, and I will add for you, the subject is strange.

"Full fathom five my father lies, / Of his bones are coral made; / Those are pearls that were his eyes, / Nothing of him that doth fade, / But doth suffer a sea-change / Into something rich and strange; / Sea-nymphs hourly ring his knell. / Ding-dong bell . . . . "

A strange life to live in a new element, long and strange before the senses can bear to say again "I hear . . . . I see . . . . I feel." Even Shakespeare does not enter the water and write of the silent life beneath all the tempests and the derelicts drifting.

But the life which stirs to consciousness again under the deepest waters is not stranger than that unknown life about which we are so curious . . . . life in the East.

To feel in it we must be of it . . . , no other way. I know no separation such as "East is East and West is West and never the twain shall meet," for on the day that I choose to wander far afield, be it to the moon or into the beds of Ocean, I may do so . . . and so also, I may go to the East and become of it any day I wish. You too. But even as there is no returning for a true lover, be the pains the pains of Hell itself, so is there no returning from India . . . . that life strange and rich which, to experience well, we must suffer. And it is for this reason I would have you all pause before you are attracted from the work you have joined me in, to listen to the exquisite fluting of the great and lovely Krishna . . . . for his sweet sad notes are but the prelude of the mighty coils of music which will be flung around all those who listen too long.

There is nothing for us to listen to . . . nothing for us yet. We Europeans and Americans are in the utmost need for we know very little . . . . we are like fools beside wise men, we Europeans and Americans standing by Asiatics . . . . and we of the theatre hammering away like slaves, we are the most ignorant of all; remember this, my good old friends, and we shall be making headway before very long.

It is not that we are not above listening . . . . but only that we are not yet in a position to listen . . . . we dare not turn an ear or an *eye away from our task.* We have yet to learn that one and one make two before we can pass to larger sums.

As it is, our pupils can barely believe us when we say, "Come, wrestle with this simple difficulty of one and one . . . . Do not echo what we have said . . . . that it makes two. See it for yourselves. And express what you have seen in your own way, not our way. Express with freedom, do not echo . . . . limiting yourselves to this simple problem. And above all, "Seek to know no more."

Why cannot you believe us? I address the eager—Be eager, but don't be taking a tiger for a pussy-cat, or a God for a 'hullo old chap.'

Why be infatuated by your own powers to the extent of dreaming foolish dreams? Why delude yourself into fancying you are capable of understanding without first feeling . . . . of feeling without experiencing . . . . of experiencing without being? For I tell you it is impossible.

And do you dare to dream you can be in a moment all that India is and not be burnt to a cinder in the tick of a clock? . . . broken and burnt and your progress hindered. . . . thrown back another ten thousand years? Will you waste the few good centuries in which your forefathers built up for you a beginning? A beginning is something; we are at that promising point now. Must you prefer Nothing to it? Do you prefer Annihilation to the chance that is before you? If so, then annihilate yourself and the toil of your forefathers in your gratified desire to see the marvel for an instant and die.

But if you are wise you will do no such thing. You will live, labour, suffer . . . if you find it part of the game . . . . and pass on to those who come a little life . . . . instead of your own corpse.

Briefly, India is dangerous to the powerless and the ignorant . . . . to us.

I am a Westerner, and you too. Our tradition of life is one which our instinct teaches us to continue. If so it is not by looking round over our shoulder or being curious about strange sights and sounds over there in the East that we shall become more enlightened. Enlightenment will come from the stones we are breaking as we sit hammering in our own jolly or dusty path. Only this . . . . we must break on and on and not pause . . . . we must labour and sweat . . . . and I promise you all India . . . . but here, in Europe, in America. And for Heaven's sake tip us a song as you work! It's that song which won't break out . . . . why not, in Heaven's name?

Can't you be jolly—can't you sing? Then whistle! Can't you whistle? Then make funny sounds . . . . can't you? Then make a face—that's Art! and that's where Art comes in in Life . . . . what it's all for. To cheer and refresh.

Do you suppose India and its brown children will laugh . . . ? no, but they will laugh if you follow after the pipe of Krishna and pose as feeling what you don't feel because you can't see, and have not lived, the life of India.

So that I understand Dr. Coomaraswamy a little . . . . enough to know that he knows I understand nothing of that noble artificiality of Indian Dramatic Technique . . . . and have enough of grace to appreciate a compliment.

I want you all to see that it is all sheer compliment, even as we should do if we saw queer things on living the life of India; for if you don't do this you'll fancy that I am half way to India and you'll drop your hammers and be racing after a spectre.

Stay where you are . . . . be as steady as you can . . . . and go on with your work.

Whenever you see an Indian work of art, tighten the strings of your helmet. Admire it . . . . venerate it . . . . but for your own sake don't absorb it. It won't do you any harm to admire it quietly . . . . the good it should do you is this, to drive you into utter despair for quite a long while; but hands off . . . . don't wish to capture a single trick of its technique . . . . don't ape it.

Dr. Coomaraswamy's translation of the Mirror of Gesture is nothing at all for you. It is dedicated "to all actors and actresses." We must disclaim any right to deserving that dedication. We must leave it to our far-off brothers and sisters in India. It is all theirs. Any Irishman will understand what I mean.

And this new book, "The Dance of Siva."

For my part I shall open it now and again as I would peep into a silent uninhabited house whose front door is open . . . . I will peep in from this side of the garden gate . . . . out of curiosity may be . . . . yet not so curious neither. It is full of strange and beautiful furnitures, carpets, flowers . . . . I see them from here. No—Curiosity is not or I should open the gate . . . . knock? . . . get no reply and creep in, one's only thought, "How pleasant for those who live in there!"

No, no, not that way, if you please. Die naturally in due time, don't ask for Siva to strike you down . . . . for it is his house. He lurks invisibly within and harms none but *strangers*. We are just . . . . strangers. Strangers, but pretty determined at home to awaken and brace up our powers and get rid of the idea that materialism is all, by realizing what materialism is.

We have for some time been battering at the sandbags behind which Commercialism and every other self-seeking growth has ramparted itself, taking us liberators for foes. For years men and women in our Theatre (to speak of the thing dearest to the Mask) have battled against these dull ogres.

Our great actors and actresses . . . . our playwrights . . . . all have prepared the way. But the path is English and is American, and it's not on the road to Mandalay that we are moving . . . . or are expected to move. Europe and America look to us, remember, to remain ourselves.

I want my followers then to love all things of the East . . . . but to really love them . . . . remembering Goethe's wise saying, "Against the superiority of another there is no defence but love." So then now you get at what I had to say.

You and I are . . . . feel we are . . . . nothing. They over there are wonderful, and we can know it, admit it, admire it, and goodnight. We love them and all their works, and just because we do so sincerely we go on along our own way.

---

Book Review. THE MIRROR OF GESTURE by Dr. Ananda Coomaraswamy. Unsigned. *The Mask*, Volume VIII, no. 12.

---

Dear Dr. Coomaraswamy.

It is a Marvellous interesting book and all that which you have translated, but here I sit in a Palace in Pisa in the room where Lord Byron wrote the greatest European poem of the last century, which has not yet been understood by Europe, let alone read, and you ask me seriously to recommend this trifle from the East to Europeans; this "Mirror of Gesture," this book of system, this receipt for enslaving men, making 'actors' of them . . . . you ask too much. We are not up to it yet.

I admire you; . . . . I am ravished by your gestures without understanding one of them, or caring a rap for any systems . . . . Eastern or western.

I am fascinated beyond description by the way you begin the séance.

Following this your text-book you shake your head up and down. You mean doubtless Indignation, Enquiry, Summoning, Threatening and all sorts of other things. But who's to guess it over here? for we frown, lower the brows, shake the head sideways when we mean some of those things, and when we mean the rest of them we make other gestures.

So you see you ask too much from the commencement. And when later, to recompense me, you assert that your waist is one of your limbs and your arm-pits another of them,[1] then you show me (and I'm no seer), that your whole system is based on the principle "heads I win, tails you lose."

No, dear and gentle Indian; I'll not play that game with you. I too want a *chance* to win.

Mind you, I haven't any doubt that "the root N I with the prefix ABHI implies—*Exposition*"; all I must remark is that your gestures expose nothing to us whereas our clowns' gestures do, spite of their lack of subtlety.

I won't speak of our great performers . . . . for some of these are so subtle that they might be fresh from Burma.

But do not take my expressions amiss . . . .

"I mean no harm" said Snook.

"But me for the pan by the sink."

(*vide 'Mask' Vol. 8 No. 2 Page 8*).

The curses of the West are many, dear Doctor. But the cussiest curse is that we are always being tempted to tell ourselves that we Westerner frogs can be as big as the biggest Eastern cow that ever strayed from the milky way.

And we succumb over and over again: . . . we are dangerously near bursting.

If we draw in one more big breath of air (EE by E) we *shall* burst.

We have other weaknesses, . . . . but conceit will be our undoing.

We must become faultless like you . . . . some day . . . . if we can, but only along a more bitter path than your artists lingered on as they created their loveliest things . . . . and after that even found some time over to make systems.

But we receive only the "Systems" . . . . the Art of Gesture does not reach us . . . . and so if we have any sense left we dare not pretend we understand.

Even in Europe some there have been who have offered systems to us . . . . perhaps since we have their works too this is less fatal . . . . but if you only knew us better I think you would agree with Lord Byron.

And with Lord Byron's words on western systems let me end: . . .

"A more amiable man in society than Mr. Hunt I do not know; nor (when he will allow his sense to prevail over his sectarian principles) a better writer. When he was writing his 'Rimini' I was not the last to discover its beauties, long before it was published. Even then I remonstrated against the vulgarisms; which are the more extraordinary because the author is anything but a vulgar man. Mr. Hunt's answer was, that he wrote them upon principle; they made part of his 'system'!! I then said no more. When a man talks of his system it is like a woman talking of her *virtue*."

1. Limbs, parts of the body and features are differently classified according to the Indian cannons of gesture than they are in Europe and America.

The book tells us that in India these are the divisions: . . .

"Limbs, *Head, hands, arm pits, sides, waist and feet. Some also say the neck. Parts of* the Body are shoulders, shoulder blades, arms, back, stomach, thighs, calves; some say also the wrists, knees and elbows.

"Features are: eyes, eye lids, pupils, cheeks, nose, jaw, lips, teeth, tongue, chin, face." You see what I mean . . . . It's all topsy-turvy for us.

The first movement of the Head is very interesting. It is called Sama (level) the movement consists of not moving; nor is the head bent or raised. It is used when wishing to express prayer, authoritative speech, satisfaction, anger, indifference, or inaction.

But at the risk of being felt to be a nuisance I must ask the Indian author by what means the dancer makes us over here understand whether he is feeling anger or satisfaction, for he has omitted to say.

Now to the Western actor or actress we critics say, "Explain to me, oh Lotus of the Strand, expound to me without any more of your bhavas (nonsense) when a door can possibly be not a door"; and indeed some of us have to become like a little child once more to know the answer.

Again, the gesture called Adhomukha (face inclined) signifies that the head is bent. It is used to express modesty, sorrow, bowing, regarding anything vile, fainting, things on the ground, bathing.

It is, in short, another language.

---

# TWO LADIES by X. Y. Z. *The Mask*, Volume XIII, no. 3, July-August-September, 1927.

---

e said: "It is the same with ladies as with dramatists— bad dramatists, I mean."

"What do you mean by that?" I asked.

"Bad dramatists nowadays believe that they are only on the road to writing a great play when they can teach something through it, and ladies—stupid ladies, I mean—are equally serious about teaching. But I do not mean dull ladies, but clever and charming ladies who become stupid thinking it all out."

"Thinking what all out?"

"Thinking how they can get their own way—bring us all up."

"And do they?" I asked, "Do they believe that in getting their own way they are teaching the others something?"

"Apparently" he replied, "for look at this story of the Princess des Ursins. Was she not quite the stupidest woman of her age, and for all this considered one of its very cleverest? And most of the other court ladies of her time — how stupid they appear in this book." He tossed it over to me.

"Have you read it?" I asked.

"Every line" he said, rising and putting on his overcoat.

"And you think I have time to read it too?" I asked, for I felt that as he had read it he might have taken the little extra trouble to review it and thereby save me the task.

"Unless you read it you won't be able to review it, and when you've read it you won't know what to say . . . . I don't . . . . so I leave it to you. It's not a history, it's a long series of novels, and not a dull line from beginning to end."

"If you were to stop a while and tell me the story in your own way and briefly, couldn't I by taking down what you say avoid reviewing the book and read it afterwards?"

He seemed to like the idea, and so, overcoat and all, he sat down at my table in the furthest corner of the Café *Giubbe Rosse* and began:

"This is the story of a fool — she was called the Princess des Ursins: no real Princess at all but a younger branch of the Trémoïlle family. A Frenchwoman — pretty — lived to the age of eighty; for the first fifty-eight years did practically nothing; — then governed Spain for about fourteen years, twice was nearly crowned queen, and held by Saint-Simon to be "illustrious" among the most illustrious of her time — and was actually a really great fool."

He didn't lean back, nor puff out the traditional three rings of cigarette smoke nor frown. His eyebrows were neither raised nor lowered: his voice was neither emphatic nor lackadaisical. He was looking steadily at the corner of the book which he had again taken up when he began to speak. This he continued to do until he had finished and he never moved. "That" I thought, "is just the concentration I should not have brought to bear on the beastly book," — for it was the fourteenth book I had had to review that week.

"She was indeed a charming woman, this young but matured lady of fifty-eight: she was beautiful as she was charming, as able as she was beautiful, as talented as able, and a great fool. She believed that she could manage people, took people for puppets, and it is of course one of the greatest follies to do that. And so from ruling Spain she fell, and in one hour. She fell out of the throne into nothing, . . . wherein she floundered and died."

"She had as puppets the King of Spain — Philippe V, that monarch who, promising as a youth, was practically an idiot after her fourteen years rule. She was his guide from the age of nineteen and she was the guide and confidante of his young wife—his first wife:—consider how great her failure that she was unable to shape him in those fourteen years. All she could do was to "boss" him, her, and the court. You know what I mean by "boss": I cannot find a better word to express precisely what she did and failed to do. We rule, we bring up, we manage or we boss. She bossed. It is wonderful how often we see women blessed with the capacity to bring up children, especially female children; also to manage some department; but seldom can they rule, and never should they boss."

"This lady was so very charming, with such honesty and truth in her disposition, that I grieve to think she fell so suddenly and that it was all through her own fault."

"This writer here"—he held up the book—"tries to find all kinds of reasons for her failure and never alights on the correct one. She puts it down to the enemies of the Princess . . . . it can only be put down to herself."

"Among her friends was Louis XIV—a curious man who never let himself be governed though the others supposed he was well under their control. A man who brought himself to do and say the right thing to everyone although another excessively foolish woman, Madame de Maintenon, for many years too many, made it more difficult for him than was necessary. Still, presumably she filled a certain need as did the many hundred others who surrounded the King. There is no doubt that he was a King, whereas Philippe V, of Spain (his grandson) around whom the Princess des Ursins buzzed, was not quite a king. Whether this made it easier for her or more difficult it were hard to say. Richelieu might have trained such a being as Philippe V—or he would have removed him. She had not, we are to suppose, ever dreamed of removing people: she was charming: she supposed she could pull the strings of anything and it would dance as she wished: she found it danced as she wished nine times out of twelve. She was playing at the game of marionettes, which in itself is a silly thing to do if you only have flesh and blood for dolls. Flesh and blood dolls are the very worst kind of puppets."

"The author of this book is always talking of puppets. I should rather compare the Princess des Ursins to a ring-master. She has that air—and she cracks her whip all the time."

"There is another woman whose book has just appeared; a certain *belle Otero*—a Spanish dancer—celebrated. You have probably never heard of her": . . . here he did lean back and puffed out some imaginary rings of smoke.

I hadn't heard of this book; I pricked up my ears:—a book by a dancer,

. . . why I could easily review *that*: but he was off on to it and I could only scribble down quickly all he said.

"This Otero . . . . a very fine woman in many ways, gives the Princess entirely away, for she says that once, when she had quarrelled with her lover Pacco or Quaco or some name like that, she left him and went to live alone in a Hotel. She says that "she liked" (I remember the words for I read them over so as never to forget them), "*I liked*" she said "*to be thought proud, wild and a little formidable but at the bottom the whole thing was a bluff.*"

"The Princess never admitted that."

"I could tell you more of this *belle Otero* . . . . a very fine woman in many ways . . . . but you had better read that book yourself."

"To return to the princess," he went on:

"Her fall was brought about by the second wife of Philippe V. The first wife was one of her "puppets"; she bossed her; she told her she was a badly dressed slut or words to that effect, bustled her, hustled her; flattered her; mentally drew on her and held her at the pistol's mouth."

"After that fourteen years went all right with that queen, though in all those years while she bossed the King she never changed him, bettered him or brought him to understand anything."

"The Queen died and a second Queen came along. The Princess went to meet this new Puppet so as to show her who was who. And like a great donkey she began immediately to bustle her and hustle her about her looks and dresses—just as she had done with the first Queen. Result, . . . in three to four minutes she was under arrest as a lunatic, the second Queen objecting to that sort of thing and, having thought of the same trick as la belle Otero thought of, (yes, a very fine woman in some ways) the Princess des Ursins was taken out of Spain the same evening."

"And all because instead of being a genuine mother or friend she was merely a boss."

"It is ludicrously tragic. And as you read this book you realize that this lady is typical of so many other ladies of that age and of this—most of them ludicrous bosses—not tragic because most ladies are not of so much worth as the Princess des Ursins."

"I have felt the utmost interest in this clever woman but she awakens in me no sympathy for her; she is so utterly insincere in her whole existence. Truthful she said she was to Louis XIV, and I think she was; and clever and—but I've told you I admire her. But for all that I consider her a fool for not knowing that if you are a woman you cannot rule a King, you cannot rule a Queen, but you may, if lucky, be a friend to both if you want nothing for yourself, not even the phrase "It was through my devotion that he did this and she did that."

"Then you want an angel . . . . " I said.

"Yes, I want an angel—and it's curious how many angels have been near kings and queens—."

"How do you know?"

"I believe": . . . he puffed no more imaginary rings of smoke but rose and went away.

I went to find the book by *la belle Otero*, that book which even I could review. It is called *MY STORY* and is by La Belle Otero. "My! what a story" would have been as appropriate a title—for it really is a great big story!

If we hadn't her word for it we might suppose it to have been written for her by a very able American journalist, assisted perhaps by a Frenchman.

There is a good deal about money in this work which makes it interesting: "in a very short time I had 340,000 pesetas to my credit" she writes: and there is more about what she calls "love."

Several fights are recorded and once she knocks another lady over with an iron chair, slightly frightening her: "it was magnificent publicity for me" she writes.

Many kind acts are recorded very simply: I have counted five. Most of them were exaggeratedly generous acts.—How intrigued I am as I read this book by what my friend has just told me of the Princess des Ursins to whom generosity I gather must have seemed to be something vulgar. Presumably it is, which is all to the good.

La Belle Otero tells stories of King Edward, of the Kaiser, of Thompson the English millionaire and of Count Kessler "director" of the Eden Museum in New York or rather its Paris agent: of Russian Grand Dukes and of Rasputin; of Baron Ollstreder, and an Assyrian host of lovers.

She is, like others who are what we call "frail," rather down on "frailty." Put it in a less Victorian way:—she is anything but moral, and down on those who are like herself, especially if they are men. She winks at Bill, calls him *Cheri* and then cries out "Why did he steal my purse?"; and of Harry she writes "he came of decent family enough but he was too fond of light girls."

If I were a light girl I should write a wiser and a sadder book. I should call it "Their story" and I should set forth in the very best phraseology at my command how sweet, how strong, how dashing, how daredevil, how terrible and awful and wonderful were their light ways. I should show how genuine was my delight in discovering others like unto me, but I should note with special pride the dastardly touches which differentiated their lightness from mine. I would not bewail in a cheerio worldly way their shortcomings, for I'd hate to be supposed to be hankering after a fame which could never be mine, for the good reason that I really considered such fame to be worth two cents at most.

I allude to the fame of the immaculate.

But this book by *La Belle Otero* is like a hundred others. I have seen it compared with Casanova's Memoirs. There is not the slightest resemblance; for Casanova's books blaze with genius and this one is not even smut with talent: but that is not the fault of *La Belle Otero*.

*The Princess des Ursins.* Maud Cruttwell. (Dent & Sons.)
*My Story.* La Belle Otero. (A. M. Philpot.)

---

Book Review. THE ELIZABETHAN JIG: AND RELATED SONG DRAMA by Charles Read Baskervill. Unsigned. *The Mask*, Volume XV, no. 2, April-May-June, 1929.

---

lory be to Charles Read Baskervill , here is a book from which the words Commedia dell'Arte are excluded. Yet it's all about the Jig and the stage and the gay times of Eliza. And about Picklehering too.

Good egg—good Charles Read Baskervill, praise be to him—*not* to have uttered the now so popular shibboleth, the *Commedia dell' Arte*. He was quite safe he felt, he could pass along without it.

369 pages all about the Jig; and about 200 more filled with queer songs, amongst them the interesting "Singing Simpkin" which is but another version of old Hans Sach's playlet which is but a blithe tale from the "Decamerone."

But why is not old Sachs mentioned as having done a version? everyone else who had a shot at it is. It's the old tale of the man in the chest and the adroit woman and the swaggering soldier and not so stupid husband.

Several old tunes are recorded.

Quite a bit of a book and all about Jigs: —

"O' my dainty Cavalilly man, / My finnikin Cavalilly man, / For God's cause and the Protestants, / I prithee le' me gang with thee, man."

She means Cavalier man, but she of the 16th century was no less driveling when she liked than any other.

---

## Marginal Notes. LA DANSE DANS LE THÉÂTRE JAVANAIS by Th.-B. Van Lelyveld. Librairie Floury, Paris, 1931.

---

[On the flyleaf in Craig's hand] Price/125 fr. 1931. Paris-/Presented/EGC

[Following the limitation] Actually only 350 were printed - says the publisher!/ possibly less says EGC.

[Unless otherwise indicated, the following notes are probably in Daphne Woodward's hand. They are summary translations of marked sections of the text on the pages indicated. Her notes undoubtedly formed the basis for Craig's review. See p. 206.]

PAGE 1: The Sanscrit words for "drama," "mimic," "actor," and the name of the chief group of Indian epic dramas, all come from the root-word meaning "to dance."

PAGE 8: In Asia, "the arts"—in the European meaning of the word—do not exist. They are simply a fundamental part of life.

PAGE 9: In India, the Dance was born of a pious inspiration, & thus became a magnificent means of expressing noble thoughts & feelings.

PAGE 10: Ritual (as distinct from theatrical) dances, disappeared from Java when Mohammedanism entered the land.

PAGE 13: The Indian Dance developed during the period when early Sanscrit dramas were given, with no décor, in temples & palaces. These dramas were chanted & accompanied by symbolic gestures.

PAGE 14: The laws of gesture were attributed to Brahma, who gave them to the Saint, Bharata Muni.

PAGE 15: In India, the Dance could only be counted as an art if the dance, like the "yogi," were capable of total abnegation—for Dance belonged first to the Gods & Godesses. / The God Shiva was called "The King of the Dancers" ("Nataraja"), or "Tândava" - i. e., "Our Master is the Dancer who, like the fire hidden in the live coal, insinuates his power into spirit & substance, & makes them dance, in their turn."

PAGE 17: The noble wisdom of Eastern Dance now only remains, to any great extent, in the Nō, & in Javanese theatrical Dance. / The Indian dancer-actor had to undergo stern discipline. He must be a puppet in the hands of the Gods. Yet, in his fixed, traditional gestures, his dance must *appear* to be perfectly natural & spontaneous.

PAGE 18: The Hindus carried their precepts into Java & implanted them so strongly that they lived there still, though almost extinct in India itself. Most of the characters of the Javanese dance-dramas are Hindu heros & heroines.

PAGE 20: The ancient Hindu tradition lays down 3 essential spiritual qualities in Dance: —the "rasa," or "poetic perfume" which penetrates the soul / the "bhâva," or emotion-feeling-produced by the "rasa" / the "Vyanjana," or force of suggestion, giving a feeling of hidden things, & releasing the imagination.

PAGE 22: The Javanese say that the Dance comes from the Widadaris—heavenly nymphs created by the Gods, & moulded from the most precious stones.

PAGE 24: There are no documents relating how Hindu civilization was carried to Java. This secrecy is attributed to the fact that Hindus were forbidden by their Gods to cross the sea: so the learned Brahmins who (judging by other evidence) must have led the emigration to Java, kept their transgression as quiet as possible.

PAGE 25: Lévi says that, in view of the importance of Dance in the Hindu religion, it is most natural that the Brahmin priests who emigrated to Java should take dancing-girls with them. / The girl-children born to the priests by the dancing-girls were trained as danseuses: the boy-children were trained as priests: so a self-contained cult was formed & maintained.

Book Review. THE RAREST DANCING IN THE WORLD.[1] *The Dancing Times*, January, 1932.[2]

his book on the Javanese theatrical dance is really two books in one: one is the book of the words, and the other is a book of pictures. The forty-eight plates will say more, to a serious dancer, than any words, and will say it more clearly. To other people, the pictures will say less. For them, the text.

On the faces of these Javanese dancers is an expression that is fretful, petulant and childlike. It is the petulance around the eyes and brows which is most marked in nearly all the dancers; and more often than not the chin recedes, giving the face quite the look of a spoilt child. According to our standards of personality, these creatures possess none whatever: as for character, they are characterless: to us they are not gracious, for they seem to show no sign of wishing to please.

They do not dance according to the rules of European dancing, for, to begin with, they keep their feet flat upon the ground. They are not like the dancers of most other lands, because they are clothed: only the feet are naked, and the arms, shoulders and face—for rarely does one cover his face with a mask, though the head-dresses worn are elaborate.

They do not grin, nor look empty nothings at the spectator: they are unconcerned by the man who "pays for his seat," or the impresario who would wish to teach them the arts of vulgarity so as to get them to *click*!

They look down, as a rule: if the head is raised up, still they look down and sideways, more often than not.

When grouping together they do not arrange themselves in such straight lines, such symmetrical patterns, that they can form the large letters, J A V A, when seen from a grand-stand, at a distance, at a tattoo—because they have no tattoo, and they do not try to imitate living letters. Their dance is dance, and to them, dance is a sacred thing, not a show.

But there we are again: the word "sacred" to them does not mean what it has come to mean to Europeans; so it is not a matter of white wings, upturned eyes, mutterings and mumblings devoid of humanity, and a general appearance of the sickly . . . nor is it expressed by savage rage or drunken whirlings, as in the dances of the Western Indians, or the dance of the Bacchantes in Greece . . . nor by an incessant wriggling of the stomach, as in another part of the world. Neither, in their dance, does the back become the front, as in the negro convention so familiar to Parisians.

There is nothing in the Javanese dance that can exclude it from being at the summit, with the rarest dancing the world has ever dreamed.

And yet it is no dream: it is a reality. Is it ready then for exploitation on the music-hall stage in London?

These are all Kings' dancers of whom I speak, who are portrayed in this book, and it is out of the question that they should appear on a music-hall stage. So the impresario, that ass who cheapens every rare thing to fit into his objectionably cheap programme, will dub them "unpractical" and "highbrow."

Mr. Van Lelyveld, in his first chapter, tells us that the Sanskrit words for "drama," "mimic," "actor," and the name of the chief group of Indian epic dramas, all derive from the root word meaning "to dance." The Javenese dance came from India—the Hindus took it to Java before India had become westernized. Once in Java, it has been preserved, so we can see what it is that India has lost. For the author says:

"In India itself, except in certain southern districts, the decay of culture and the European influence have destroyed all but a few vestiges of an art of rhythmic movement. Only in Java does the theatre still exist in its most perfect form . . . the dance in its original stage: symbolic, expressive, and wonderfully beautiful."

What would the Scotch say, for example, who know how to dance their reel, if the silly sort of imitation Scottish dance that we see at a music-hall were to be held representative of their grand national dance? What is the good of having bled with Wallace if, some five hundred years later, your descendants, "the Sisters Wallis," become a side-show with a dancing bear?—for then a good deal more than sixpence has gone bang. Such a happening proclaims that the whole country is ready to go bang. I am told that the Scots have preserved their glorious dances, to the honour of their race, and that people who would degrade our English stage do not search for Dianas among the artists' models in Skye.

The preservation of the Indian dance in Java reminds me how useful—right away from beautiful or noble or anything else—how useful the dance is. It serves, as a straw does, to show which way the wind blows. It is such an easy, useful little thing to preserve a dance. A dance is like a good barometer in a house—you know when to take out an umbrella in time to avoid a drenching, or when to take out a sunshade. It is such a sensitive little instrument, the dance, that it can tell you with precision when your nation is just going a little bit too much to the right, or a little bit too much to the left. Whether on perceiving the first decline of their dance, the Javanese will realize that their country is about to enter a crisis in its history, and will be able to avert that crisis, is a question that I cannot answer. The author of this book, who has observed the coming to Java of the cinema, the wireless, and the other idiocies of our beautiful civilization—most of which have contributed to the disastrous situation from which we are just emerging—the author knits his brows. He doesn't like the look of it at all.

The rules and conditions of the Javanese dance vary a good deal in the different provinces. In Jogya (where the Sultan's brother, Prince Arya Souryadiningrat, has done much to preserve and support the dance) women and girls take no part in the theatrical dances. At Solo, on the contrary, not only the women's parts, but some male rôles, are taken by girls. At both Jogya and Solo, the young princesses take part in certain ceremonial dances which are religious rather than theatrical; and the dance plays a great part in the education of all these children of royal and noble families.

At Jogya, the theatrical performances last for several days sometimes, and certain rôles have to be doubled. At Solo, the performances are short.

There are no special theatre buildings—the performances are given in the open air, or under a roof with open sides; until recently no platform was used, but these are now beginning to be adopted.

The costumes are very splendid, and there is little or no décor, though a backcloth is now sometimes used.

These theatrical dancers are never professionals, and many of these too are the children of the princes and nobles.

Each gesture in a dance expresses a certain action or emotion, and when a point of the story is to be emphasized, the gestures which explain it are repeated several times. The Javanese spectators, even the children, know and understand every movement made by the dancers . . . except that the meaning of certain gestures of the hands has been lost during the centuries.

The Javanese dancers do not point their toes; the foot is placed flat on the ground, and lifted horizontally. When the foot is raised, the body remains upright, and the knee of the other leg is bent.

The eyes follow the direction of the hands and feet. The head is carried at the same angle throughout the dance—its position on the neck does not change, even if the head has to be violently flung back. The nobler the character a dancer is representing, the more does he bend his head, in token of his simplicity, modesty and thoughtfulness. In each rôle, the position of the head, like the movements, is laid down by tradition.

The author says:

"If we grant the possibility of imitating, with grace and suppleness, the outward forms of this dance (as certain western dancers of great ability have successfully done in public, after much study) it is none the less certain that these *tours de force* can never reach the subtle beauty of the original. The difference in physical structure is, in itself, an overwhelming obstacle. Such interpretations can never be anything but mechanical copies, lacking the inspiration of the Oriental soul, which can neither be imitated nor learnt."

A warning. It is strange how many intelligent European and American dancers take pictures, photographs, vase-paintings, statuettes, and imitate these, no matter what the period or what the land of their origin—and become Egyptian, Chinese, Indian, Persian, Scandinavian, Spanish or what not.

How sick we are of seeing the so-called "Greek poses," the so-called "Egyptian gestures," and the others! Some even go so far as to put on Egyptian dress when imitating these Egyptian gestures, or Spanish dress when pretending to be Spanish. This is all utter folly. But so much of modern European dancing is, to my way of feeling, utter folly—and when it is professedly foolish, then we are all right. The dancing clown is so genuine, the dancing faun of to-day so false. But though the clown is genuine, he ought not to be the only dancing figure, as he is to-day. Is not our fraudulent civilization able to find one genuine partner for this clown?

1. *La Danse dans le Théatre Javanais* by Th.-B. Van Lelyveld. (Librairie Floury, Paris.) 1931.
2. [Reprinted in *Dance Index*, Volume II, no. 8, August, 1943.]

# PART IV.

GORDON CRAIG ON MODERN DANCE

## ISADORA DUNCAN SIX MOVEMENT DESIGNS. The Insel-Verlag, Leipzig, 1906.[1]

## INTRODUCTION.

Much Noise, and a deep Unrest
Sadness and Discord
Is this in any way the final estimate of the whole?
The Reality?
Is it then so certain that Life is made up
of four Absurdities?
Is it not far more certain that Life is made up of
Four Beauties
of Calmness Joy Harmony
Rhythm the truest Reality.
And what of the expression of all this Art?
Must Pandemonium and Ugliness
ever stand for Strength?
Must Restlessness be made the Symbol of Life?
Must a noisy and discordant Sadness spread
itself over the Loveliness of all?
If these are questions, I am not one of the Questioners.
I have no doubt whatever
I see Calmness and Beauty both the Strong and the Sweet
advancing now with perfect ease
All makes way for this spirit
Nothing can hinder it.
Three marks of a pencil, or three hundred
It is ever the same Picture
A note sounded, or a fall of notes,
It is the same Song.
A step, or a hundred steps
It is the same Dance.
Something put down
a Record
Something uttered on that divine theme understood
so easily, and only with ease

that theme which commences
*"I AM HAPPY . . . ."*
and which ends in
*". . . . it is Beautiful"*
This is the theme she dances
Not yet has she depicted a Gloom or a Sorrow unbearable
For ever it seems Sunlight with her
The little Shadows themselves are found out
and move away as she passes
This is the great power.
She comes of the lovely family
The great Companions
That Conquering Race which has held up the
World so that it might spin without difficulty.
The courageous Giants
the Preservers of Beauty
the Answerers of all Riddles.

1. [In *Dance Index*, Volume II, no. 8, August, 1943, George Amberg's translation of the German version (translator unknown) appeared. Amberg's translation also appeared in Paul Magriel's *Isadora Duncan*, Henry Holt and Company, New York, 1947.]

---

REALISM AND THE ACTOR. AN INTERNATIONAL SYMPOSIUM by J. S. [John Semar.] *The Mask*, Volume I, nos. 3 & 4, May-June, 1908.

---

he series of visits which the Sicilian Players are paying to all the European capitals, exhibiting an unfamiliar phase of realism in theatrical art which is almost primitive in character, has once more called public attention to certain questions as to the relation between realism and the stage. Believing that we could best serve the interests of the theatre by collecting and publishing expert opinions on Realism and the Actor we framed three questions to which we solicited answers from some of the students of the Theatre. We wondered whether

anyone would reply in the affirmative to the second question, "In your opinion should the Actor be allowed the same liberty in his expression of the Passions as is permitted to the Writer or the Painter?", for we recalled to mind the many subjects or moods which the poets and painters have treated realistically and we wondered whether anyone would hold that the same liberty should be permitted on the stage; liberty, first in choice of subject and secondly in treatment. We mean, of course, those subjects which the masters of painting and literature always chose as their favourites, . . . . those religious moments in the lives of the saints, those profane moments in the lives of the demons and those all too "human" moments in the lives of men and women.

We call to mind some of those moments: — The Annunciation; The Last Supper; The Birth of Eve; The Expulsion from Eden; The Nativity; The Crucifixion; The Agony in the Garden; The Last Judgement; The Birth of Venus; Perseus and Andromeda; Samson and Delilah; Lucretia; The Creation of Man; The Triumphs of Bacchus; The Birth of Pan; Salome and John the Baptist; Judith and Holofernes. These questions, with the replies sent, are to be found below. We may perhaps be excused in saying that our questions are made as simple as possible, so that the mind of the English reader shall not be confused. The outcry raised in some of the English journals against the Realism of the acting of the Sicilians, and of Signora Mimi Auguglia's performances in particular gives us reason to believe that it was time to have a clear definition of what Realism in acting consists of, and whether it is a wise and beautiful thing to see upon a stage, shown in the same way as we see it in Painting and Literature. The Three Questions are as follows:

(1) Do you consider Realism in acting to be a frank representation of human nature?

(2) In your opinion should the Actor be allowed the same liberty in his expression of the Passions, as is permitted to the Writer or the Painter?

(3) Do you think that Realism appeals to the General Public or only to a limited section of Playgoers?

We call to mind the wonderful books we have read: The Books of St. Matthew, St. Mark, St. Luke and St. John; the Vision of Heaven and Hell by Dante; The Temptation of St. Anthony by Flaubert; The book of Genesis, The Thousand and One Nights; The story of Gargantua, and many more, and it remains for us a very grave and difficult question and one to which we can answer neither yes nor no, as to whether these should serve as themes for stage representations, no matter whether the treatment be realistic or idealistic.

But because we can as yet give no answer, it makes it all the more interesting to solicit replies from those better equipped to speak. From these replies we gather that the majority are in favour of the same liberty of expression for the stage and its actors as that possessed by the painters and poets, and that they are eager to see upon the stage the frank realistic representation of plays founded on the stories from the New Testament, from the stories of Venus, Jupiter and the Deities of the ancient world, and from such themes as those treated by Correggio, Titian, Hogarth, Burns, Michelangelo, Blake, Whitman, Goethe, Cranach, Rembrandt, Jan Steen, Goya, Velasquez, Manet, Whistler, Verlaine, Tolstoi, Botticelli, Boccaccio, Dante and an innumerable collection of poets and artists of the world's history; that they would consider it an excellent thing if such themes were allowed to be placed before the public in the modern theatres. We would put but one other question to those who have answered the second question in the affirmative, and it is this: . . . . "Do you approve of cutting out certain passages from the works of Shakespeare as being unfit for the ears of the General Public and have you ever done so yourself, . . . . and why?" We hardly expect any answers to this question though we should welcome the further opportunity of going more deeply into an important, and, to us, a very serious and difficult problem.

---

## THE QUESTIONS.

---

(1) Do you consider Realism in acting to be a frank representation of human nature?

(2) In your opinion should the Actor be allowed the same liberty in his expression of the Passions, as is permitted to the Writer or the Painter?

(3) Do you think that Realism appeals to the General Public or only to a limited section of Playgoers?

(1) Do you consider Realism in acting to be a *true* representation of human nature? What else can be true or . . . . frank?

(2) By "truth" and "frankness" the word "*allowed*" cannot appear: these things are a common *right* which no one can gainsay. For here nature asserts herself and establishes her right and so proclaims the "*law*" and *real* laws we obey, we cannot direct them!

(3) What a question. You might as well ask if there *is* such a thing as *a limited section* of *Playgoers*! Shakespeare is real . . if the actors are not, and does *he* not appeal to all. The pioneer of an unknown thing, by his discovery establishes a fact. The Sicilians can I think quote this. A figure in wax, however well it is made, does not give us the same sensations that the real thing would: or, could it be so well produced that our senses, (through the impression made upon the mind) would respond to the imitation as to the real. In any case the law (written or unwritten) is that no imitation of whatever kind can possess the value of the real. Why then should "acting" play a better part than the rest? Art is the imitation of nature, or of man's handiwork; never can its value equal that of the real. By value one means its worth in truth, not money, for the latter misleads yesterday, today and tomorrow. There is no doubt that real feeling, really expressed, can never be replaced nor confounded by its imitation, however perfect that imitation may be.

[Only Miss Fuller's comments are reproduced as she was the only dancer to reply.]

Foreign Note. England. By R. S. [Rudolf Schmerz.] *The Mask,*
Volume I, no. 6, August, 1908.

our request to report whether the Theatres show signs
of careful or hasty work finds me compelled to reply,
Hasty work. Haste, in fact, characterizes the entire
world of the Theatre. They seem to be working against
time. I questioned some stage hands the other day.
"Plenty to do, Sir," they answered, "to get ready in
time; but it will be all right on the night." That is typical of the whole
Theatre. So long as they are "ready on the night" it doesn't much matter
*how* it's ready.

On many a first night I have been to lately the actors have not known the
words of their parts. Perhaps this is one of those details in which the
manager may be inaccurate, . . . of that I am not able to speak; the scenery
and general management of the stages reveal much hasty work. What
happens to be good is good through happening.

Miss Isadora Duncan and "twenty Parisian dancers" have been here this
month, and here again haste predominates, for surely it was only *over
haste* which caused Mr. Frohman to describe twenty poor little German,
Belgian, Polish and Dutch girls as "Parisian Dancers." These little girls
have been trained in Berlin and have visited several cities in Europe where
they have exhibited their games; they may have danced in Paris, . . . but
this does not make them "Parisian dancers."

And surely it was only *over-haste* which made Mr. Frohman announce
on the posters that the music was from Gluck's INPHIGENIA instead of
IPHIGENIA.

According to "The Stage," a reliable authority on all matters pertaining
to vaudeville, Mr. Charles Frohman is going to be still more hasty in
America. "The Stage" announces that Mr. Al Levering, who is Charles
Frohman's right-hand man at the Aldwych in London, suddenly turned up
in New York lately and is making arrangements for the appearance of Miss
Isadora Duncan there, professedly at one of the theatres, but as a matter of
fact, "The Stage" has every reason to believe that Mr. Frohman is contemplating an excursion into the vaudeville field, and to that end is quietly
making arrangements for Miss Duncan and a few others[1], for preliminary

experiments, which, if successful, will be enlarged upon. With this end in view several artists have been approached, with regard to the supply of high-class acts.

Miss Duncan in the vaudeville field is the most colossal idea which Mr. Frohman ever invented; but it also shows *haste*.

Mr. Frohman describes Miss Duncan as "The sensation of the Continent." This also shows *haste*. We may shortly expect such notices as the following: "Mr. Frohman presents Madame Duse, the Rage of the Earth." and "Mr. Frohman presents Miss Ellen Terry, the Mirth-provoker of the World" .... that is to say, if Madame Duse and Miss Ellen Terry permit such vulgarity.

This *haste* in matters of art has been directly imported from America. It is spreading over Europe. Art will in time be taught in the schools by hustling tutors who will tell their pupils that Art is hustling mesmerism. Twenty Parisian Dancers!!! Tremendous, Mr. Frohman, simply tremendous! ... But isn't it swindling the public?

1. Who can these "few others" be? . . . Most mysterious. Possibly the same "Twenty Parisian dancers" warmed up again, this time probably described as "Forty Moorish dancers"? .... Or may we expect the Napoleon of the Theatrical world to present in one and the same theatre on the same evening Miss Duncan, the White-eyed Kaffir, and Sandow?

Foreign Note. London. By R. S. [Rudolf Schmerz]. *The Mask*, Volume I, no. 6, August, 1908.

he scene used by Miss Isadora Duncan, which everyone has taken for the work of Mr. Gordon Craig is not by him, but is rather a poor imitation of his work. We should have thought Miss Duncan the last person in the world to have been satisfied with an imitation.

Foreign Note. Brussels. Unsigned. *The Mask*, Volume I, no. 12, February, 1909.

he Theatre here is as fashionable as ever, the Art of the Theatre as unpopular. Often we have shocking attempts to imitate the work of individual artists who visit us from time to time.

This was the case when Miss Isadora Duncan danced here some time ago. The opera went mad for a while. It made its ballet girls costume themselves in things which resembled night dresses more than Greek robes, and the ballet master, evidently bent on the sincerest form of insult, made the poor ballet dancers more miserable by forcing them to prance about in a manner more distrait than buoyant, . . . and the result was villainous.

Fancy sixty or seventy chic girls, thoroughly at home in frills and tights, having to discard both, . . . for bareness and bedroom wear! The poor dears took it amiably enough, but so sadly! They felt so ashamed for once, and the audience so full of pity. We were all horrified here, for we love our old-fashioned ballet with its foolery and its frills, and its fine, if fading, echo of a noble century.

If the master of the ballet has the desire to bring back the "Greek Dance" (whatever that namey thing may be), he might spare us his experiments for a few years, and in the meantime find his Greek girls, instil into them, (if he knows it himself), the Greek belief, make them dance to Greek music, and so do the thing more thoroughly. If it should take him ten years we should not complain, and perhaps our children would rejoice.

Still, Brussels has little to complain of as a rule, and if the "Greek Cult," . . . that is to say, the imitations of the performance of a beautiful personality,[1] threatens us for a while, the clouds vanish, all the sooner by the assistance of the many serious and learned essays and books which come to us often enough.

To these can be added the lectures given here by Mr. Jean Jacques Olivier, one of the first of the living Theatrical Historians, whose interesting study of the actor Lekain, & other books relating to the 18th Century Theatre in France, form so valuable a contribution to Theatrical Literature.

1. [We suppose our correspondent to refer to Miss Isadora Duncan. —Ed.]

Foreign Note. London. MISS LOIE FULLER AT "HIS MAJESTY'S." Unsigned. *The Mask*, Volume III, nos. 10-12, April, 1911.

iss Loie Fuller has for some unaccountable reason accepted a little engagement at His Majesty's Theatre to help in some production. It has not transpired what she will be asked to do, but from certain indications it can be gathered that the task will not be an arduous one nor the engagement for more than a few days.

Magazine Review. Unsigned. *The Mask*, Volume IV, no. 2, October, 1911.

he *Forum*, published monthly by Mitchell Kennerley, New York, is always interesting.

The most notable among recent contributions have been by Mr. W. B. Yeats, whose fine play, "The Green Helmet" appeared in the September number, while to the August number he contributed a long essay on "J. M. Synge and the Ireland of his time," which should be of especial interest to Americans just now since they will so soon have the opportunity of seeing some of Synge's plays acted by Mr. Yeats's own company from the Dublin Abbey Theatre.

The last number includes also an article by Gaspard Etscher on the "Renaissance of the Dance" as exemplified in the art of Miss Isadora Duncan.

Mr. Etscher writes enthusiastically and intelligently, but he is surely incorrect when he attributes to Miss Duncan the abolition of footlights, stating that "It is to her love of nature that we owe the alteration she made in the stage-lighting "

"She diminished very much, as much as possible" he goes on, "the importance of the footlights, which are so irrational and produce so often ugly shadows, throwing from the nose a black triangle on the forehead."

We believe, however, that we are correct in saying that this doing away with the footlights was not due to any initiative of Miss Duncan's, but was one of the first changes made by Mr. Gordon Craig when he began to stage plays in London ten years ago, and that the American dancer has been but one among the many who have imitated him in this as in his other methods of stage production.

---

NAKED WOMEN ON THE STAGE by Jan van Holt. *The Mask*, Volume IV, no. 4, April, 1912.

---

e have from time to time in this journal spoken, probably with prejudice, in favour of the use of Masks. As veils for the face, hiding its weaknesses and revealing what is in the soul of the poet, masks have always seemed to us a gain. And at the same time we have always regretted (probably with prejudice) the gradual unveiling of the bodies of persons on the stage, which practise we failed to see brought any gain to the Art.

The ladies in pink tights had grown into a convention and suggested the Farce of things, but ladies without them grew objectionable and suggested nothing but the bathroom and "La Vie Parisienne," a charming little journal to be found at the hearth of every cocotte.

And if the ladies and gentlemen who take off their shirts, stockings, trousers, *und so weiter,* for us on the stage gave us frankly to understand that a new episode in "La Vie Parisienne" was about to be revealed to us for our amusement we should be better able to accept the performances.

But this is anything but the case. There is much solemnity about these undressings. Gods are evoked, masters of music, painting and sculpture are dragged in to perform the parts of high priest, and then the victim sacrifices herself in all the solemn splendour of the café chantant.

And all this is done, it is said, in the cause of Beauty and Art. Now to see what it has led to. I quote from the *Daily Mail* of March 9th in full.

---

*FROM OUR OWN CORRESPONDENT.*
*BERLIN, FRIDAY.*

---

"The Parisian dancer Adoree Villany, who dances without clothing, and who was charged with giving an immoral performance, was prosecuted by the Munich police in connection with a series of performances given last November before an invited audience of painters, sculptors and Academicians. The final performance was broken up by the police, who invaded the theatre and carried off the dancer to the station.

"The case came up for trial yesterday, and ended in the acquittal of Mlle. Villany and her theatrical managers, the co-defendants. The jury held that Mlle. Villany was serving "the higher interests of art" and the question of an offence against public morals was therefore irrelevant.

"Half a dozen of the most eminent artists of Munich went into the witness-box to testify to the artistic satisfaction which they derived from watching Mlle. Villany.

"Professor Kaulbach, the most celebrated German portrait painter, described the dancer's performance as "thoroughly artistic and respectable." The professor had taken his wife to the performance, and she, too, found it unobjectionable. Professor Petersen, president of the Munich Artists' Society, said that he would be happy when such performances could be given for the masses, instead of to a select artistic audience. Such an advance in culture would be a universal blessing, and public morals would not be jeopardised by giving the public an opportunity of admiring the beauty of the human figure.

"Professor Keller, another Academician, flouted the "ignoble conduct" of the police in interfering with "so chaste a séance." He said that the action of the police was equivalent to placing artists beyond the pale of moral society.

"The public prosecutor asked the Court to fine the dancer and the two managers £10.0.0 each, and to send them to gaol for twenty days each, but their acquittal followed after the jury had been out only a few minutes."

Now no one upon earth is going to pretend that this sort of thing will benefit Art one scrap, and we are not going into the question as to whether it is good for our morals. The whole episode is a revelation of the extent the tremblers will go to for the sake of money and civic pride.

On the one hand we have the Dancer, her theatrical managers, and their witnesses, Professor Kaulbach, and his wife, Professor Petersen, President of the Munich Artists' Society, and Professor Keller. These are out to make money.

On the other hand we have the Judge and jury composed of Bavarians wild with anger but prepared to go to any length rather than admit that Berlin and the Kaiser were right.

Neither side was out for truth.

And now let us glance at each of these amazing groups piecemeal.

(1) Miss Villany / Evidently a pretty young woman; evidently a perfect painter's "model"; evidently quite honest in her desire to make as much splash, noise and money as possible without the bore of posing to one man.

(2) The Theatrical Managers. / These business men are not working for Art or Philanthropy. You cannot blame them for exhibiting a naked woman. They are at liberty to go even further in this line if it is not illegal. Why not? and who is going to find fault with them?

(3) The Witnesses; Professors Kaulbach, Keller and Petersen. / In our opinion it is these gentlemen who are obviously through and through culpable. To begin with they ought to know that a painting of a naked woman and the exhibition of a naked woman in public are two quite different things; but if they don't know that it is only a matter of ignorance. They ought to know that the masses, . . . . that even a select audience . . . . do not understand such exhibitions. They ought to know that anything so obviously out to make money by such means cannot be quite honest.

But may be, as I say, these witnesses are ignorant.

Is it from ignorance that they gave such vile evidence? Let us look a little closer into the matter.

How do Messrs. Kaulbach, Keller, Petersen and Co. make their money? Let us realise that and we shall find the weak spot at once.

Messrs. Kaulbach, Keller and Petersen make money by painting or carving nude figures. Most artists paint or carve nude figures; it is an old custom handed down to us from ancient times when men and women dressed so that the human form was in part revealed. It is a custom utterly out of date and out of place; but no matter; let us accept it as a custom which has been kept up.

Now these Munich Professors when called as witnesses were up against a difficult proposition. If they said that naked ladies should not show themselves in public the jury would ask them why that which could not be shown in Public could be shown when Painted by the said Professors: and of course these particular Professors would not know what to answer to such a question; and, though there is an answer, and an entirely satisfying one, had it been given the jury could never have grasped its meaning.

The Professors saw this clearly. They had patronized the performance of the naked dancer; they must therefore say it was great art or all would be lost . . . . commissions . . . . reputation . . . . life itself. So they swore it was "thoroughly artistic and respectable" (respectable old Munchen kerls); that they had (one of them) taken their wives to see the show (for their wives like to live also . . . . and like to dress prettily (queer) and entertain; all this takes money) and that it was "ignoble" of the police to interfere with "so chaste a séance": and the jury opened their mouths and sang of one accord, "It is in the interests of the Highest Art."

---

## INTEREST.

---

That's it. Pure per centage.

And the Judge and jury, . . . why did they also sing this tune?

Well, do you know Germany? I was there the whole of last year and found out one curious thing about it which is not sufficiently realized in England.

In Germany there are many states, and two states in particular; Prussia and Bavaria. Prussia is in the north, and chilly; Bavaria is in the south, and warm . . . . (if wet). Yes, Bavaria, Munich in particular, is clammy.

Well, Berliners and Muncheners just hate each other and the Munich man loves nothing so well as to jeer at the Berlin man's exaggerated "morality," at his lack of "temperament," at his ignorance of what is Art. So whenever he can he tells the whole of Germany what Art is and how it is not the "proper" thing that Berlin and the German Kaiser would have it.

He may be right . . . . or wrong. That is not the point here. But he has made Munich the Paris of Germany and he has to think like a Parisian . . . even if inspired by the Café Luitpold.

So when it comes to such a question as this where a naked woman is concerned, professors, jury, judge and all, turning their superior faces towards the north with significant sniffs toward Friedrichstrasse pronounce the exhibition "moral . . . artistic . . . Humpf."

Could it have been prevented? Could Munich have been saved having to decide?

It could: and the weakness of the whole episode is the weakness of many other such episodes in the history of this pretty town.

Let me explain.

Whenever a cute business man or woman has wanted to make money in Germany by exhibiting, in public, parts or the whole of some dancer's or model's person they have one method and one only. They go to Munich; they see reporters; they announce that they have a great ART work to show.

They then take their bait, the said model or dancer, and lay it before the chief Professor of Art in the town. They find him at his studio; he is possibly painting from a model at the time. They ask the Professor if they may see his pictures: . . . "oh, how noble! what power, what beauty!" They then humbly ask permission to be allowed to show the Professor their art . . . and the girl is thereupon trotted out and performs her nude or semi-nude dance before the Professor.

He, being painter or sculptor, sees in the girl a fine specimen of physical beauty, and, as he is used to such exhibition in his private studio, he sees nothing unusual in what is before him.

The girl then fascinates the artist and asks him if he will form one of a committee for the small informal meeting of artists to be held at the Kunstler Haus or Artists' Club before which she desires to perform. "Certainly, my dear" he answers, and lends his name to the thing.

The impresario now packs the Gladstone bag and proceeds with the Professor's promise to see other Professors.

They fall into the trap more easily. "Has Professor . . . . lent his name to it? then certainly so will I." Five or six names are collected; the performance is announced; the reporters are seen again; are told what the Professors have said; all goes well; the town is caught. The performance takes place; the police come in; the Professors are indignant; the impresario chuckles; the girl is enjoying the luxury of success.

But this is not Art: . . . . this is smart business at the expense of public, artists and art alike. This is one of the most monstrous tyrannies we are obliged to put up with because Professors have forgotten that Art is not nature nor nature Art and that what is seemly here is out of place there.

But it is a good thing that the *Daily Mail* brought up the matter, for the methods employed by these travelling performers who traffic in nudity under the guise of it being Fine Art needed being revealed.

JACQUES DALCROZE AND HIS SCHOOL by John Balance.
*The Mask*, Volume V, no. 1, July, 1912.

ou probably have never heard of Dalcroze. You've heard of Maud Allen: . . . well, that's not it; You've heard of Del Sarte? that's not it either; You've heard of Isadora Duncan? . . . . well, that's nearer it, and, to do M. Dalcroze full justice, in his teaching he reaches nearer to Miss Duncan's ideal than that of one of her imitators or one of her masters.

But then Dalcroze is himself no originator. There seems to be really no exquisite reason why he should be except that we like a man to think and feel for himself. If a woman derives her inspiration from a man its only natural; she adds a personal touch which is common to her sex and somehow that staggers us all . . . . as it very rightly should do. We are all of us always staggered by that sex; the gods were even staggered. Jupiter reeled; Apollo, . . . well, that's different, for,

"is not even Apollo, with hair and harpstring of gold
A bitter God to follow! a beautiful God to behold"?[1]

Apollo . . . creator of Form, bringer of Light, Music; the impersonal God, the God who burns up the dross; burns Isis, has power over Osiris. Come now, here is an inspiration which counts. And in him we have the God before whom even the staggering impertinence of the fair sex comes to a standstill. The tiptilted noses droop beautifully again, and the ladies make way for the true artists once more to advance and reveal the power of Apollo.

Dalcroze knowing this claims that his art is Apollonian. Alas, it is not.

Instead it is the real old Theatrical article served up very neatly. For Apollo never asked for a parade of womanly charms in his service. "A bitter God to follow." Women don't follow after Gods that offer bitterness, for there are very few women who know how to make beauty and goodness out of what spreads itself as bitterness on the earth. No, Venus, or some more pleasant Deity is their favourite. And as Dalcroze fills his school with girls he empties it of Apollonian possibilities and lets the Cyprian slip into the Fold.

M. Dalcroze's girls are just delightful. No one who sees them exercising or watches them as they watch their master, can doubt for a moment that they are true and sincere worshippers of Venus. She it is who coos over all at Hellerau: . . . a distinguée, nice and pretty modern Venus; modern because, unlike all the other Deities, she *will* be "in the fashion." Although a quite brainless, soulless Goddess she is intelligent. . . . I once had a dear little pussy cat called Topsy, and what that creature couldn't do! . . . but to the matter in hand.

Under the inspiration of Venus modernized into something at once healthy and chic M. Dalcroze advances to instruct his many promising pupils in the art of Rhythm. Gymnastics, Dancing and Dramatic Gesture are practised in doors, . . . or out doors . . . . for M. Dalcroze has a delightful and vast open air courtyard designed by the architect Heinrich Tessenow who doesn't seem to have wasted an ounce of his material or an inch of his space.

I can't speak too highly of this whole building. It is made for the purpose to which it is to be applied, and it is a real working place. And what energy and enthusiasm the subscribers to the whole affair have shown!

Into this building Dr. Dalcroze dumps his girls, and sets them swinging their arms and legs and bodies. Outwardly all is perfect, for the girls are just the perfectest girls that ever girls could be. Inwardly there is nothing . . . .

I mean, of course, comparatively nothing. For inwardly there are hearts, beating awfully prettily, and emotions chasing one another, and beliefs all butterfly-like playing easily at Bo-Peep: . . . and there are very pretty little dances, and such a nice feeling of good breeding and pleasant hours spent. And there's just the prettiest of houses near the school where the girls are kept and fed and where they exchange those lovely confidences which girls alone know how to exchange without having given anything.

The head mistresses of the school are most intelligent ladies of much refinement and thoroughly capable, and no one could desire a more perfect directress than Frau Mabel-Riees.

And yet the net result of the whole effect is *nothing*.

Individuality is lost in this school. And that is rather a grave matter, because they employ the individual even as the carpenter employs wood or the goldsmith gold.

Herein lies the root-evil of the whole matter. Girls are employed like so much marble or gold . . . . and Dalcroze, like Michaelangelo, hacks away at them, turns them, bends them . . . . and of course they like it.

Excellent! excellent that any and all girls should like being bent and turned by a man; . . . it is an old virtue of theirs, but it has the disadvantage of it no way conducing towards the production of a work of art.

It has been lately pointed out,[2] and for the first time so far as I know, that a work of Art can only be made "from those materials in which we can calculate" and it has been shown that "man is not one of these materials" because "the whole nature of man tends towards freedom." And therefore as "Art only arrives by design," to make use of the bodies of men and women can only end in creating something accidental. If this has but lately been proclaimed as a principle it has for centuries been realized by every artist, great or small from East to West as a truth.

The girls whom M. Dalcroze shows us in the frontispiece to this book are awfully pretty and charming: they spring up into the air like the dearest of nymphs . . . but they don't bear looking at besides even the smallest statue by Donatello or by Yeshin-Sôdzu. It is Venus versus Apollo, and she loses the throw.

Compare these dear little dancers with a different and a less spiritual work of art; put them beside the figures carved and coloured in the sixth century before Christ by the master at the Acropole and their Goddess deserts them . . . . for Dionysus peers out through the Temple doors.

So let us remember; the old Laws hold good, and if the grandest Law of Life is Liberty, the grandest Law of Art is Slavery. The artist himself is a servant . . . he is the servant of God and he is commanded to go and select any material which creation can yield him; but he must not make use of man, woman, child, bird, beast[3] or any other living thing in his attempt to make a work of art. These things are free agents and must be left free; these are already formed, already fitted with life: to touch these, to take these with intent to use them as material of a work of art would be to eat of the Tree of Life that is forbidden. . . . . That one tree only, . . . and theatrical people have disobeyed.

M. Dalcroze is not exactly a theatrical person; he is a musician. He comes promising to release us; he only binds us all more selfishly and more cunningly than his predecessors. As master of gymnastics and director of a well-ordered establishment for young ladies we are all in favour of M. Dalcroze. As a teacher of art we consider him entirely lacking in conscience, bringing false counsel of a very dangerous kind, . . . . that ancient advice of the serpent with its lithe and sinuous gestures, "Ye shall not surely die, for God doth know that in the day ye eat there of your eyes shall be opened and ye shall be as Gods, knowing good and evil."

And it is to women that the good fascinating, harmless M. Dalcroze appeals. They are to be goddesses again, . . . through the power of Rhythm and by the grace of Dalcroze.

He would have been right to make such an offer but for one small thing . . . . woman.

Let us remember that against the Laws of Nature and against the Laws of Art it is forbidden to rebel, and he who does so shall not prevail, and his disobedience shall eternally plague him.

Come then, let us move on; let us strive to give birth to a new art of the Theatre; but let us learn first the Laws, however stern they may be, and surely forbid ourselves that which Nature has already forbidden us.

1. Swinburne. "Hymn to Proserpine."
2. In "On the Art of the Theatre," by E. Gordon Craig.
3. Performing Animals are every whit as eligible to be called artists as are either Actors or Dancers, yet no one so far as I can recall has claimed for any troupe of performing elephants or dogs what Dalcroze claims for his troupe of girls. Nearly everyone realizes that the practise of training living things to perform obediently before the public is merely a harmless if objectionable sillyness which appeals only to those in quest of the peculiar and unnatural, . . . well then? . .

Book Review. MODERN DANCING AND DANCERS by J. E.
Crawford Flitch, M. A. Unsigned. *The Mask*, Volume V, no. 1,
July, 1912.

his is one of those useless books. The writer is an M. A.
and the author of "Mediterranean Moods."
If this book has not quite the Monte Carlo touch it has
some of the oppressiveness of the Mediterranean's Li-
byan mood. I never could abide the sirocco, but when it
comes tasselled and begowned as an M. A. then it is
doubly relaxing.

Why write a book about Dancing at all unless you know all about the
art?

There are some scraps of good journalism in the book, but journalism at
fifteen shillings a copy is rather expensive.

The reproductions of photographs are common and the eight coloured
things in the book pretending also properly to represent two arts are
doubly awful.

Book Review. THE EURHYTHMICS OF JACQUES
DALCROZE. Unsigned. *The Mask,* Volume VIII, no. 12.

e cannot see why it is that this book about this System
"Rhythmische Gymnastik" has come out in England
. . . . and what Professor M. E. Sadler means by still
pushing German goods in England at this day is incomprehensible. Because even if Germany has as
much right on earth as any other lunatic, it is not the
time, nor is England the place, to encourage any but our own lunatics.

In this book we find that Herr Dalcroze of 1913 has now become Monsieur Dalcroze. Detestable if incomprehensible. Herr Teichmann becomes Monsieur Teichmann of Bâle.

The ladies in bathing drawers have not changed anything, so little was there left to change . . . . except some of their poses and their too intense, if always charming, facial expression.

Monsieur Dalcroze says nothing different from what Herr Dalcroze said. He does not approve of the "Russian Ballet and their 'L'Après-midi d'un Faune' " though he is good enough to approve of "several" of the plastic interpretations of Miss Duncan . . . . in a foot note: but his aim is the same as it ever was, . . . . to turn out a number of Isadora Duncans if by hook or crook he possibly can.

Anyone who has seen Monsieur Dalcroze's early books, before the genius of Isadora Duncan illumined three quarters of Europe and M. Dalcroze into the bargain, will have noted that his movements, costumes and whole system had the appearance of being what the Germans call *gemutlich*; that means comfortable.

Monsieur Dalcroze saw that these woollens really wouldn't do. So he removed some of them; then some more . . . . and then another little bit, seeing no harm; and at last made his pupils really comfortable; . . . but still he was unable to give them a scrap of the genuine thing which they think they are to get . . . . and the genuine thing is the power of expression.

However we must admit that for servant girls or programme girls it should be an admirable school to go to: . . . . can't you see Fanny entering with a tray tip-toe Mercury and realising something which M. Charles Blasis aimed at in 1829? . . . I suppose you know his book? . . . quite interesting. "The Mask" should really reprint it with the pictures.

And now that one comes to think it over a moment longer, why should not a school or two be started in England taking M. Charles Blasis and M. Del Sarte as guides? They wrote such good books, too. Did you never hear of the books of Del Sarte? . . . America has. Americans in some of the States were brought up on Del Sarte.

The effect was, I believe, that it made young ladies walk better than before . . . . which is most deceptive. Tell me, don't you like a rat of a woman to walk like a rat, so that we shall not mistake her for a lady or a blessing when we meet her? The worst of these 'systems' is that they baulk expression. No longer shall we say "here comes such and such a nature," . . . but we shall be aware that here comes a trained Dalcrozian. That ultimately . . . . I admit only ultimately . . . . will tell against the lady who adopts his systematic beauty at so much a lesson. And they are dirt cheap.

Men soon begin to see under that sort of mask.

I am one of those who think that individual expression in life is what we must preserve; therefore I think Dalcroze is a nuisance.

Except, as I said, for servant girls, programme sellers, waitresses and all and any who are or want to be in uniform pattern.

If Monsieur would guarantee to train none but the servants of the public, then might not we hope to see governments and local bodies taking up this system and stereotyping hundreds of females per day? . . . Democratic any how.

I have turned once more to the book to see if I am not doing injustice to Monsieur Dalcroze . . . . I am not.

No . . . no . . . . the results achieved are insipid: . . . he may be right in his theory . . . . but not right as rain: . . . and the artisticness of the whole thing would be right enough for those groups in America or even England or Germany where groups of ladies thrill, gush or *schwerm* over things they take to be *uplifting,* "perfectly lovely" or *reizend:* but for any place not befogged by doubts, or at any period when people are at last trying to awaken to realities, it is out of place and it is out of date. And Isadora Duncan is still a living influence.

---

FOLLOW THE LEADERS. Unsigned. *The Mask*, Volume IX, 1923.

---

 e are winning—and don't forget it for a moment.

It was in 1908 that "The Mask," representing Mr. Gordon Craig for England, Miss Isadora Duncan for America, M. Adolphe Appia for Switzerland, Herr Reinhardt for Germany, M. Stanislawsky for Russia, Signor Toscanini for Italy, Mr. W. B. Yeats for Ireland, Madame Yvette Guilbert, for France, the late Wyspiansky for Poland, and the theatre artists of Holland, of Spain, of Austria, stood firm, — if alone in this — and cried out the words *"The Artist as Leader and no other."*

To this declaration we still adhere.

A few of you have hesitated and shuffled, but most have been true and remain so.

Those who have shuffled can now look around and see if what we said was not true and destined to prevail.

The Artist has been leading for some years now, — no longer alone. Many have followed and more are following every month. All over Europe and America men have been stirred and things are moving.

Patience, — more confidence — more endurance — more good humour; more loyalty to your leaders; — more adhesion to them — and you will win with us.

Foreign Notes. ONCE ST. PETERSBERG; PARIS. Unsigned. *The Mask*, Volume XI, no. 2, April, 1925.

 ome delightful pictures of Isadora Duncan's immense school of the Dance, at last permanently founded (at least so we pray) in the city which we always remember as St. Petersberg, recently appeared in "Commoedia," Paris. As head instructress of these pupils, some thousand to guess from the crowd of *Jeunes filles* on the banks of the stream in picture b, stands Irma Duncan.

What, a daughter? Bless your heart no — and yes. She was once upon a time a little German girl in the most middle-class surroundings in the town of Hamburg (I think); worked as she works now, faithfully and well, only perhaps without ever having seen a theatre or the big world or heard music. Now she has seen all; and, remaining faithful and working well, is not altered, . . . . only happier. Was it not worth it all?

And there are some odd folk battling all their lives to prevent the spread of the dance, the theatre, and all which is happy, believing that all which is grey and pinched is better for their souls.

A hundred times better if they have no fidelity and are merely farthing egoists.

But even if this great dancer only found one being worth its freedom it was well done to have let loose a hundred to their destruction. That is what still has to be learnt by some people. So, brave Irma.

As a matter of fact, out of a hundred pupils I believe Isadora Duncan can count as many as five successes, . . . and I think that is a triumph.

*        *        *        *

At the Vaudeville Madame Ida Rubinstein was recently again playing "La Dame aux Camélias" in her original way. She advertised the scenes, costumes and furniture as: "Decors and costumes of the period from the designs of M. Alexandre Benois. Furniture and Accessories are real works of art loaned by private collectors. New stage setting by M. Armand Bour."

Which recalls to me a passage from that little known book by Mr. Gordon Craig, "The Theatre Advancing," in which he contrasts a permanent and a temporary theatre, and speaks of the sham properties of the ordinary playhouse as being excellent for a theatre which has no ambition to endure.

Madame Rubinstein possibly feels that real works of art (even though but loaned for the occasion) render her Vaudeville one of the first permanent Theatres. But alas, this is not all we look for in the way of permanence.

The Vaudeville Theatre itself is but a temporary playhouse judged by the standards of "The Theatre Advancing," and the play, "La Dame aux Camélias" a play for a few days.

Notions of permanence are curiously ephemeral nowadays; still, a pose of permanence should deceive for a moment. What could be more charming, and who could convince us better than Madame Rubinstein.

# ON A BOOK ABOUT ONE OF OUR ENGLISH ARTISTS: MARGARET MORRIS. *The Mask*, Volume XII, no. 4, October, 1926.[1]

iss Morris's book[2] I have not read, but I have read Mr. L. St. Senan's review of her book which appeared in the "New Criterion."

Mr. St. Senan compares pretty Miss Morris with M. Diaghileff. Was it to damn the Russian impresario that he did that? I can conceive no other intention. If you compare a rose with a plate you are obviously having a sly, if absurd, dig at the plate. If you compare even a radish with a fine antimacassar you are not laughing at the radish, and Miss Morris is after all a pretty English rose.

Had Mr. St. Senan compared Miss Morris with any other *danseuse* — with Miss Allen, or Miss Ruth St. Denis, for example — he would have done a little better. Self-trained dancers must be compared with other self-trained dancers . . . . not with machinery.

Mr. St. Senan tells us that M. Diaghileff has "made history in the art of the theatre not once but over and over again." He has done no such thing. He has caused several groups of dancers to make a success over and over again. He has that knack — he is really a good impresario. But he is not the Chevalier Noverre. Only Isadora Duncan has "made history" in the Dance of this century.

Critics grow a little confusing who, for no particular reason, compare plates and flowers. M. Diaghileff does not dance, does not sing, does not act, does not, I am told, even whistle. He manipulates those who dance, those who train dancers, those who design scenes, and those who direct orchestras.

He has been probably the first to lend the Impresario something which in appearance looks very like the true artist. In any other age M. Diaghileff would perhaps have attempted diplomacy and become *Valet de chambre* to a prince, — a great personage like M. Bachelier, *valet de chambre* to young Louis XV. His personality lends a grace to the European stage which was not possessed by M. Astruc or Phineas Barnum. I know of another theatre man who seems possessed of even more indifference, even more certainty about what he is doing; he is an Italian impresario, but he works less in the limelight than M. Diaghileff and seems in no way to be the great man nor to desire such a celebrity.

Such men can be compared for one compares them with Mr. Cochran and with M. Herbelot; but none of these can possibly be compared with Miss Morris.

Miss Morris is a very excellent dancer, suffering because Mr. St. Senan and his kind will not make a little effort to stand by her and her English faults and qualities. Is she too technical?—is she too precise?—is she too light?—is she too heavy? I'm sure I do not know. But whatever she is, we could have had a Ballet of our own long ago if, instead of being ashamed of our own dancers, we had stood up for them all a good deal better. Miss Morris might long ago have developed if we had encouraged her. We did not; we never do encourage our artists, not even when critics are throwing bricks at them.

I suppose it is bad form to encourage since it is considered good form to be ashamed of them. Good form or no, it is anyhow damn bad behaviour and shows a wretched spirit to drive our stage artists, who would experiment, into finding their own little theatres and paying for them, or more or less paying, out of their own meagre purses.

For there are patrons of the Arts in London; oh, yes, they will give an artist £100, even £200 (if the artist worries sufficiently); and for that they feel themselves privileged to say to London "Yes, I am supporting her art" or, "That is my special charity."

Special fiddlesticks.

If Miss Morris is not better developed as a dancer (and Mr. St. Senan seems to feel she is not) it is his fault and the fault of those he listens to and echoes, and the fault of all those wonderful "Patrons" of the Arts in London.

How the sensible folk in London allow them to block up the road when people are trying to get on, I find hard to understand. There they are, smiling their eternal smile of self-satisfaction while they down all that is English—if it have some talent and independence—by supporting it too feebly. Miss Morris, if she is independent, is so in spite of them.

I need not expect her to do what Taglioni did in order to appreciate what she does . . . . in order to see what she could do if properly supported.

If she was first of all driven into a pseudo-artistic set it is the fault of our English critics, who fail year after year to combine and demand in a group what they are too timid to demand individually, . . . fair play, fair training, fair pay and fair opportunity for all English artists who are beginning.

Who wants merely praise or blame from critics? What critics are made for is to see first of all that the conditions under which artists are working in London are at least as good as the conditions of the East end slums.

The conditions are worse.

Who comes to enquire — to help? The Prince of Wales? . . . the Duke of York? No, the Bishop of Rumtifoo.

Scepticism enquires, reports, grins, turns its back, and art is prevented.

But M. Diaghileff, you say? Ah, M. Diaghileff!!! M. Diaghileff is from Russia; he has talents all of which I have acknowledged, all but one . . . . the art of raising the wind. He has that art assuredly. If Miss Morris had it you'd all be at her feet tomorrow.

Are we to suppose that Miss Morris can raise even £ 50 easily, we who can draw our cheques for £ 1000 as easily as we can call a taxi and say "to the Russian Ballet"? No one has a notion how much good material is lost to the arts in England because of the sheer poverty of the artists — and their inability to pay their way.

You cannot quite wear down a William Blake—he has a pencil and can afford three new brushes when he sends out for his porter — and he has a friend — one. And two rooms. But you can even make a William Blake tedious by throwing him back year after year on his last resources:

On his one friend / two Rooms / and three new brushes.

In England we make mistakes often because we don't know. We have killed and continue to kill our artists because we didn't know. If we go on doing this we shall wake up one morning and know right enough and know exactly twenty-four hours too late. We shall have tried to kill the wrong artist and he will object.

I repeat that the conditions under which our artists work in England are worse than the conditions of the worst English slums.

Daily we hear of young artists who want to put an end to their existence: — they see that no one wants their work as it is — when it is good. Sometimes by God's luck some good being happens to pass along — buys a picture — or an engraving — and the lad is saved. But it's touch and go. I know several cases of this wearing down of the artists.

When they are more solid and can stand more, (Miss Morris for example) the folk think it a cue to put a greater strain on them. So they pelt them with plates, Diaghileffs and other bric-à-brac.

You go to the wrong people to enquire as to the condition of the English

Artists. They tell you that all is quite well and the artists rather spoiled than otherwise. That is an untruth.

I ask for the sixtieth time in this journal for fair play for the artists—and decent pay. I ask for something to be done to dam the rush of amateurs—mostly society ladies and gentlemen—who imagine that a Miracle has happened and endowed them suddenly with powers of expression equal to that of Rachel, Fanny Elssler, Jenny Lind or Miss Elinor Wylie.

They push forward and shove rudely into places which are not theirs and are not free. American impresarios assist them:—it is such a draw to have a real Society bird, as Mr. James Glover calls them, in place of the genuine nightingale.

I ask that these people be very distinctly given the cold shoulder—and your artists a warmer welcome. It is the only fair-play thing to do.

1. [Reprinted in *Dance Index*, Volume II, no. 8, August, 1943.]
2. Margaret Morris Dancing: by Margaret Morris and Fred Daniels. (Kegan Paul, Traubner, Trench & Co.)

---

Book Review. THE AMERICAN BALLET by Ted Shawn.
Unsigned. *The Mask*, Volume XIII, no. 1, January, 1927.

---

r. Shawn has divided his book into chapters on The spiritual Basis; The Sources of thematic Material; the classic European Ballet tradition, how it helps and how it hinders; Social dancing; American Music and composor; Dancing and nudity; Dancing for men; Dancing in church; Dancing and the Theatre; and The Dream.

There is a Preface by Mr. Havelock Ellis, who writes: "The path of the genuine artist in dancing today is rather like the path to martyrdom. The world is prepared to appreciate the dancer, but the world has not yet prepared a stage, and still less a temple, to receive the dancer"; which seems to us, after twenty years thinking about it, to be overstating our needs. "There is" Mr. Ellis goes on, "the concert hall ready for the musician, and there is the opera house where the ancient formal Italian ballet is permitted to figure as a mere interlude, but otherwise the dancer must fight with all sorts of vested and traditional interests, and in the end submit to an often heart-rending compromise, in which the artist's conception is lost. It is inevitable; it must happen in the new birth of any art. But the time is coming for the next step."

There are a good many photographic illustrations, but all seem to represent Mr. Shawn, Miss St. Denis and their troupe; we look in vain for one which shows us that greatest figure of the American dance, . . . indeed, of the new spirit in the dance in a far wider sense; there is, in fact, no picture at all of Isadora Duncan, which seems a strange omission.

Mr. Shawn, it is true, does not ignore Miss Duncan. He refers to her not infrequently; but bracketted with, and secondary to, Miss Ruth St. Denis. "Just as the first great waves foretell the flood to come, so came the first pioneers, Ruth St. Denis and Isadora Duncan": . . . . "This renaissance of the dance which is now taking place, and which we all recognize, owes its beginning to the pioneering of two great American dancers, Ruth St. Denis and Isadora Duncan": . . . . and so on, and so on.

Now in a book which is so saliently a piece of propaganda for the Shawn-St. Denis ideas and practice it is natural that Mr. Shawn should wish to give prominence to his own companion. But then he should surely have called this nice looking volume "The St. Denis-Shawn Ballet"; and not "The American Ballet"; for, in a work bearing such a title, we naturally expect a large part to be given to the work of the greatest of them all, and, as has been insisted on by "The Mask" since 1908, there are not two greatest but only one.

No history of the American dance, or of the dance at all in its noblest sense as manifested in the last thirty years, can be worth serious consideration, which does not do justice, and pay adequate tribute, to the greatest exponent and the most inspired modern protagonist of the Dance.

It is doubtless the democratic spirit which would always raise on stools all the surrounding figures lest a central figure should overtop them; but, personally, we dislike the artificial process of levelling up even in ordinary and civic affairs, and infinitely more so in Art.

The truth that Miss Duncan is herself does not render Miss St. Denis and Mr. Shawn any less than they are: and a due sense of proportion, an understanding of that primal inspiration to whose power the requickened life of the Dance is due, would have lent not only a grace, but also a definite value, to Mr. Shawn's book.

Book Review. ISADORA DUNCAN' [sic] RUSSIAN DAYS by
Irma Duncan and Alan Ross Macdougall. By F. M. Florian. *The
Mask*, Volume XV, no. 3, July-August-September, 1929.

his is a touching book of remembrance by the most
faithful pupil any man or woman could wish to have,
assisted by as faithful a secretary, for Mr. MacDougall
was secretary to Isadora Duncan for many a day.

It tells something interesting to him who may chance
to have known Miss Duncan. It once more bears tes-
timony to her intense distrust and even hatred for organization. In the
future, a stranger, eager to understand why she did as she did, will be able
to explain to himself—if not to the world—the reason for her seeming
egoism, her apparent lack of discipline, her supposed habit of terminating
friendships, provided he bears in mind her contempt for organization. He
will have to trace this hatred for organization to the right source before he
will arrive at the reason behind most of her acts. The reason will be found
to be quite unreasonable, and Isadora Duncan will then cease to be a
mystery, without anyone being able to explain her.

Yes, I doubt whether anybody will ever discover the secret, and so her
name will become even more of a legend than it is already. They will erect
statues to her, and more statues to her; and these monuments, unless
something happens to stop the tendency, will all by then have something
sorrowful and tragic in them . . . all very unlike her. Round her is growing a
grave legend—thoughts associated with death and tears linger where her
name is spoken—which of all things is the most ridiculous, since this sad
figure was but a dummy put up—and put up by herself—to draw the fire
of the enemy. On one statue I would like to see the words, "She fooled
them to the top of her bent"—and under the words, in bas-relief, a copy
of her book.

I once met Miss Duncan—it was in a train, going to Zurich,—and I had
one of the most interesting conversations with her that I have had with
anyone I have ever met. I had been in Paris interviewing President Wil-
son, Mr. Lloyd George, and Clemenceau, and was going to meet a far
more extraordinary man than any of these, . . . the then unknown Signor
Mussolini.

Miss Duncan never hesitated in talk, gesture, or idea, as many girls do—and Miss Duncan, you will recall, was always a girl—essentially young and, to use a poor word, "idealistic." It is as though I had called Lord Reading, "always a boy" and "up in the air"—but so he was—so he is.

I listened to this girl then, not as I would listen to a worldly woman—this girl whose speech never halted—who seldom blushed—yet who was all girl—who skipped woman, as it were, and became—something more: I listened and I heard her utter things which the world calls mad.

Some things she said made me alive to her hatred for organization although she was full of schemes which included a considerable amount of organization—but I perceived she hated it.

Everything she said after this took on the most original complexion. Her unconcern that her school had recently been scattered to the four winds—an indifference which flowed like a deep undertide, even while she bewailed her loss. She bewailed in unconvincing tones—she was not born to bewail—she was only born for joy—and the joy in her was evident to me. She told me grievous things—I could not grieve with her for under all was Joy.

I began to realise—I say—that she it was who broke up her school so often; she who prevented America giving her a million to establish a school there, and that she knew what she was doing when she broke things up—she was saving the thing she treasured more than the world.

As compensation she gave to the world some performances. Of one of these she wrote (but not in a book), "the Lady what dances, danced all over the place . . . . the yellow dog and the gas man liked it and so apparently did all the Kings and the Queens in the audience—it was full of Imperial Loges and Kings and things like that—the lady what dances was in an awful rage and danced horrid at all the people—then she went to the dressing room and fought with the other lady."

Besides performances she gave the world a book—memoirs—and here again she knew what she was doing and gave it nothing—threw dust in its eyes and it has felt really flattered.

That is why I call the Miss Duncan who is known to the world, her dummy. The real being will never be known—as for the girl, . . . who knows?

Book Review. ISADORA DUNCAN by Arnold Genthe. By l.l.
[Lois Lincoln.] *The Mask,* Volume XV, no. 3,
July-August-September, 1929.

r. Mitchell Kennerley has produced a good plain book of remarkable photographs by Mr. Arnold Genthe — twenty-four studies of Isadora Duncan, nine of which I recognize. In a brief but able Foreword Mr. Max Eastman claims her as an American.

Surely when all's said and done she was without nationality.

Until nations jealously protect and support their artists, artists can have no nation — they then belong to the world.

It will not do for a nation to treat with indifference any artist they wish at death to claim as their child.

Isadora Duncan was treated shamefully by America, and America no longer has a shred of claim on her.

But this book . . . a tribute to her genius by Genthe . . . . is really well worth getting.

MISS ANGNA ENTERS by D. P. [Drury Pervil.] *The Mask,*
Volume XV, no. 4, October-November-December, 1929.

have never seen this lady perform, but everyone seems to speak well of her. . . . I hate to discover that I have said what someone in "The School for Scandal" says of Joseph Surface. There is some critical use in the line, when applied to any celebrated successful performer: the performer must have stooped rather, bent a little, been of a coming-on disposition for *every* one to find the performer wonderful. What a ridiculous creature the spectators form themselves into—that monstrous thing called an audience; fancy being disposed to stoop to it.

I always like a conquering actor better than a winning actress, for the reason that he comes *at* them—he doesn't bend to them: and indeed, for all I know, Miss Enters may be like Mrs. Siddons and do just that; I would even be prepared to believe that she ignores them entirely—that she is so concerned with her art of composition that she never gives them a thought. If so, she will be certainly one of the unique persons of the stage.

I very much wish that those who write about performers would cease to talk of them as artists, would invent a new name for them, if they are not content with the word "performer," and would refer to what they do by using any other word except that of "art." Miss Enters seems to be a dancer, and, so far as I can gather, her dance is more like that of Emma Hamilton, and much less like that of La Taglione. I can almost suppose that what she does is rather more acting than dancing. She seems also to dress up a great deal: she likes to look each part and she has a number of them. We are told that "She has a gift of facial expression" and that "had she employed the most perfect speaking voice in the world, she would not have added one iota to the effectiveness of her presentation." All critics praise her to the skies; but it is a little bit embarrassing to find one of them saying "It is not dance, it is not drama, it is divination." That won't do, and that is why I want to see her to discover what it is.

# ALL VERY FITFUL. *The Dancing Times*, July, 1932.

*It is Miss Irene Mawer's book that has suggested to me the following reflections.* [1]

antomimists have more often mimed the funny moments of life than the tragic ones. How is that?—for in life the funny moments are all a matter of talk and nothing is done, whereas in the tragic moments all is done, and in silence.

"Don't stand there chattering—do something," is what you'll hear over and over again when some accidental or deliberate deed panics everyone, and they begin to ask how it happened, why, and who did it.

On witnessing a comic pantomime which has some clearly defined story, we often wish that the people in it would speak. There seems no good reason for being so tongue-tied—whereas in a tragic pantomime the silence fits well. Tragedy should be surrounded by comparative silence: and perhaps that is why some people wish that *Hamlet* would talk less and get on with things—though in this particular tragedy, surely talk suits the whole situation so well that the more he talks, the more comic tragic it becomes.

But certainly the public do feel oppressed by too much talk in most Elizabethan, French and Greek tragedy. Not so in the short No plays of Japan, where the values of dance, scene and costume, mime, and of masks, have all been well understood and employed by the dramatist-actor.

There is no good reason why a tragedy should consist of words, and words alone. Eight thousand words are not the very stuff to lead up properly to a tragic climax consisting of one minute of horror, and that after this, another eight thousand words come in well to express the pity which should, can, and does follow upon the tragic act. There should be always one theatre in every land where lengthy tragic recitation could find many hundreds of people happy to listen to it and, understanding it, feel satisfied. And there should be one theatre in every land where tragic pantomime would satisfy as many people. But these are the two extremes of theatricals—and neither is to be found to flourish in England; so there is no one theatre for either.

We are all for a variety show. Too much of anything except variety is apt to bore us after three or four minutes. That is why we only like the Shakespeare plays well cut down, flashily tricked out in finery and plenty of pretty music, and with enough intervals to make the evening enjoyable. We couldn't stand the Greek plays even if Aeschylus and Euripides could be born again in England and re-write them into some new tragic idiom: we don't like to think when we go to a theatre, and we don't want to feel—we want to enjoy ourselves. It has been so for years—and it has been said so for years. Even spectacles like "The Miracle"—which, though I've never seen it, I am told was impressive, well done and tragic—even such affairs bore us in England. And it appears that to produce them costs so much money that it doesn't pay. "Casanova," "White Horse Inn," "Waltzes from Vienna" cost more; but as they are not intense, the public enjoys them. I saw "White Horse Inn," so I know what it is they enjoy, after Sir Oswald Stoll has got them into the building. He never gives them anything "artistic"—that awful blight of the present-day theatre in England—he gives them frank, straightforward, slap-dash stuff—that stuff we all love so much, when done professionally. The downright newspaper gives it us too; and the cinema, of course, gives it us.

And I believe some semi-artistic souls in London are actually blaming Sir Oswald Stoll for being astute enough to know what the big public likes to have. The British public has rejected over and over again all that is genuine in the art of the nation; but it has always hated that which was semi-artistic, and it has always loved the good old tawdry stuff—and as it likes it, it should have it.

When a great writer or painter or actor does set himself against this tendency towards the good old vulgar, he finds in our land a certain amount of vague support *from a few people*. A few people were loyal supporters of Shakespeare and Irving—Gilbert and Sullivan—Ruskin and Rossetti; but half of the people who hung around these artists and their work, were grumbling and cavilling. All very fitful.

This is why Miss Irene Mawer's book, "The Art of Mime," will not have the same large sale which it would have had in other lands—our people don't want art and they don't want mime.

But though they don't want it, the book will give numbers of students to the dance and pantomime the liveliest of pleasure—they will be glad that it is a readable book, that it's well illustrated and soberly bound, and they will jump at the opportunity of getting, for seven-and-sixpence, a brief history of this most ancient desire to mimic everything—and also getting, free of charge, a series of lessons for which they would have to pay at least twelve guineas.

1. "The Art of Mime," by Irene Mawer. (Methuen.)

## MEMORIES OF ISADORA DUNCAN. *The Listener,* Volume XLVII, no. 1214, June 5, 1952.

 have something to say about Isadora Duncan. In fact I have a good deal to say to her: but that can wait and take its place in my memoirs. The something I have to say now is that she was the first and only dancer I ever saw—except for some in a street in Genoa and some in a barn near York.

Isadora came to us in the first years of this century. When she died it seemed to some of us that dancing ceased. Dancing and ballet dancing are two separate things. Ballet dancing had been flourishing for at least 300 years, but remember this: dancing is as old as the human race. I have no reason to take ballet quite so seriously as do certain enthusiasts of the last thirty years. Ballet may have been a fine, strong plant in the seventeenth century, when Monteverdi in Italy and Ben Jonson in England were alive to write music and verse for these rare spectacles—not money-making spectacles but given at royal and ducal courts. For the general public in those days were quite happy to be out of it, and publicity agents were not being paid to work up the business at court. The public in those days danced together as they do today—not in large winter gardens or skating rinks at half-a-crown or five shillings a head entrance fee, but among themselves for pleasure. It therefore enjoyed its jigs and other jolly dances, and left ballet to display itself in the not very large rooms of very fine palaces.

The public preferred to enjoy things in a homely way; the public had not been taught by publicity agents of every kind to consider itself somebody. It loved a dance—ballet was rather ridiculous to it, not that the public ever said so in so many words, for its opinion was never asked. Neither was money needed: its presence at court was out of the question. The dancers therefore did not have to please any public, and could dance as their masters and the poets and composers decided they should do. Critics were not present to write them up or write them down in next morning's newspapers. All therefore was perfectly safe; the dance might do as it pleased and might hope to please a few.

But this century, it may not do that; all sorts of different people's interests have had to be considered. All became therefore very unsafe. Into this dangerous world leapt Isadora. The world raved about her for several years, as it will rave, and often ignorantly; and then it actually forgot her. People called her a great artist—a Greek goddess—but she was nothing of the kind. She was something quite different from anyone and anything else. I always thought how Irish she was, which means, how full of natural genius which defies description: but she had more than that. Yet she had the tip-tilted nose and the little firm chin, and the dream in her heart of the Irish who are so sweet to know. And in her eye was California, and this eye looked out over Europe and thought well of what it saw.

What more she had, no one will ever describe. She was a forerunner. All she did was done with great ease—or so it seemed, at least. This it was which gave her an appearance of power. She projected the dance into this world of ours in full belief that what she was doing was right and great. And it was. She threw away ballet skirts and ballet thoughts. She discarded shoes and stockings too. She put on some bits of stuff which when hung up on a peg looked more like torn rags than anything else; when she put them on they became transformed. Stage dresses usually transform the performers, but in her case it was these bits which actually become transformed by her putting them on. She transformed them into marvels of beauty and at every step she took they spoke. I do not exaggerate.

I shall never foreget the first time I saw her come on to an empty platform to dance. It was in Berlin, the year 1904—please make a note of that, somebody says it was 1905—the month December. Not on a theatre stage was this performance, but in a concert-hall, and you know what the platforms of concert-halls were like in 1904.

She came through some small curtains which were not much taller than she was herself; she came through them and walked down to where a musician, his back turned to us, was seated at a grand piano; he had just finished playing a short prelude by Chopin when in she came, and in some five or six steps was standing by the piano, quite still and, as it were, listening to the hum of the last notes . . . . You might have counted five, or even eight, and then there sounded the voice of Chopin again, in a second prelude or etude; it was played through gently and came to an end and she had not moved at all. Then one step back or sideways, and the music began again as she went moving on before or after it. Only just moving— not pirouetting or doing any of those things which we expect to see, and which a Taglioni or a Fanny Ellsler would have certainly done. She was speaking in her own language, not echoing any ballet master, and so she came to move as no one had ever seen anyone move before. The dance ended, and again she stood quite still. No bowing, no smiling—nothing at all. Then again the music is off, and she runs from it—it runs after her then, for she has gone ahead of it.

How is it that we know she is speaking her own language? We know it, for we see her head, her hands, gently active, as are her feet, her whole person. And if she is speaking, what is it she is saying? No one would ever be able to report truly, yet no one present had a moment's doubt. Only this can we say—that she was telling to the air the very things we longed to hear and until she came we had never dreamed we should hear; and now we heard them, and this sent us all into an unusual state of joy, and I sat still and speechless.

I remember that when it was over I went rapidly round to her dressing-room to see her, and there too I sat still and speechless in front of her for a while. She understood my silence very well; all talk being unnecessary. She was tired after her dancing, and was resting. No one else came to see her. Far, far off we heard applause going on. After a while, she put on a cloak, and shoes and out we went into the streets of Berlin, where the snow looked friendly and the shops still lighted up, the Christmas trees all spangled and lighted, and we walked and talked of the shops. The shops, the Christmas trees, the crowd—no one heeded us. Time passed, time went on.

Some weeks later on she thought she could found a school of such a dance; or she said she thought so. She had forgotten what her much-loved poet Whitman had said: 'I charge you that you found no school after me . . . . ' Very cautious was that poet, and he often uses this word 'caution' in his books, as you will have noticed.

Isadora caused the rash enthusiasts to imitate her, to do it well or to do it badly, but she laboured very long to create a school, talking much for very many years about it all, getting girls into a schoolhouse and putting her sister Elizabeth (a very clever woman) to train them. The first result of this showed well; I saw this first showing at a matinee at the Kroll Opera House in Berlin, where, after dancing her own dances, turning towards the wings she called her little pupils to come to her and please the public with their little leapings and runnings: as they did, and with her leading them the whole troupe became irresistibly lovely. I suppose some people even then and there began reasoning about it all, trying to pluck out the heart of the mystery. But I and hundreds of others who saw this first revelation did not stop to reason, for we too had all read what the poets had written of life and love and nature, and we did not reason then; we read, we wept, we laughed for joy. And so it was at the Kroll Opera House that day—we all wept and laughed for joy. And to see her shepherding her little flock, keeping them together and specially looking after one very small one of four years old, was a sight no one there had ever seen before and, I suppose, will never see again.

This is something she did towards forming a school, just as Blake's first two verses in the 'Songs of Innocence' are but something; the whole great singing follows. And as surely did the whole great dancing of Isadora follow after these first wild, lovely steps. Unlike seeds, schools are things of peculiar slow growth; but in this way for ten or more years she projected the dance for us to take with us in our heads and 'in our heart's heart, Horatio.'

Was it art? No, it was not. It was something which inspires those men who labour in the narrower fields of the arts, harder but more lasting. It released the minds of hundreds of such men: one had but to see her dance for one's thoughts to wing their way, as it were, with the fresh air. It rid us of all nonsense we had been pondering so long. How is that—for she said nothing? On the contrary, she said everything that was worth hearing; and everything that anyone else but the poets had forgotten to say. Yet here was a divine accident.

How did she do it? Ask a poet how he makes his verse. Yeats answered: 'I made it out of a mouthful of air.' He is right. You may find that an unpractical answer, but do you get any further if he tells you, like Baudelaire, 'I made it always by reading the dictionary?' 'Words, words, words'; it is about all the poet has to work with; so give your son a dictionary if he fancies he will write verse. But tell him, also, what Yeats said. Yet you think by sending your girl to a ballet school you will help her to dance. You will not; you will hinder her. What must she do then? She should do what Isadora did: learn what it is to *move*: to step, to walk, to run; few people can do these things. Did it ever occur to you? First the thought, then the head, then the hands and feet a little, just move, and look around, watch all that is moving. Tell that to your daughter. For dance comes with movements; but there are no first, second, and third positions unless you are drilling for a soldier, though after all each dancer will make his own first, second, and third positions if he wants to, but they must be *his own*.

How long did it take Isadora to move? About five minutes (that is no answer, yet is the only true one anyone can give); and then she taught herself how to move this way, that way, every way. But not according to the teaching of Noverre, or of Blasis or Petipa or any of the famous ballet masters. This took her many years to learn. But I believe that that forgotten man, Del Sarte, helped her through his book. Once I found a copy of this book in her room when I was looking for a trunkful of books I had lent her. I did not find the trunkful, so I took this one. Many thousands of people in America and France studied this book by Del Sarte, and yet very few of these thousands ever gleaned any secret from its pages. A word or two to a genius like Isadora is always enough, whereas one hundred thousand are thrown away on duffers.

What is it she lacked? What was it she had? She had calm. She had no vanity. She had no cleverness—by which I mean no clever little tricks of the trade—little or no understanding of the arts, a great comprehension of nature and perhaps rather too much ambition.

I have heard Christian Bérard say that he only saw her dance in 1926, or thereabouts, when she was no longer slim. 'Fat,' he said, without a shade of contempt or criticism. 'Quite big—fat.' He added this: 'I never saw such movement in my life—a transformation took place when she began to move.'

He and I were in a small and empty restaurant on the Boulevard St.-Germain, when I asked Bérard if he had ever seen Isadora. It was the first time I met him. He was not given to excessive solemnity, though he was one of the most serious of the artists of his day, the day which ended far too soon. He was a very great stage decorator, though 'decoration' in his case is somehow the wrong word, for his thoughts were to create places on the stage which had not been seen before; and this he did, places peopled with figures not seen before either. Other people have written and will write of his work; not, perhaps, as it deserves, but having seen him at work they will be able to write more knowingly than I can speak of it here. Yet his artistry pervaded the performance of Giraudoux's 'La Folle de Chaillot': he did not merely design the scenes and costumes, that is simply nothing, for having the good Jouvet as his *metteur en scène*, who was also the master of the theatre in which the work appeared, he had perfect liberty to let his imagination play freely, and Jouvet let it play freely. So that almost every move of the figures in the second act was his, as was each costume and each yard of scenery, of course, and all these he caused to act as no other artist has done to my knowledge. It was design ever changing and always keeping a unity, split up as the parts were, a dress here passed a dress there and achieved designs as it went, passing at such and such an angle through such and such a light. This never ceased in that act—and I have admired no bit of *mise en scène* more.

So when the admirable Bérard spoke of Isadora Duncan, and with such gentleness, and only yesterday, when nearly all Paris has forgotten her, it said a great deal to me; and may these words about her say something to you.

# INDEX

nformation in square brackets has been inserted by the Editor, either variant spellings used in the text or from other readily available sources. Craig's pseudonyms are treated in the same manner. "M." may not be an initial letter, usually it represents the abbreviation for *Monsieur*.

Duncan, Elizabeth, 249
Duncan, Irma, 234, 235, 241
Duncan, Isadora, xiii, xiv, xv, xvi, xvii, xix, xx,
    xxi, xxii, xxiii, 83, 86, 87, 89, 90, 107,
    111, 115, 136, 179, 181, 182, 213, 218,
    219, 220, 221, 222, 227, 232, 233, 234,
    235, 236, 240, 241, 242, 243, 247-252
Duncan, Raymond, 106
Duport, Mme., 178
Duse, Eleonora, xxi, 43, 49, 219
Duthé, Mlle., 117, 118, 128, 133, 134
Duveen, [Joseph], 144


Eastman, Max, 243
Edward VII, 202
*Edward Gordon Craig*, xxii
Edwardovitch, Edward [pseud.], xix, 146,
    147, 148, 190
Egypt, 62, 63, 67
Egysthus, 98, 99, 100
Elijah, 167
Elizabethan Dance, xix, 203
*The Elizabethan Jig and Related Song
    Drama*, 203
Elizabethan Stage Society, 7
Ellis, Havelock, 239
Ellsler [Elssler], Fanny, xiv, 112, 167, 168,
    239, 249
*Encyclopaedia Britannica*, 182
*Enemies of Society*, xxiii, 159
Engelhard, Marice, Ch., 65
England, 43, 60, 62, 65, 66, 78, 89, 90, 94,
    101, 137, 143, 145, 148, 149, 161, 163,
    167, 231, 232, 233, 238, 246, 247
English Folk Dance, xix, 144, 190-192
English Folk Dance Society, 144
*The English Folk Dance Tradition*, 144
Enters, Angna, xix, 243, 244
Ervine, St. John, 147
*Essays of the Year, 1931-32*, 71
Esshin, 95
Etruria, 67
Etscher, Gaspard, 221
*The Eurhythmics of Jacques Dalcroze*, 231
Euripides, 5, 246
Europe, 147, 189, 192, 194, 195, 197, 218,
    219, 232, 248
*The Everlasting Gospel*, 101
*Exhibition of Dutch Art*, 162

Exposition of Turin, 181
Exter, [Alexandra], 142


*Fabulae Atelanae*, 68
Farnese, 129
Fauré, [Jean Baptiste], 183
Ferrara, 129
Fitz James, 132
Flaubert, [Gustave], 48, 49, 92, 215
Flitch, J.E. Crawford, xxiii, 231
Florence, xv, 65, 93, 129
Florian, François M. [pseud.], xix, 241
Fokina, Vera, 179, 181
Fokine, [Michel], 90, 97, 98, 100, 101, 136,
    179, 182
Fontana, Carlo, 150
Foote, Samuel, 164
*The Forum*, 221
Fouquier, 130
Fragonard, [Jean Honoré], 118, 124, 128
France, 62, 66, 81, 137, 145, 169, 176, 177,
    220, 233, 251
France, Anatole, 4-5
*A Frenzied Greek Bacchante*, 170
Frohman, Charles, 218, 219
Fuller, Loie, xix, 217, 221
Furst, Adolf [pseud.], xvii, xix, xxiii, 60


Gandhi, [Mohandas K.], 169
Gardel, Mlle., 178
Gardiner, Ralph, 144
Garollo, Prof., 178
Garrick, David, 97
Gauguin, Paul, 86
Gautier, Théophile, 167, 168
Gay, John, xii
Genova [Genoa], 120, 150, 190, 191, 247
Genthe, Arnold, 243
George I, 67
George II, 67
George III, 67
Germany, 137, 169, 225, 226, 231, 233
Giannetti, Pietro, 150
Gilbert, [William Schwenck] and Sullivan,
    [Arthur Seymour], 246
Gillicudy, Mr., 134
Giorza, Paolo, 151

# THE MASK

NEW
NUMBER

JUST
OUT

# Gordon Craig
## defends
# Russian Ballet

**ORDER AT ONCE**
**7 JOHN ST. ADELPHI** TELEPHONE
REGENT 1601